Can We Unlearn Racism?

CAN WE UNLEARN RACISM?

What South Africa Teaches Us about Whiteness

Jacob R. Boersema

Stanford University Press

Stanford, California

STANFORD UNIVERSITY PRESS
Stanford, California

Printed in the United States of America on acid-free, archival-quality paper

Library of Congress Cataloging-in-Publication Data

Names: Boersema, Jacob R., author.
Title: Can we unlearn racism? : what South Africa teaches us about
whiteness / Jacob R. Boersema.
Description: Stanford, California : Stanford University Press, [2021] |
Includes bibliographical references and index.
Identifiers: LCCN 2021018464 (print) | LCCN 2021018465 (ebook) |
ISBN 9781503614765 (cloth) | ISBN 9781503627789 (paperback) |
ISBN 9781503627796 (epub)
Subjects: LCSH: Whites—Race identity—South Africa. | Whites—
South Africa—Attitudes. | Racism—South Africa. | Post-apartheid era—
South Africa. | South Africa—Race relations.
Classification: LCC DT1768.W55 B64 2021 (print) | LCC DT1768.W55
(ebook) | DDC 305.809/068--dc23
LC record available at https://lccn.loc.gov/2021018464
LC ebook record available at https://lccn.loc.gov/2021018465

Cover design: Angela Moody

Typeset by Kevin Barrett Kane

Contents

Preface

I arrived in South Africa in 2007, twenty-five years after the American anthropologist Vincent Crapanzano visited apartheid South Africa in the early 1980s. Crapanzano produced the first ethnographic study of White South Africans, *Waiting: The Whites of South Africa*.[1] Whereas previously most White ethnographers had studied the racial other, Crapanzano turned the ethnographic lens on White people. By observing them and talking to them, he sought to reveal the workings of White power. Crapanzano wanted to know "what the effects were of domination on everyday life—not the everyday life of people who suffer domination but of people who dominate." He sought to analyze "the discourse of people who are privileged by (their) power and, paradoxically, in their privilege victims of it."[2] In a *New York Times* book review, South African novelist J. M. Coetzee complimented Crapanzano's interpretation of "the process of deception and self-deception, yet without loss of human warmth."

It has taken me over a decade to write the first ethnographic study of Whites *after* apartheid and strike a similar balance. I wish to begin this book by acknowledging that in the process of writing it, I wrestled with approaching my subjects with clear-eyed critical engagement but also with empathetic understanding. Through that struggle, I've learned that one needs both perspectives to reveal the enigmatic and sometimes counterintuitive mechanics of Whiteness, power, privilege, and race.

The fact that I've gained this dual viewpoint and written this book was never a forgone conclusion. During my research, I traveled far and wide across three continents to understand the story of White South Africans, but as a White, male, European, I traveled just as far in my comprehension of race to discover my own positionality. Indeed, it took the full span of writing this book—a decade—to altogether come to grips with how much I was both an outsider and an insider to this community. It was only after the book had been revised many times over that I landed upon using the word "We" in the title. I include myself in the audience of the book, asking myself its core question of what South Africa has to teach us—White people from the Global North—about racism.

As a European sociologist, I was never trained as a race scholar. At the University of Amsterdam, the center for the study of race and ethnicity had closed in 1995, almost ten years before I even arrived at the university. The Dutch race scholar Philomena Essed, who wrote *Everyday Racism*, left the university the day I arrived, after many years of public criticism of her work.[3] The chair of the Department of Sociology took a stand against the framework of my study during a conference to say that he preferred ethnicity to race as an analytical concept: "Race was so unclear," he argued. My supervisor said that racism was too loaded a term to be useful in research, and in both sociology and the humanities he is in good company. American historian George Frederickson writes in his *Racism: A Short History* that even during his work on White supremacy in South Africa he thought racism to be "too ambiguous and loaded a term" to describe his subject effectively."[4] Race scholars, nonetheless, have argued even longer that sociological thinking in terms of nationalism, ethnicity, class, and gender must not discount the importance of race and racism as well.

Similarly, growing up in the 1980s and 1990s in the Netherlands, my idea of race was bound up primarily with the Holocaust in Europe, which limited and twisted my understanding of how race works. I was taught about racism more as a specific historic event—"the Holocaust"— rather than a global story with many subplots that extended back centuries. My first exposure to another model came extraordinarily late in my education—when I conducted fieldwork in Rwanda, where Belgian colonizers had racialized the Hutu/Tutsi difference and thereby sowed the seeds for the genocide that left almost a million dead in 1994. I came to understand that race and racism have a plethora of local histories and global connections. But how exactly they had been used to become a marker dividing humanity and—more important—how they continued to be used in this way was not yet clear to me.

Race, I was taught at university, is not a biological fact but a "social construct," and therefore it doesn't exist. European scholars sometimes use this to legitimize the position that race must not be used in the analysis, which makes it difficult if not impossible to study racism (as if money is not also a social construct, and yet it clearly exists and has consequences!). It wasn't until I immigrated to the United States that I learned that American scholars have compared the way race shows up in the social world with witchcraft.[5] Witches never actually existed, but as a social phenomenon, witchcraft was real in its effects. Race is a fiction too, but racism is real. Thinking about race as "racecraft" helped me as a researcher to shift my focus from race as something that is or is not real to thinking about racism as something that racists do: that racism is real in its effects and in its actors. In this way, this book is as much a product of my journey to the United States as of my journey to South Africa.

During my fieldwork in South Africa, I had oscillated between being an outsider and an insider to my subjects—and had moments when I felt I was in both positions at the same time. As a researcher from the Netherlands working in South Africa, I was an outsider because I was not South African or Afrikaner; I was coming from the metropole to study the former colony. However, the historical ties between my country and the people I interviewed were close, and I was also White and male. I was painfully confronted with the privileged access provided to me when a school refused a master's student of mine who was from Sudan similar access to the school for research. There was also the language: I gained exceptional access to this community because of my ability to understand and read Afrikaans. Even my Christian upbringing worked in my favor, as many White South Africans I spoke to were deeply religious. As a researcher, I felt this unique entrée enabled a rich understanding of how and why White Afrikaans-speaking people think and interact as they do, how the world looks from their perspective.

Writing this book, however, I reconsidered the meaning of my Whiteness and maleness in my rapport with White South Africans. I realized that my race and gender were one reason why I had originally struggled to see the importance of race in what White South Africans did or talked about—many of the things they did and said appeared normal to me.

Reflecting on my own racial socialization, knowledge, and racial blind spots helped me to establish a better balance between critical engagement and empathetic understanding. My position as an outsider with an insider understanding allowed me to paint an intimate portrait of White South Africans after apartheid. But my long journey toward becoming a race scholar who is reflexive of his own positionality also enabled me to do something else: to show how intimately and how inextricably race is interwoven with the everyday lives of White South Africans.

As a consequence, I believe, the story I tell in this book is a more truthful story about White South Africa that provides lessons for us all. Early misconceptions I had in my research approach ultimately provided their own insight: rather than ignore my racial positioning and dismiss my educational shortcomings in writing this book, I was able to use them productively to construct a more complete narrative about White South Africans after apartheid. It is a story driven by empathetic understanding of the challenge White South Africans confront but that also elucidates the politics of race at the heart of this challenge.

Acknowledgments

The only person who will be happier than I am that I have finished this book is my wife, Nathalie Le Du. Throughout the ten years it took me to write it (and rewrite it), she supported this project in countless ways, and it would be a crime to start these acknowledgments with anyone else. I'm extraordinarily lucky to have married such a lovable genius—she plays many roles with intelligence, creativity, and incredible stamina. As I was writing this book, she became a mother and a publisher, but she continued to make time to encourage me, apply her editorial skills to my work, and quite simply help me become a better writer and thinker.

The final version of this book was written between the births of our son, Lev, and our daughter, Rella, and it would have been impossible to complete it without the joy they brought into my world. Nothing has been more uplifting and rewarding than joining the family chaos after hours of solitary writing. I wish to thank them for bringing so much needed happiness and balance to my life.

The seeds of this book were planted early. I was seventeen years old when I discovered *The Murderers Among Us* by Simon Wiesenthal on my parents' bookshelf, and I went on to write my high school thesis on this holocaust survivor and famous Nazi-hunter. Wiesenthal's work raised a question that captivated my young mind and never left me: How should one respond to a collective moral crime in the midst of one's community? Besides stocking nearly a library's worth of books in our home, my parents, Anthonia Margaretha Bremmer-Boersema and Jan Boersema, provided an unshakeable foundation for all of my intellectual explorations, and I am grateful for their love and support all these years. I would also like to acknowledge the unending support of my sisters, extended family, and friends. They kept me afloat through it all with their love and faith—and edits. And I want specifically to thank my mother-in-law, Barbara Le Du, for the many hours and days she took care of our son Lev.

Inspired by my history teacher, Menno Ten Berghe, I traveled with my mother to Vienna, the capital of Austria, to interview Simon Wiesenthal—my first interview as a researcher, and by far not my last—whose ideas about the importance of justice instead of revenge and thirst for education continue to inspire.

A decade later I traveled to the small country of Rwanda to join the oral history project of Belgian researcher Philip Verwimp and conduct research on the genocide. Every day, I took a motor taxi with my translator to the field site, a hill dotted with small clay huts and banana trees, to interview community members. I sat with survivors, bystanders, and perpetrators in their small huts and documented their stories about what had happened in 1994, when almost 800,000 Rwandans were murdered in the genocide. My indebtedness to these Rwandans is immeasurable, and my interactions with them taught me a great deal about my responsibility and privilege as a researcher. I am grateful Philip offered me this unique experience, which also taught me the power of fieldwork, living history, and storytelling.

My research experiences in Rwanda inspired me to apply to the doctoral program in development studies at the University of Amsterdam, where Prof. Isa Baud and Dr. Johan Post accepted my application; I'm still thankful to them both. The Department of Geography, Planning and International Development provided me with an intellectual home, and many initial ideas for this book were generated through conversations with my colleagues there. I sincerely thank Barbara Oomen, who acted as an early guide while I found my way in academia and whose research on transitional justice provided a new critical perspective on South Africa. I'm also grateful for the welcoming community of PhD scholars, including Perry Hoetjes, Ellen Lammers, Anna Laven, Robert Rölling, and Hebe Verhest. Finally, Mario Novelli's passion for education and critical theory taught me a great deal about the role of education in addressing conflict, reconciliation, and injustice; he also generously introduced me to two exceptional South African scholars, Crain Soudien and Jonathan Jansen.

My first period of fieldwork in South Africa was a success in large part owing to the following individuals at the University of Cape Town. I am thankful that Crain Soudien was the first professor I met at UCT. His exploration of how we could unlearn the logic of race helped me shape my own ideas about unlearning racism. My focus on White South Africans was undoubtedly inspired by the work of Jonathan Jansen, who showed how a focus on White youth could tell a larger story about all White South Africans; I am grateful to him for having joined my PhD committee. Similarly, Melissa Steyn's work on Whiteness as ideology proved pivotal to my own thinking, while Hermann Giliomee and Marlene van Nieuwkerk also helped me immensely to make sense of South Africa during that first trip; all deserve my thanks. Perhaps most crucially, I met a group of young scholars that included Thomas Blaser, Tom Devriendt, Marianne Kriel, and Christi van der Westhuizen, whose work helped to shape my own thoughts.

During that first trip, I religiously carried Antjie Krog's books with me, and to this day I continue to be inspired by her ideas about humanity's capacity to change. I was also fortunate to meet two of her children, who charitably opened their homes to me and shared their views of post-apartheid South Africa. I will be forever thankful to them for the amazing hospitality they showed me.

Between my first and second periods of fieldwork in South Africa, I switched from development studies to sociology. I am immensely grateful to Jan Willem Duyvendak, who took a risk with me at this critical juncture and introduced me to the craft of sociology. Perhaps most consequentially, Jan Willem introduced me to James (Jim) Jasper and assisted me in a successful application with the Prins Bernard Cultuurfonds to study with Jim at the CUNY Graduate Center in New York City. In Jim I found a true mentor, who helped me navigate the wondrous world of American sociology while also demonstrating to me in practice, when it came to the study of culture and emotions, how to combine theoretical rigor with an empirical, pragmatic approach. I also wish to thank Jim, John Krinsky, and other participants in the Politics and Protest Workshop for helpful comments on a draft chapter for this book. Thankfully, I also made two cherished friends at CUNY, Koby Oppenheim and Stephen Ruszcyk, who have supported the development of this book over many years and continually provided insightful comments and guidance.

During my second period of fieldwork in South Africa, I met many South Africans who helped me with my research in both small and large ways; I am deeply indebted to them for sharing their time, knowledge, and networks. I especially appreciate the high school students who bravely opened up to me and the school management that unselfishly opened the doors of their schools to me. I am also grateful for the hospitality and access that the South African trade union Solidarity provided me; I thank Flip Buys and Dirk Hermann, in particular, who allowed me to join their research department and participate in meetings and activities. The leadership of the Afrikaanse Handelsinstituut provided an equally warm welcome, and I am truly grateful for their help, the access they provided, and the time they offered me.

After I finished my PhD in the Netherlands, I found a welcome place as a postdoctoral student at the Rutgers Institute for Health, Health Care Policy, and Aging at Rutgers University. I wish to thank my supportive supervisors, including Deborah Carr, Peter Guarnaccia, and David Mechanic, and especially my personal supervisor Allan Horwitz. My cohort of postdocs also included wonderful colleagues, including Amy Almerico-LeClair, Carolina Hausmann-Stabile, and Zoe Wool. I also had the privilege of attending a class by Eviatar Zerubavel, who taught me how to "think with" theorists and introduced me to his work on collective memory. Thankfully, Zaire Dinzey-Flores also became my colleague; her imaginative work on race, class, and gated communities pushed my thinking on race and urban developments in South Africa.

At Rutgers, I was fortunate to be introduced to ethnographers of Whiteness that helped me develop this book. Richard Schroeder and David McDermott's work on Whiteness in Tanzania and Zimbabwe, respectively, helped me to see the particulars of South Africa in sharper focus, and Janet McIntosh's brilliant ethnography on White Kenyans was a true inspiration for this book. Together with the gifted historian Danelle van Zyl-Hermann, who was writing her own book on Whiteness in South Africa, this newly developed network proved crucial in the development of the ideas for this book. Danelle's intelligence, wit, and loyal support make her a fabulous colleague and fantastic friend. Her many historical insights, nuanced theoretical ideas, and deep knowledge of South Africa have made this a much better book.

Yale University's Center for Cultural Sociology provided me with a second academic home during my postdoc years. There, Jeffrey Alexander, Philip Smith, Frederick Wherry, and above all my supervisor Ron Eyerman provided the warmest of welcomes. Ron's deep knowledge of critical theory and his interest in cultural trauma were tremendously beneficial for developing my thinking. I wish to thank the participants of the Center for Cultural Sociology Workshop and the Whitney Humanities Center Workshop, "The Trauma of the Perpetrators? Politics, Ethics and Representation," for their helpful comments on draft chapters of this book that I presented. I also learned a great deal and tremendously enjoyed the company of other fellows, including Shai Dromi, Till Hilmar, and Dicky Yangzom. I specifically wish to thank Thomas DeGloma, who encouraged me to pursue this book project. The welcoming community of cultural sociologists at Yale enhanced my respect for sociological theorizing and helped me embrace a meaning-centered analysis in my work.

This book, however, is not a work of cultural sociology but a book about race from a cultural-sociological perspective. No community was more helpful in transforming me from a cultural sociologist into a race scholar than the colleagues, PhD candidates, and students of Columbia University. After my postdoc, I had the privilege to teach at Barnard College and Columbia University, thanks to the kind invitation of Debra C. Minkoff. At Barnard, I met Jonathan Rieder, whose ethnographic study on the White Jewish and Italian communities in New York in the 1980s was a great inspiration for this book. At the Race, Ethnicity, and Migration Workshop, led by the welcoming and always helpful Van C. Tran, I presented a draft chapter for this book and received crucial feedback. The comments of Mignon R. Moore and her suggestion to engage with Michael Omi and Howard Winant's book *Racial Formation in the United States* proved pivotal in developing the framework for my study. And, since nothing teaches you more than becoming a teacher yourself, I must thank the whip-smart students from my seminar Race in the Global World—particularly Corwin McCormick and Noah Schoen—who read and reflected on part of this book.

As I was teaching at New York University, this book found its final form, in large part to the scholars I met there and around the world. I was fortunate that Malte Reichelt hired me (and subsequently Jeff Goodwin and Jeff Manza) and that we became good friends. The amazing sociology students at NYU taught me as much as I taught them about ethnography, interviewing, and what makes a good sociological book. I specifically want to thank Raven Barnes, Michael Bearman, and Songzhi (Era) Wu for the stimulating discussions. I had the privilege to meet and learn from the formidable race scholars Chrystal Flemming and Jean Beaman, whose work on racism in Europe and the United States provided an essential comparative perspective for my own work on South Africa. Stimulating conversations with the Dutch scholars Markus Barkanol, Sinan Çankaya, and Paul Mepschen on both sides of the Atlantic helped me tremendously to develop my own thinking about Whiteness, and two Dutch friends who visited New York, Jessica D'Abreu and Seada Nourhussen, taught me more about my own Whiteness than I care to admit. I am grateful for the opportunities that Katja Uushakala offered me—first in Helsinki and later in Edinburgh—to present my work, where Catie Gressier also helped inform my thinking about Whiteness in Africa.

During the final years of working on my book at NYU, no one was more helpful and supportive than Ann Morning. She encouraged me to contact Marcela Maxfield at Stanford University Press, who put her trust in me as I wrote this book and provided exceptional guidance, together with her team at Stanford including Sunna Juhn, Gigi Mark, and the excellent Christine Gever. I also want to thank Peggy Perona and specifically Marci Adilman, who for the last ten years has made every iteration of this book better with her wonderful edits. Ann Morning and Deirdre Royster also invited me to present draft chapters of this book to their courses on race and Whiteness, and the continued feedback was essential. For the day-to-day banter and support, as well as keen comments on draft chapters, I also wish to thank my favorite office buddies, Zawadi Rucks Ahidiana-Massac and Dina Bader. They made those last window-less writing months in the office so much more cheerful and even fun.

This book could not have happened without the contributions—great and small—from the above individuals and institutions. I will be forever grateful to all those who encouraged me to dream such a big dream, to begin climbing this mountain, to persevere through many drafts and challenges, and finally, at last to publish it. Last but not least, I'd like to thank you, the reader, for your precious time, for opening your mind to this work, and for educating yourself on this crucial topic. I look forward to continuing the conversation with you.

Can We Unlearn Racism?

White without Whiteness

"NO ONE IS BORN hating another person because of the color of his skin or his background or his religion. People must learn to hate, and if they can learn to hate, they can be taught to love. For love comes more naturally to the human heart than its opposite."[1] In the summer of 2017, former president Barack Obama responded to the racist violence in Charlottesville, Virginia, with a series of tweets quoting former South African president Nelson Mandela. Obama's tweets became some of the most "liked" tweets of all time.[2] At a time of crisis in the United States, when White supremacists marched through the streets of the American South, the former president turned to South Africa for the promise of change.[3]

Mandela believed that racism was something you could unlearn. In the final paragraphs of his autobiography, he writes, "The oppressor must be liberated just as surely as the oppressed."[4] He defines the racist—"a man who takes away another man's freedom"—as "a prisoner of hatred; he is locked behind the bars of prejudice and narrow-mindedness." When he became president, Mandela saw it as his mission to liberate *both* the oppressed and the oppressor. This work was not finished, he concluded. "For to be free is not merely to cast off one's chains, but to live in a way that respects and enhances the freedom of others. The true test of our devotion to freedom is just beginning."

During my fieldwork in South Africa, White South Africans repeatedly referenced the idea that racism was something you could unlearn. When I visited a school in Cape Town, a young, White Afrikaans-speaking girl told me that people always asked her if she had "transformed" yet. A boy in her class told me that as a White South African, you are always seen as a racist, but that he said, "Wake up, smell the coffee! The old South

Africa: that was racism—the Verwoerd years, apartheid. In the new South Africa, if you are not going to change, you will not survive." Older White people also told me about unlearning racism. I spoke with a middle-aged White man who worked at Eskom, the South African electricity company. He assured me that he was no longer a racist. "I have learned my lesson." It seemed then that White South Africans believed they could change and unlearn racism.

The longer I listened to the stories of White South Africans, the more the idea captivated me: Can we unlearn racism? If so, how does it work? And where is it happening? To answer these questions, I tell two stories in this book.

The first story is about unlearning racism as a social and cultural *process* happening in present-day South Africa. I wrote this book because, while many people believe we can unlearn racism, few have asked *how* it actually works. As a sociologist, I was inspired by autobiographical accounts of individuals gaining insights into their own racism as well as sociological studies about racism as an ideology, but I wanted to bridge the gap between these genres. Our individual challenges to unlearning racism are deeply shaped by economic and social forces; thus, our individual ability to unlearn racism differs from person to person, organization to organization, and setting to setting. Additionally, White South Africans need to forge a new cultural narrative about who they are and who they are not. This chapter opens with an exploration of the way South Africans imagined unlearning racism as a collective challenge, a uniquely South African idea they saw neither limited to "coming to terms with the past" nor solved by embracing the ideal of nonracialism. Rather, White South Africans saw unlearning racism as a goal of reconfiguring Whiteness away from an ideology of White superiority and privilege and toward something else: to be White without Whiteness.

Whiteness presents us with an alternative way to think about racism and the challenge to unlearn it. The second story I tell in this book starts in the second half of this chapter with an analysis of the social logic of unlearning racism by redefining Whiteness. However, I found that Whiteness is no substitute for racism as a concept, because racism has always had an anti-Black and pro-White component; Whiteness only reveals one half of racism. I consider the way Afrikaner nationalism historically created Whiteness and examine how Whiteness develops beyond White nationalism today.

In the midst of this story, it's important to ask: Why has academia hardly explored unlearning racism? American academics historically have been skeptical of the idea of unlearning racism, and their skepticism has been confirmed by the recent rise of White nationalism in the United States. On the contrary, South African scholars were perhaps too optimistic, skipping over unlearning racism to unlearning race completely. The exception has been Whiteness scholars, who hoped that by making Whiteness visible—the historical construction of it and the way it continues to confer privilege on people who identify as White—White South Africans would do away with it.

However, I demonstrate that racists often reinvent racism by misappropriating antiracist strategies. And indeed, South Africa's White minority now uses a new racism that I call *White identity politics*. White identity politics is the process of adopting the language of marginalized communities originally intended to promote multiculturalism and minority rights, and then reimagining identity politics and group rights for the benefit of White people. These campaigns seek to normalize White South Africans as "just another group" among the many minorities in South Africa to mask their privileges. This conclusion to the second story allows us to see the future of Whiteness beyond White nationalism and to confront the question of how to truly unlearn racism now that Whiteness is being normalized.

South Africa teaches us that Whiteness is a flexible and durable ideology that is not easily undone by exposing its workings. The country demonstrates the limits of the antiracist strategy built on the idea that making Whiteness visible—marking it—leads to abolishing it. One reason for this is because Whiteness has always been entangled with how White people think and feel about their nation, ethnicity, culture, language, and most important, themselves. Thus, White people normalize it rather than disentangling it. Abolishing Whiteness cannot happen before White people disentangle their Whiteness from these other constructs and ideas about themselves. Does the rise of a new racism in South Africa mean that White South Africans are not unlearning racism, or even that we *cannot* unlearn racism? Such a conclusion would be too rash. My aim by interweaving the two stories in this book is to do justice to White South Africans' individual efforts to unlearn racism while not losing sight of the bigger sociological picture of how racial hierarchies are being reproduced. Perhaps my focus on the social logic teaches us more about why people *cannot* unlearn racism rather than about how they can. While this message may be frustrating, it must be counted as progress too.

Racism's Last Word

South Africa has not always been a symbol of moral transformation. At the end of the twentieth century, the world viewed South Africa as the epitome of racism. The French philosopher Jacques Derrida called it "racism's last word."[5] The United Nations called apartheid a crime against humanity. Apartheid South Africa became the embodiment of a racist state, for the most part as a result of the largest antiracism movement in the world: the global anti-apartheid movement. In the 1970s and 1980s, this movement turned the apartheid regime into the outcast of the international community. The decades-long movement was successful in withdrawing US investment from apartheid South Africa. In the end, this disinvestment campaign helped to pressure the South African government under President F. W. de Klerk to embark on negotiations that ultimately led to the dismantling of the apartheid system.

Despite their more recent differences, the United States and South Africa share a long history of colonial settlement, slavery, civil war, and White supremacy. Both countries were colonized by European powers, which dominated indigenous populations and instituted systems of slavery. During the nineteenth century, each country embarked on a civil war in part about the fate of slavery. After the civil wars, the warring White factions achieved reconciliation over the backs of Black people as each country reconstructed a racist system based on White supremacy: Jim Crow segregation emerged in the United States and Afrikaner nationalists implemented apartheid. American sociologist Pierre van de Berghe has described these as *Herrenvolk democracies*, countries democratic for the master race but tyrannical for subordinate groups.[6]

What is distinctly different about the two countries is also important for understanding unlearning racism: White people have always remained a small minority in South Africa. When White capital tried to develop both countries into industrial nations, South Africa did not have an abundance of White workers and thus continued to rely on the coercion of African labor to succeed. In 1900, the White minority consisted of 20 percent of the population; by 2000, this segment had shrunk to just 5 percent.

The consequence of remaining a minority was that Whites in South Africa were able to lift all Whites out of poverty, but this came at a much greater cost. Apartheid was a far more pervasive system of control over nonwhite people in South Africa than segregation in the American South. Apartheid was a system of institutionalized racial segregation that existed in South Africa from 1948 until 1990. Via the National Party (NP), Afrikaner nationalists ensured that White citizens had the highest status in a rigid racial structure of stratification, followed in descending order by Asians, Coloureds (mixed-race people), and Blacks. Racial segregation had a much longer history in South Africa than official apartheid, or *apartness*, but this new arrangement extended segregation to the whole of society and organized racial relations, rights, and privileges through a series of legislative acts. There was "petty apartheid" and "grand apartheid," two systems that coexisted. The first entailed the segregation of public amenities and events—a system roughly similar to the Jim Crow laws in the American South—but grand apartheid, which included ethnic cleansing and the deportation of millions of South Africans, rested on a different racial logic. Grand apartheid was a unique and violent system that tried to control nearly every facet of life and severely limited the personal and political freedom of millions of Black South Africans. And grand apartheid was enforced with brute force.

To create the illusion that Whites were the majority in South Africa while still using Black labor, nationalists forcefully removed 3.5 million people from cities and the countryside. The "Bantu population," the apartheid term for Black South Africans, were to live in nine newly created "Bantustans," which together encompassed only 13 percent of South Africa's land surface. Additionally, the apartheid government curtailed the movement of nonwhites through a pass laws system. The new "Black nations," another term for Bantustans, each had its own "ethnic minority" with its own culture, political system, and economy, but in reality these nations were engineered to be wholly reliant on White South Africa. White supremacy was cast as the "separate development" of nations. In this sense, South Africa had its own version of "separate but equal," the American legal doctrine that justified racial segregation in the American South. South African sociologist Harold Wolpe called apartheid "racialism without racism," a system of racially defined discrimination and exploitation (racialism) not justified through an ideology of racial superiority (racism) but through cultural difference.[7]

Economically, apartheid was extremely beneficial to White South Africans. Although not all Whites profited in the same way from this system of racial and economic exploitation, they all benefited. By the late 1980s, South Africa was one of the most unequal countries in the world. The White upper class that accounted for 12 percent of the population earned 45 percent of the national income.[8] In urban areas, White South Africans lived in neighborhoods that were physically separated from the rest of the population.[9] White neighborhoods were prosperous, with good municipal infrastructure, while everybody else lived in poorly serviced areas known as townships, with dilapidated and inadequate infrastructure and where poverty, drugs, and gangs were rife. The population density of Black townships was up to sixty times higher than that of White suburbs.[10] Moreover, 30 percent of the population lived below the international poverty line of two dollars a day.

When Nelson Mandela was released from prison in 1990, the image of South Africa began to change radically: the country came to symbolize the possibility of change and an end to racism. Mandela both embodied it and proselytized it. In 1993, Mandela and de Klerk were each awarded the Nobel Peace Prize. "South Africa has been the symbol of racially conditioned suppression," the Nobel committee said. "Mandela and de Klerk's constructive policy of peace and reconciliation also points the way to the peaceful resolution of similar deep-rooted conflicts elsewhere in the world."[11] Many saw South Africa's first free election a year later, which elected Mandela as president, a triumph of democracy and the beginning of a transformation—of unlearning racism.

A South African Idea

Given this history, what does unlearning racism mean to South Africans today? Some people feel they have unlearned racism if they no longer use *kaffir*, the Afrikaans equivalent of the American "n-word." Other people argue that socializing with co-workers of color counts as unlearning racism. And yet others seem to imply that what symbolizes their change is a new belief in South Africa's cultural diversity. Individually, South Africans present a great variety of stories, but they agree that unlearning racism is a collective challenge, and they share three specific narratives about how it works.

Truth and Reconciliation Committee

The first is the Truth and Reconciliation Committee (TRC). South Africa installed a court-like restorative justice body after apartheid as part of the political compromise between de Klerk's National Party (NP) and Mandela's African National Congress (ANC). Its goal was to expose the apartheid regime's gross, systematic violations of human rights and contribute to healing in South African society and to the construction of a new, shared national identity. Indeed, the hearings between 1996 and 1998 revealed the racist crimes and brutality of the apartheid regime, as well as the official web of government lies and deception officials spun to conceal it. The premise of the TRC's work was that truth could heal a divided nation; its work was seen as complementary to political negotiations and settlement. Archbishop Desmond Tutu, chairman of the TRC, credits its work with providing a framework for the cultural and moral restructuring of South African society.[12]

The TRC presents one way of thinking about unlearning racism in South Africa: the idea that Whites would change by "coming to terms" with the crimes of the past. This idea of confronting historical atrocities has its origins in the thinking of German sociologist Theodor Adorno. He argued that after the Second World War, the Germans were unable to move forward because they had not addressed the crimes of their past.[13] Postwar Germany figured as an important reference point, and the ANC leadership consciously modeled the TRC as an alternative to the justice-by-trial in Nuremberg after the Second World War in Germany. Indeed, reconciliation, forgiveness, and *ubuntu*—the Nguni Bantu term meaning "humanity" or "I am because we are"—became powerful new ideas for imagining a new beginning for all South Africans.[14]

When the limits of the TRC's approach to addressing racial inequality became clear—it failed to effectively deal with reparations to victims of apartheid—the country looked to the United States for inspiration. At the official presentation of the final report in 1998, South Africa's deputy president, Thabo Mbeki, expressed his frustration with the TRC's inability to address apartheid's systemic racism and the continuing inequality. In his "two nations" speech, he decried the continued racial inequality in South Africa, borrowing a metaphor from the American political scientist Andrew Hacker, who a few years earlier had described the United States as a country of two nations: one White and rich, the other Black and poor.[15] When President Mbeki succeeded Mandela in 1999, he borrowed another American idea. Inspired by President Clinton, he launched a yearlong effort: "Combating Racism: A Nation in Dialogue." At the conference that concluded the year, Mbeki said: "If White South Africa is fearful of the future because of what it might lose, Black South Africa looks forward to the future because of what it will gain."

White without Whiteness

The South African writer Njabulo Ndebele offered the idea of Whiteness as an alternative way to think about racism and the challenge of unlearning it. He was among the many critics of the ANC's politicization of racism in the South African political context. The ANC was in power—President Mbeki received 66 percent of the popular vote in 1999—but the focus on racism reduced the party to complainants, he said, as if it had no capacity to act. In the 1970s, Ndebele had been part of the Black Consciousness Movement (BCM). This student movement, led by Steve Biko, called on Black South Africans to fight apartheid independently from White people and to build a positive Black identity.[16] Ndebele contended that the focus on racism after 1999 often served political expedience rather than concern about Black lives. He criticized the ANC but simultaneously called on White South Africans to change their "culture of Whiteness." For him, this process was fundamentally about finding a home in Africa. White South Africans needed to come out from under the umbrella of global Whiteness. Following Ndebele, the writer Antjie Krog also cautioned against the political uses of racism. In *Country of My Skull*, her highly acclaimed book about the TRC, Krog had emphasized the need for White South Africans like herself to change, because apartheid's perpetrators were, as she put it, men of her race.[17]

Ndebele's and Krog's ideas of deconstructing Whiteness and reconstructing what it means to belong in Africa suggest that we might define unlearning racism as becoming White without Whiteness, as White South African without the ideology of Whiteness.[18] Krog sees it as a process of cultural and corporal change. She uses the extraordinary image of the sole—*tong*, or tonguefish, in Afrikaans—to capture the depth of transformation that is needed. As the sole matures, it experiences a metamorphosis: one eye migrates from one flank to the other; its skeletal structure changes; its nasal and gill openings shift position; and on its upper side a dark pigmentation develops.[19] In her second book, *A Change of Tongue*, the tonguefish reference reflects her poetic sense of the need for a new cultural vocabulary. However, the fish's physical adjustment also points to her emphasis on corporal transformation: how to make the body and skin compatible with South Africa's new reality. For Krog, Whiteness is in the way you walk and gesticulate—it is embodied—but it is also in your words and thoughts. She feels her Whiteness is inextricably linked to her Afrikaner culture and identity. Hence, she closely scrutinizes her cultural and emotional reflexes. She consistently emphasizes in her work the need to learn and unlearn.

What does White without Whiteness look like, specifically in Africa? In *Begging to Be Black*, the final book of her transformation trilogy, Krog finds resolution in the "Blackening" of her Whiteness, in which Blackness stands for Africanness. Her belonging in Africa, she realizes, is conditioned on her efforts but also on the acceptance of Black Africans. She writes: "I want to be part of the country I was born in. I need to know whether it is possible for somebody like me to become like the majority, to become 'blacker'? And live as a full and at-ease component of the South African psyche."[20] In the African context, Krog claims, divesting from

"Whiteness" can be thought of as moving toward "Blackness." Just as the African American writer Toni Morrison claimed that American means White in the United States—American identity was White, according to Morrison, because its ideals only applied to White people—Krog contends that African means Black in South Africa.[21] Krog does not seek a Black identity by becoming "Blacker," in the American sense, but she wants to learn a more African way of understanding and belonging in Africa. For Krog, White without Whiteness means to truly belong in Africa.

Nonracialism

Nonracialism is the third way in which South Africans understand unlearning racism. It is an antiracist ideology that developed in the 1950s and confronted how the apartheid state constructed races, nations, cultures, and ethnicities to justify apartheid.[22] As American political scientist Michael MacDonald explains, Afrikaner nationalists initially described apartheid's racial logic as racialism, as if it had nothing to do with racial stratification.[23] Apartheid was supposedly not based on White superiority, as segregation policies had explicitly been previously, but on Africans being racially and, later, culturally "different."[24] Total segregation would provide Africans with "full opportunities" to develop according to their "own" cultural norms. Racialism was a cynical manipulation of American anthropologist Franz Boas's theory of cultural relativism: the idea that all peoples have equally developed cultures. Opponents to apartheid understood how Afrikaner racism was not primarily rooted in personal psychology or social relations but in state power. Nonracialism meant the undoing of apartheid's racism. Opponents of apartheid targeted its underlying logic of racialization. They knew racism continuously reinvents itself to justify and mask state practices to legitimize racial inequality.

In South Africa's post-liberation political order, nonracialism remains a popular term, but South Africans struggle to define its meaning or use its legacy effectively for unlearning racism. Mandela made a strong political push to have it included it in South Africa's new constitution, adopted in 1996, where the term is only implicitly defined as formal equality before the law. The ANC struggled to further develop nonracialism beyond a vague sense of antiracism and formal equality.[25] Moreover, this ANC ideal did not prevent it from using apartheid racial categories after apartheid to promote affirmative action programs and other policies to achieve "racial equity." Opposition parties like the Democratic Alliance co-opted nonracialism for their own brand of color blindness, which stressed the dangers of racially based redress policies. Academics have interpreted nonracialism abstractly, as doing away with all racial categories and race thinking, thereby focusing on the literal meaning of nonracialism and not on its original function as an antiracist ideology. It is commonly used to celebrate diversity and multiracial democracy, and its connotation of antiracism—its rejection of racism and racialism—has been lost.[26]

However, nonracialism has been challenged from various directions, most prominently by the Rhodes Must Fall movement in 2015. This student movement presented a withering critique of South Africans' ideas about reconciliation, racism, and nonracialism that had taken hold after 1994. The young activists emphasized the unequal outcomes of Mandela's project of racial reconciliation. They critiqued the "everyday racism" at the university—to use Dutch sociologist Philomena Essed's term—at the supposedly transformed liberal institutions such as the University of Cape Town. They saw the ideal of a nonracial society used to promote color-blind racism and falsely claim that race no longer mattered after apartheid. They called for decolonization of their university and challenged academics who thought abolishing the concept of race could effectively fight post-apartheid racism. They drew on Biko and on anticolonial scholar Frantz Fanon to racialize the South African debate about inequality. For the new generation, naming Blackness and Whiteness was seen as essential to understanding the experience of racism and to effectively fight against it. They popularized a number of new concepts, such as Black pain, to challenge White South Africans about the continuing problem of racism in the country.

The wake-up call of the protest movement drew its force from the continuing high levels of economic and racial inequality in South Africa, despite twenty years of democracy. Since 2014, South Africa has been officially ranked as the most unequal country in the world.[27] White South Africans' lifetime work-related earnings on average are four times higher than for Africans.[28] The number of South Africans living under the international poverty line has remained at 30 percent since 1994.

The Rhodes Must Fall movement grasped an essential truth about the struggle against apartheid: As an antiracist slogan, nonracialism had a function, not just a meaning. The anti-apartheid movement adopted it strategically to expose and undermine apartheid's racist logic of "racialism without racism." The Rhodes Must Fall movement understood that after apartheid, new kinds of racism must be met with new antiracist strategies. Nonracialism needed a living legacy, not a dead orthodoxy. While racism was no longer rooted in state power, it had reinvented itself in other social structures, like the education system and the economy. The Rhodes Must Fall movement exposed the limits of how South Africa had thought about unlearning racism after apartheid. To understand the true liberatory potential of nonracialism, we must analyze the process of unlearning racism anew.

The Social Logic of Unlearning Racism

Unlearning racism is a dangerous idea. We must not be naïve about claims of having unlearned racism and White people's potential ability to reinvent it. As I listened to White South Africans, I found a complex and uneven portrait of the transformation from apartheid to democracy. The White minority acknowledges that they will never have political dominance again and that they must adapt to being a less powerful minority. I heard many who felt that their skin color forever ties them to a history of racial domination and privilege. They benefited from a structurally unfair system, and they feel stigmatized by it. But they do not see themselves as bad people and want to feel good about being White and South African. The risk for White South Africans unlearning racism is thinking they have already moved beyond it.

Unlearning racism can only be analyzed together with newly emerging racist ideologies and structures of post-apartheid South Africa. Racism is foundational to South Africa, but it has also changed in character over time. Racism is about the relationship between the cultural aspects—racist beliefs and meanings—and structures of racial domination, as Fanon wrote.[29] During apartheid, the Black liberation movement thus understood racism as always changing. They analyzed racism from a cultural perspective: as a concept to be understood ideologically in the relationship between cultural meanings and societal institutions. Their ideology of nonracialism was born out of the acknowledgment that their antiracism strategies could only be successful if they challenged how racism continuously renews itself.

Whiteness is a helpful term by which to analyze unlearning racism. The problem is that Whiteness in South Africa is more than a racial identity and a way of knowing the world. Whiteness has historically become meaningful because it is based on relations of power. As American legal scholar Cheryl Harris has argued, Whiteness is a social construct, predicated on White dominance and Black subordination.[30] During apartheid, Whiteness meant full citizenship and economic security, offering employment guarantees, protection from poverty, and capitalist exploitation. Even to Whites without power, money, or influence, Whiteness offered the psychological benefit of feeling superior and secure. These wages of Whiteness (to use American sociologist W. E. B. Du Bois's term) were available to all White South Africans regardless of class position. Whiteness after apartheid might no longer be sanctioned by state power, but whether it continues to be anchored in institutions such as the economy or education remains an open question. South African scholars' treatment of Whiteness as a substitute for racism fails to acknowledge their interrelationship.[31] Whiteness gives White people a stake in racism; this is what makes unlearning racism hard.[32]

White South Africans' experiments with unlearning racism offer us a look at the risks, possibilities, and limits of this idea. My starting point is how South Africans imagined unlearning racism—collectively and individually—but I use my sociological toolkit to analyze it. Exposing the perils of misunderstanding nonracialism is thus as important as exploring the possibilities of rethinking unlearning racism through Whiteness. Determining who is unlearning racism and where unlearning transitions into reinventing racism might teach us an important lesson about how we must or must not imagine unlearning racism, and how we can move forward from it.

This book is the first ethnographic study of White South Africans after apartheid. During my three years in South Africa, I spent many months living with, talking to, and observing White South Africans. As I visited schools, neighborhoods, and workplaces, and interviewed more than 150 South Africans, I explored how White South Africans confronted the legacy of apartheid in their daily lives. For all their different views and opinions, what ties them together is that societal forces, such as the economy, urban structures, and educational institutions, shape their struggle with race.

Unlearning racism, I found, is a social process. It is not about a "change of heart." It does not happen at a single moment or in a specific place. It is something people do together and is shaped by structural and cultural forces—but not determined by it. People's racial knowledge, beliefs, and outlook develop in interactions with others and their context.

The story begins in 2000, when most scholarship on the political transition in South Africa ends.[33] By the late 1990s, South Africans viewed the democratic changes in 1994 as an elite transition from apartheid to neoliberalism, through which Whites continued their economic dominance. The White elite had forced the ANC to give up its socialist program and adopt economic policies that sustained the privilege of the White minority. In 1998, the ANC government launched a new, ambitious program of Black Economic Empowerment (BEE) and affirmative action, a color-conscious program to redress apartheid's inequalities and redistribute wealth. It defined all nonwhite people as "Black people."[34]

To examine the structural forces that affect people's ability to unlearn, I analyzed institutional change and White South Africans in the settings of their work, home, and school, as I wanted to know how unlearning racism might be different for individuals depending on the institutional setting. Sociologists have argued that people experience race and racism differently in the political, work, and educational spheres, where relationships are hierarchical, as opposed to their neighborhoods and families, where relationships are more equal.[35] But we know little about how these different institutional spheres interact in people's lives. To understand the cultural forces at work, I analyzed the public debate and the private narratives developed by White organizations that represent White people's collective interests. Unlearning racism is not a moment of "seeing the light."[36] To appreciate its social logic, we must analyze the structural and cultural basis of this process.

This book pushes back against the dominant *individual therapeutic model* of unlearning racism. Black feminists, such as bell hooks, have expressed their skepticism about the impact of this model because of its focus on a cathartic experience.[37] I challenge the idea that unlearning racism can only be thought of as an act of willpower or an intentional process that people walk through individually and willingly (it cannot be forced upon people).[38] However, history teaches us that this is a false belief: people have often confronted the challenge of unlearning racism by necessity. I do not dismiss the power of personal narratives of transformation. American educator Mark Warren effectively mined them in *Fire in the Heart: How White Activists Embrace Racial Justice* for powerful lessons on how change happens.[39] These stories are revealing, but the narrow focus on seminal experiences tells us that individuals unlearning racism is not enough for racism to cease to exist.

The title of this book asks how we can unlearn racism because it must also be a collective question. This book does not offer an alternative *social model* of unlearning racism. Instead, I provide a careful assessment of unlearning racism as a sociological idea and evaluate the success and limitations of South Africa's experiments with unlearning racism as a society. Unlearning racism always happens through the interplay of societal forces and individual choices, as well as along race, class, and gender lines. I could only conclude that different collectivities struggled differently to unlearn racism and with various degrees of success. I also discovered newly emerging forms of racism beyond White nationalism.

Beyond White Nationalism

South Africa allows us to think about Whiteness beyond White nationalism, an ideology that remains dominant in the West.[40] Afrikaner nationalism has long been analyzed as an ethnic movement, not a White movement. In this study, I emphasize how Afrikaner nationalism was constructed on top of an ideology of White supremacy.[41] Nationalists used ethnicity and Whiteness to unify people, but they did not always succeed. To outsiders, the White nationalism of Afrikaner nationalism often appeared unified, but in fact it never was: it was fragmented, although nationalists worked hard to make it whole. White nationalism was deeply divided along racial, class, and gender lines. It never captured—as a unitary ideological belief—White South Africans' racist beliefs, as it meant different things to different groups of Whites. Despite the divisions, White nationalism served to bind and protect Whiteness by force and uplift. To analyze unlearning racism after apartheid, we must understand the making and unmaking of White nationalism.

Afrikaner nationalism was a successful intellectual movement in the early and mid-twentieth century that turned a diverse group of Afrikaans-speaking South Africans into a White ethnic group who called themselves *Afrikaners* (which is Afrikaans for "Africans") to express their allegiance to Africa. It promoted a nationalist identity for all Afrikaans-speaking South Africans—at least those whom they deemed White. Through its newspapers and other outlets, the movement created an imagined community of Afrikaners with a heroic past and a moral purpose. The National Party won the 1948 elections in part because they opposed South Africa's involvement in the Second World War against Nazi Germany, but also because they proposed apartheid as a more rigorous solution to what White South Africans termed the "Native Question."[42]

Sociologists invented apartheid. As I learned while writing this book, many leading South African social scientists in the nationalist movement were trained in the Netherlands (where I was born). The South African sociologist Geoff Cronjé received his PhD at the University of Amsterdam in the Netherlands in 1932.[43] The South African writer J. M. Coetzee called him "the mind of apartheid," a reference to his ideological influence and his manic obsession with preventing "race mixture" in South Africa.[44] Cronjé earned a reputation as a *rassesosioloog*, or race sociologist, and he remained influential throughout his career, leading various government committees in the 1950s. Hendrik F. Verwoerd, the architect of apartheid, was a Dutch-born sociologist.[45] As South African president in the 1960s, Verwoerd greatly expanded apartheid, after he first designed it as minister of native affairs in the 1950s. Before he was a full-time politician, however, Verwoerd was the first professor of sociology in South Africa at Stellenbosch University. Scientific racism has its roots in anthropology, but sociologists created, designed, and executed apartheid.

The global rise of social science was steeped in White supremacist thinking. What has been obscured by academic debates in South Africa over Verwoerd's explicit distaste for racial eugenics in American sociology and Cronjé's specific admiration for Nazi Germany is how racism in Afrikaner nationalism took a specific form that was rooted in racist assumptions at the heart of modern sociology.[46] In the 1920s, so-called White men's countries saw the problem of "White poverty"—a seemingly benign but deeply racialized cause—through the lens of global Whiteness and anxieties about racial domination. In the United States, this White anxiety translated into White solidarity through philanthropic projects from the Carnegie and Rockefeller Foundations.[47] Scholars have pointed specifically to the study of Carnegie's *Commission of Investigation on the Poor White Question* for its role in shoring up global Whiteness through American support to South Africa's White nationalism.[48] American Africanist Tiffany Willoughby-Herard has demonstrated how social scientists, sponsored by foundations, used the poor White problem to manufacture Whiteness and racialize ethnic, class, and gender identities.[49] These scholars used the racial logic of White vulnerability, which constructed poor Whites living in mixed neighborhoods as a cultural anomaly that needed to be separated, disciplined, and economically lifted up.

Afrikaner nationalists turned this global Whiteness project into their own racist dream of dominating nonwhite people and disciplining poor White people. They co-opted *the* poor Whites to make them *their* poor Whites.[50] Nationalists could not see poverty without seeing race; their concerns consistently interwove Whiteness with class. The worst thing that could happen to a poor White person, they claimed, was losing their Whiteness. They wanted to unite different economic groups in their political coalition—commercial farmers, industrialists, businessmen, and organized labor—and the "poor White problem" proved a potent mobilizing issue. As a political project, it allowed Afrikaners to tie ethnic mobilization and their ambiguous Whiteness to a robust American Whiteness, the rising symbol of global Whiteness. Nationalists like Verwoerd saw poor Whites, who often lived in mixed neighborhoods in close proximity to nonwhites, as evidence that White society was vulnerable to disintegration. They were a source of embarrassment, shame, and guilt.[51] The

Carnegie Commission offered nationalists an opportunity to turn their White shame into nationalist pride. Their mission became to prevent poor White Afrikaners from "degenerating" toward Blackness, first by advocating state intervention, social welfare, and apartheid laws to separate the races, and later by executing government policies. Ultimately, apartheid's racial categories would solidify race as a matter of social standing and way of life—mixing Whiteness with class.[52]

Afrikaner nationalism became synonymous with White male interests and aspirations. Nationalism was about *het Volk*, the people; the Afrikaner family was thought of as its cornerstone, and the "Afrikaner man" its steadfast and noble patriarch. National manhood as an ideal of citizenship was built on intersecting ideas about nation, race, class, and gender. In 1938, Afrikaner nationalists staged the one-hundred-year celebration of the Great Trek, commemorating the time of White settlement of South Africa's interior, with a large ethnic festival that included wagons named after each male *Voortrekker* leader. In the 1940s and 1950s, Cronjé continued to reach back to the masculine ideal of the *Voortrekker*. This noble patriarch embodied to him "the highest spiritual values of the young and energetic Boer nation": morality, *Volk* pride, racial consciousness, and love of freedom.[53] Cronjé also identified threats to the patriarchal family structure. One danger threatening the morality of the *Volk*, the stability of the family, and the economic standing of the Afrikaner man was alcoholism.[54] Specifically, alcohol abuse among poor White men living in mixed neighborhoods led to a special kind of male deviancy: *rasvermenging*, or miscegenation. Cronjé warned against *gelykvoeling*, or feelings of equality with nonwhites. The thinking of these nationalist sociologists demonstrates how racialized their nationalist concerns were about the social problems of poverty, family structure, and manhood. To apartheid sociologists, all social problems were ultimately racial problems.

South Africa defined unlearning racism as a national challenge, but this does not mean that White Afrikaans-speaking South Africans relate to this challenge in the same way. Race, class, and gender intersect in unlearning racism. White nationalism is no longer a political movement after apartheid, but it continues to exercise its power through the way it has shaped the cultural archive. Afrikaner nationalism tied race, class, and gender closely together, with race being its firm foundation. The unraveling of nationalism exposed the racial, class, and gender interests and identities along which it was constructed. Ideologies of Whiteness and patriarchy at the heart of Afrikaner nationalism have become visible. After apartheid, he who used to be called *the Afrikaner* has become a *White, Afrikaans-speaking, upper- or lower-class man*. What it means to be a White man has changed. Given White people's possessive investment in Whiteness—the way apartheid produced tangible material results for people who imagined themselves to be White—this ideology might be harder to unmake than nationalism. South African scholars such as Krog emphasize that Whiteness is lived through culture and ethnicity. This idea challenges popular American notions of Whiteness as nothingness. American race scholars argue that Whiteness has been so long the unmarked default in the United States that White Americans struggle to give it meaning. If in South Africa Whiteness and ethnicity first need to be disentangled, as Krog suggests, this also raises questions about whether the end goal of unlearning racism must be the abolition of Whiteness. Thinking beyond White nationalism means we must be open to the possibility of a new kind of Whiteness.

South Africa has always been a bellwether for how racism developed globally. The worldwide fascination with "the Afrikaners" continues to present a distorted picture of Afrikaner nationalism, which mythologizes its origins, exoticizes its tribalism, and mystifies how Afrikaners' rivalry with the British Empire rested on White supremacist logic. This allows American and European scholars in particular to portray Afrikaners as different and distant from themselves. As a European-trained sociologist working in the United States, I ask in this book what South Africa can teach us about Whiteness. South Africa must not be analyzed through the lens of exceptionalism. Afrikaners are like us—they are like you and me. This is why I ask: *Can we unlearn racism?*

Unlearning racism is a challenge confronting Whites around the world, but post-apartheid South Africa provides a unique lens by means of which to analyze it. In the 1990s, the country captured the world's imagination because of the promise that change and transformation were possible. Moving beyond White nationalism, South Africa helps us understand the trappings, trajectory, and challenges of unlearning racism. If we understand what it means to unlearn racism and the various barriers and pathways each step poses, we will have important lessons for the global fight against racism in a world where racism still dominates much of the economy, education, housing, and culture. Indeed, US history provides an example of how racism persists even when structural changes attack its roots. The civil rights era brought about a revolution in race relationships in the 1960s, but segregationists preserved and refined segregation through White flight with dire consequences for the Black minority. The first Black president of the United States, Barack Obama, embodied hope and change for the twentieth-first century, but the populist White nationalism of President Donald Trump dashed any dreams of a postracial future. During critical periods in American history, racism was reinvented but not unlearned.

From Unlearning Race to Unlearning Racism

To sociologists, a focus on racism as something that can be unlearned might come as a surprise. The disciplinary tradition is to focus on racism as a social problem. As there is a long tradition of American sociologists studying race and racism, Black sociologists such as W. E. B. Du Bois were at the helm of this movement, motivated by Black liberation and the moral impetus to end racism. Sociologists studying race and racism have been concerned variously with racist ideology and its history, racial inequality and its origins, and the various forms of institutional racism in housing, education, the law, the labor markets, and other institutions. Most race scholars in the United Sates conclude that racism is reproduced and transmitted to the next generation. The ostensible absence of the process of unlearning racism in the United States seems to legitimize scholars' lack of attention to the process.[55]

South Africa provides the promise of a different story about racism, a story rooted in the long history of the ideology of nonracialism in the anti-apartheid movement. It was sustained through the global antiracism movement against apartheid, which helped to end the last White supremacist regime in South Africa. It continued during the hopeful days of a mostly peaceful transition to democracy and the adoption of a new South

African constitution that firmly expressed the country's commitment to nonracialism. The TRC further solidified the narrative of a country on an exceptional path in coming to terms with its racist past and working toward racial reconciliation. This process of reconciliation also provided an important contrast with the United States' racial history. In South Africa, the White minority handed over political power. They will never enjoy political dominance again—they must now adapt. South Africa's political project was unthinkable without the belief that unlearning racism was possible.

Despite the appeal of this story, sociologists have been hesitant to examine the idea of unlearning racism. After apartheid, the ideas of change and transformation were central themes in the academic literature on South Africa.[56] However, few South African scholars directly connected the possibility of change with the question of racism. For some sociologists class has become more important than race after apartheid. Scholars inspired by Marxism argue that the dividing line in South African society is no longer the color line but the class line.[57] The political economist Patrick Bond, who served in Mandela's government, speaks of the shift from racial apartheid to class apartheid.

Scholars who focus on race tend to emphasize racial identities over racism. At the conference "The Burden of Race? 'Whiteness' and 'Blackness' in Modern South Africa" in 2001—the first South African conference specifically focused on race—all presentations were on racial categorization and not a single one on racism. It is race that is presented as a burden and not racism.[58] Researchers prefer to explore the possibility of new forms of political, ethnic, and racial identity rather than new forms of racism.[59] If racism is addressed, academics argue that it has become a contested concept and too vague to use analytically.[60] One exception at the "Burden of Race" conference was South African sociologist Xolela Mangcu, who argues that there is nothing necessarily undesirable about "race thinking" and talked the conference organizers into adding a question mark to the conference title. Mangcu, who works within the Black Consciousness tradition, argues that in a nonracial society, "race" should be celebrated as the basis of positive social and cultural identities.[61] However, the majority of South African academics emphasize unlearning race rather than unlearning racism. They take a utopian approach in their efforts to imagine a nonracial society without race.[62]

The exception has been academics who looked at White South Africans after apartheid through the lens of Whiteness.[63] Whiteness scholars turned the spotlight on a group of people who had previously endorsed the racist ideology of White supremacy, reversing a general academic tradition that saw race primarily as a trait of nonwhite people. During apartheid, the leader of the Black Consciousness Movement (BCM), Steve Biko, had already chided White liberals, whose "natural passport to the exclusive pool of White privileges" made them unreliable allies.[64] Black liberation theologists had questioned whether White allies were motivated by White salvation or Black liberation.[65] South African writer J. M. Coetzee introduced Whiteness in *White Writing* as "the concerns of people no longer European, not yet African."[66] However, South African scholars also followed American scholars who had focused on the social construction of Whiteness in the United States, as an ideology and identity of racial superiority—constructed to justify discrimination against nonwhites.[67] After apartheid, the study of Whiteness allowed scholars to explore the subjective experiences and meaning-making practices of White South Africans as they confronted racial democracy. As a concept, it offered a new way to analyze White people's agency and intent, and to conceptualize change.

As South Africa's way to theorize unlearning racism, the promise of Whiteness as analytical concept must not be undone by replacing racism with Whiteness, because they are not the same. American political scientist Ashley Jardina has demonstrated that the way in which White Americans think and feel about their Whiteness is distinct from how they think about racism.[68] Yet this claim obscures how Whiteness and racism are intertwined beyond the individual level and how at the social level it is their relationship that is interesting. Racism is defined by an asymmetry of power, not an equal relationship between "Whiteness" and "Blackness." Whiteness, American historian Barbara Fields writes, must be analyzed in the context of society's racial order and the work that is being done by White people to maintain it. Similarly, American sociologist Joe Feagin argues we must analyze how White people think about themselves (Whiteness) together with how they think about Black people (racism), while not losing sight of the systemic and foundational aspects of this White worldview.[69] For the United States, Feagin finds the White worldview to be stable across time. The question I raise is whether White South Africans' Whiteness ideology might have changed since the end of apartheid.

To analyze the changing meaning of Whiteness and racism, I use *racial formation theory* in this study. American sociologists Michael Omi and Howard Winant's starting point is that "race" is a social construction, an unstable complex of cultural meanings that is always changing because of political contestation. They introduce the concept of "racial formation" to capture "the socio-historical process by which racial categories are created, inhabited, transformed, and destroyed."[70] The state, they argue, plays a central role in shaping racial categories, meanings, and realities, although it is not the only site of struggle. Different actors try to politically and legally reorganize the state through "racial projects," a concept that captures how organizations, institutions, and state agencies together or alone advocate or resist racial policies and practices. Unquestionably, racial formation theory is applicable to South Africa. During apartheid, the country had a rigid system of racial categorization, and the ANC government continued to use apartheid's racial classifications for its color-conscious policies of affirmative action and Black economic empowerment to achieve racial redress. I use racial formation theory to analyze how Whiteness as a racial category changes meaning over time, but I also use Winant's suggestion to combine the concepts of Whiteness and racial project into "White racial project" to analyze how formerly Whites-only organizations shape and resist racial policies.

What I add to this theory is that I also analyze struggles over the meaning of racism after apartheid.[71] American historian Ibram X. Kendi argues that Americans' limited definition of racism was a result of a concerted effort by the conservative movement to narrow the meaning of racism, and that we must identify those whose interest it is to actively produce restricted definitions of racism.[72] In South Africa, racism had also become contested.[73] The struggle over the meaning of racism is intense because of the ANC government but also because South Africa has hate-speech laws. In the United States, the First Amendment to the US Constitution protects free speech. In South Africa hate speech is specifically excluded from the protection of free speech in the constitution. Because the South African state and its affiliated institutions have this active role, political contestation after apartheid about racism has been particularly intense.

The New Racism: White Identity Politics

South Africa's White minority after apartheid adopted the language of "White identity politics" to articulate new claims about Whiteness and racism in the public sphere. I use this term to conceptualize how White South Africans, through White racial projects, have strategically politicized their collective White identity and adopted the language of marginalized communities. Paradoxically, White South Africans tried to normalize Whiteness as visible, assertive, and embodied by using the particularistic language of identity politics. White identity politics must be understood not as unlearning but as a newly emerging form of racism. This new racism can be defined as the promotion of White racial self-interest though the downplaying of White privilege, racial inequality, and institutional racism. People who practice White identity politics claim that White people have an equal right to protect the collective interests of their own group. However, the argument that White people are a normal group—like all other ethnic and racial groups—is strategically used to deny, mask, and minimize the existence of White privilege. White South Africans purportedly have unlearned racism through the normalization of Whiteness, but instead defend their privileged position in this new way.

Scholars claim that Whiteness in South Africa became visible and marked after apartheid. It is more accurate, however, to say that Whiteness became differently visible and marked after apartheid. Afrikaner nationalism was always visibly White nationalism, despite the apartheid government's efforts to hide it. What happened after apartheid with Afrikaner nationalism is that the White minority adopted the language of White identity politics to articulate their claims in the public sphere. White men learned to manage their newfound visibility and embodiment through positioning it in the public sphere as traumatized, injured, and in pain—a language borrowed from the identity politics of marginalized groups. The practitioners of White identity politics want to make White identity legitimate again, at a time when Whiteness has become synonymous with racism. They are focused on the cultural rather than the political sphere, so as not to be defined as overtly political and invite scrutiny. They claim that every group—including the White group—has a unique history and the right to affirm their collective identity and defend their self-interests. White identity politics has overtaken Afrikaner nationalism as the dominant form of racial politics.

White groups use White identity politics to assert Whiteness as normal and go on the political offensive. All White groups normalize Whiteness, but there are similarities and differences between elite and populist discourses, which become visible if their different forms of White identity politics are compared.[74] What is similar is that the elite and working-class White organizations both reach back to the time before apartheid to structure their White racial project, as if a more innocent Whiteness can be recovered from South Africa's days of racial segregation. What is different is that the White elite practice White identity politics by strategically accommodating racial integration through embracing selected members of the nonwhite elite. The populist White working-class Solidarity Movement uses the strategy of "White minoritization" to culturally refashion the White population as a minority that is vulnerable and threatened. White people have always been numerically a small minority in South Africa. But populists use this demographic fact to culturally adopt the language of marginalized minorities to defend White privilege. This populist move tries to increase legitimacy through soliciting sympathy. It highlights the defenselessness of White bodies and downplays White privilege and racial inequality. Paradoxically, populists present the White minority as victims of the new democracy—not the perpetrators of White supremacy in the past—to make new political claims about their needs and rights. They claim that their minority must be treated like all other minority groups who defend their self-interest, while demanding special rights for Whites. Ultimately, all White identity politics is about the transformation of White shame into pride and making White people feel normal again.

As Whiteness became marked in a different way after apartheid, White South Africans felt it differently. Whiteness is about cultural knowledge but also about knowledge in the body.[75] "White embodiment" is a concept I define as the White body's way of "being in the world," to capture how Whiteness is inscribed in the body. White South Africans have long cultivated their Whiteness and racial dominance in physical displays and mannerisms that signal confidence, ease, and entitlement. In post-apartheid South Africa, this White embodiment is challenged in desegregated spaces such as work and school and produces strong feelings. White embodiment pushes the analyses beyond what people say to understand as well what people's feelings tell us about the relationships among institutional racism, Whiteness, and intent. After apartheid, old institutions changed and new institutions were created. Because Whiteness is not only experienced but also exercised inside institutional environments, for example within a gated community, new forms of institutional racism are built on White embodiment.

The idea of White embodiment complicates South African theories that seem to equate unlearning racism with White identity change. The concept of White identity is essential to analyzing White people's intent to unlearn racism. However, White identity change is a necessary but not a sufficient condition for unlearning racism, which entails more than the development of a positive White identity narrative about diversity and multiculturalism. The process of unlearning racism cannot be limited to identity change because Whiteness has deeply shaped people's experience and perspective on their place in the world. Whiteness is an ideology not just an identity. What is needed to unlearn racism is cultural change. Ultimately, unlearning racism is a process deeply tied to White people's sense of superiority and privilege: economically, culturally, and corporally. It is a challenge deeply anchored in White bodies. Twenty-five years after apartheid, the problem of White embodiment is one of the reasons Whiteness has been reinvented as something ordinary.

The rise of White identity politics presents a challenge to the analysis of unlearning racism. Practitioners of White identity politics developed an argument specifically targeted to deflect accusations of Whiteness and racism. One might conclude that White South Africans have unlearned racism, when it comes to the kind of racism that is defined by explicit hate of nonwhites or White supremacy defined as White oppression and domination of other races by state power. As a new ideology of racism, White identity politics is supplanting *color-blind racism*, because in a White minority context it more effectively deflects the charge of racism. Race scholars have demonstrated how racists time and again adopt anti-racist language to reformulate racism. American sociologist Eduardo Bonilla Silva has shown how, after the civil rights movement in the United States, color-blind racism became the dominant racial ideology through which Whites defended the American racial order.[76] This ideology perverted Martin Luther King Jr.'s moral claim that people must be judged by "the content of their character rather than the color of their skin." They used this argument against race-based policies to address racial inequality. In South Africa, color-blind racism briefly seemed to succeed the White nationalism of apartheid, as academics in particular popularized nonracialism-as-color-blind-racism at elite universities.[77] White identity politics is different from color-blind racism in that it stems from a newly articulated, explicitly racialized viewpoint. It equates cultural and political claims of White people with those of other groups. In South Africa, White people no longer have the political power to demand segregation based on culture, nor the authority to impose the color-blind racist argument that race does not matter. Instead, they defend their outsized racial interests by claiming as a group to be similar to everybody else in order to deflect obligations to confront their continuing privilege and dominance.

South Africa is an extreme case of White identity politics, but a closer look at the travails of its White minority provides us with a new perspective on Whiteness and racism in the West. In the United States, Whiteness has long been portrayed as unmarked and invisible. Researchers saw White group identity in the United States as politically less prevalent and less potent as a minority group's sense of identity. Instead, they argued that White Americans rely on color-blind racism to deny racism and White privilege, and opposed policies to address racial inequality. But we might also anticipate a shift in the West when it comes to Whiteness and racism. In the United States, political events such as the presidency of Barack Obama, the Black Lives Matter movement, the rise of Donald Trump, and population projections that Whites will be a minority by 2042 are changing this. Various commentators predict a shift toward new White

American identity politics. The South African case offers rare insights and learning opportunities for the United States and the larger world.

A History of Whiteness

There is a long history of White supremacy in the West using South Africa as an alarm bell for the vulnerability of global White hegemony.[78] In 1893, British-born Australian historian Charles Pearson wrote and published *National Life and Character: A Forecast*, which became an international sensation.[79] In the book, Pearson portrayed the White race as under siege. His apocalyptic predictions became popular around the globe—US president Theodore Roosevelt even wrote Pearson a personal note in praise of his book.[80] Pearson was specifically concerned about political and demographic developments in South Africa. He thought the country was destined to become "Black" and advocated for the White minority to form a united front in order not to lose power. Pearson's book is just one example of a broader literature that focused on the crisis of Whiteness in the world at the dawn of the twentieth century.[81] The rise of White identity politics at the beginning of the twentieth-first century can thus be located in a century-long history of Whiteness in South Africa, in which Whiteness was made and remade.[82]

South Africa only became a true "White man's country" as a result of the South African War between the South African (Boer) Republic (SAR) and Great Britain between 1899 and 1902. In the end, an international coalition led by the United States brokered a peace between the White factions to secure the future of Whiteness in the country. The direct reason for the war was a dispute about the political rights of British citizens living in the SAR, but the underlying cause was Britain's wish to exercise more control over the gold discovered in 1886 in the Boer republics. The dispute also had a racial dimension, as people of color had more rights in the British part of South Africa than in the SAR. During the conflict, especially because of their strong critique of the racial laws in the SAR, the British hinted to Black Africans that they might be rewarded with political rights after the war for their support. Instead, the British and Boers reconciled and made lasting peace by prioritizing White unity and the shared goal of White rule at the cost of the rights of people of color in South Africa.

In 1910, the South African Party led by General Louis Botha came into power and introduced a series of laws that discriminated against nonwhites, institutionalized racism, and laid the foundation for the segregationist policies that would eventually become apartheid. However, Afrikaner nationalists were not satisfied with Botha's government. In 1914, they formed the National Party (NP) with General J. B. M. Herzog as leader in an effort to become independent of the British Empire. Herzog had left Botha's government because he deemed South African interests more important than those of the British Empire and was opposed to Botha's "one stream" policy to merge the two White "races" into one people. Inspired by European nationalism, Afrikaner nationalists thought of themselves as a distinct ethnic group with their own language (Afrikaans) and religion (Calvinism). Seminal to their version of nationalist history was the "Great Trek" of the 1830s, when an estimated group of fifteen thousand "Boers" migrated inland from the Cape. These Boers moved to the frontier mainly because of disagreement over the abolition of slavery by the English authorities in the Cape Colony. The Boers—also known as *Voortrekkers*, or settlers—presented themselves as the founders of the sovereign states in the heartland of South Africa.[83]

The new South African government did not consider all people of European descent equally White. Up to the 1920s, the White working class and the White poor were excluded from rights, but then the government started to see them as a way to keep the racial hierarchy in place.[84] Aware of the competition between White and Black workers, the government feared "racial deterioration" and a White "descent" into Blackness, which to them meant that Whites would live with Black South Africans in similar conditions. However, the incorporation of the White working class and the White poor into South Africa's White supremacy system followed different trajectories. The White working class waged many labor struggles for job protection and "White rights," through which they developed a distinct White identity that was inseparable from their understanding of the racial order and their aspiration to be included in White society.[85]

In 1924, the National Party and the Labour Party together formed the Pact Government, which installed a wide range of social and economic policies that formed the basis of the South African welfare state and improved conditions for the Afrikaans-speaking White working class. The new pension policy was a crucial pillar in the "civilized" labor policies, which were designed to favor employers using White labor and establish a clear racial hierarchy.[86] As a result, Black South Africans, already devastated by land expropriation, forced migration, and coercive employment, were further disparaged as "cheap labor" and "unfair competition" to Whites. Thus, government policy normalized racial discrimination, lower salaries, and poorer living standards for Black Africans.

Together with the international community, the South African state aggressively co-opted the White poor to strengthen the boundaries of Whiteness and legitimize anti-Black violence. The government perceived a risk to White supremacy, as the White poor intermingled with African people and sometimes worked as subordinates to Black Africans. White Americans and Europeans viewed South Africa as a laboratory for racial knowledge and experimentation, and assisted in the uplift aimed at shoring up "global Whiteness."[87] In 1932, the Carnegie Corporation published its study on poor Whites in cooperation with the South African government, which analyzed poverty among White South Africans and made recommendations about racial segregation. The government raised the living standards of poor White people through social assistance to achieve "civilized standards of living," a euphemism that indicated a standard that was "not Black" and above that of the native African population. Yet the government's uplift of poor Whites also resulted in stigmatization and repression through stereotyping the poor as deficient Whites. Ultimately, the South African welfare state was a racist response—alongside racist policies such as racial segregation, disenfranchisement, and labor exclusion—to *swartgevaar*, or Black peril.[88] The White political elite projected their racist anxieties onto the White poor, who embodied demographic, political, sexual, social, and economic threats.

In the 1930s, the Afrikaner nationalists started to envision a radicalization of White supremacy through the policy of apartheid.[89] The traumatic defeat in the Boer War stimulated Afrikaner nationalism—which until then was a small and elitist movement—to become a vital populist movement. In the early twentieth century, British media had portrayed Boers and Afrikaners consistently as not White enough. British writer

Rudyard Kipling, the bard of empire and writer of *The Jungle Book*, depicted the Afrikaners consistently as "degenerate" and less than White in his writings on the Boer War.[90] Afrikaner nationalists successfully used poor Whites as an issue to politically attack the British and exploit racist fears, even as White poverty was disappearing through industrialization.[91] The nationalists presented the Afrikaner as one *volk*, or one people, that fought against *samensmelting* (amalgamation) with the English and *gelykstelling* (equalization) and *rassenvermening* (miscegenation) with Black Africans. Specifically, sociologists such as Verwoerd explained the "degradation" of poor Whites "scientifically" to prove that Afrikaans-speaking poor Whites were not inferior "human material" but part of the *Volk*. In 1934, Verwoerd helped organize a *Volkskongres* (people's conference) on the poor White question and in its slipstream turned this problem from national cause to nationalist rallying cry. He blamed poor Afrikaners on a capitalist system dominated by English and Jewish interests, and on Black workers, who supposedly undercut the Afrikaner worker.[92] The Second World War further radicalized Afrikaner nationalists, who painted the expanding African working class as an urgent threat to Whiteness and ultimately made the White Afrikaans-speaking population receptive to apartheid.[93]

Apartheid

After the election in 1948, the National Party, led by D. F. Malan, implemented a legislative agenda in rapid succession that institutionalized segregation and the apartheid policy of "separate development." Apartheid nationalized, modernized, and "rationalized" a patchwork but extensive system of racial segregation already in place in South Africa. Grand apartheid extended a system of exploitation, domination, and segregation to all institutions of society. With great violence, disregard for human life, and long-lasting consequences such as poverty and hopelessness, they forced nonwhite people into Bantustans, or Black homelands. This policy of "ethnic political independence" (for each of the eight ethnic groups identified) set up a complex machinery of government and institutionalized relations between the state and the reserves. Apartheid was never just about racial segregation or preventing *ras-menging*, or race mixing. It built on the system of racial segregation adopted under British rule, but it went far beyond it and could better be described as systematic ethnic cleansing.

The apartheid program introduced by the NP after 1948 never had a single plan of design or developed in a linear fashion.[94] For example, plans to control the movement of African labor from rural to urban areas developed only slowly in the 1950s because race ideologues and business interests were not always aligned. Nevertheless, in the 1960s the NP under Verwoerd successfully pushed for a more comprehensive segregationist and authoritarian program. It included policies for race registration, group areas, anti-miscegenation laws, separate and unequal public amenities, Bantu education, media censorship, militarization, and a growing police state. Despite there never having been a blueprint for apartheid and its emergence being fragmentary and gradual, its policies transformed South African society far beyond labor policies.

Apartheid's racial logic was different from segregation. South Africa's apartheid government needed to deny its ideology being racist after the Second World War. The United Nations' Universal Declaration of Human Rights and UNESCO's report on the "Race Question" had renounced racism, the term that had become popular during the war to describe the anti-Jewish policies of the Nazis. The NP defended its apartheid political platform through cultural racism, not through any other ideology or biological racism. Responding to international pressure, it presented apartheid as a policy in the "mutual interest" of both the White and nonwhite population. Black Africans, the government said, had a different culture and different needs, and such government claims were backed up, supposedly, by scientific evidence, scriptural injunctions, and the "unique" historical experience of Afrikaners.[95]

In response, opponents of apartheid started to use nonracialism in the 1940s to challenge the new logic of racialization that justified apartheid. The Non-European Unity Movement (NEUM) was an innovative Trotskyist group that once claimed to be the premier liberation movement.[96] The label "Non-European" was to unite at the national level South Africa's main groups of Africans, Coloureds, and Indians. It rejected race-based organizing and the concept of race itself.[97] In the 1950s, nonracial democracy was popularized as an alternative to White liberals' ideas of a multiracial society, implemented around this time in countries such as Kenya, which provided only a qualified franchise for nonwhite groups.[98] Nonracialism also effectively forged an alliance between Black and White anti-apartheid fighters, specifically between the ANC and the White-dominated Communist Party.[99]

The 1950s and 1960s were the heyday of apartheid.[100] Apartheid and Afrikanerdom drew White Afrikaans-speaking South Africans together into a tight-knit political community committed to White supremacy. The apartheid system enhanced Afrikaners cultural distinctiveness and their common interest. Through state-sponsored welfare and employment programs, the Afrikaners economically caught up with the English-speaking White group.[101] After the Second World War, the economy boomed and White privilege seemed secure. As prime minister between 1961 and 1967, Verwoerd sustained South Africa's post–Second World War economic growth, which lifted all White Afrikaans-speaking South Africans out of poverty to solid White middle-class status. The coercive but relative peace in the 1950s and 1960s helped the economy grow, but it also came at a tremendous price for the Black population.

Black resistance to apartheid grew in the 1950s. The ANC began 1950 with a new commitment to militant mass action and tactics of boycotts, strikes, and civil disobedience. New groups joined the ANC, which had been founded in 1912 to bring all Africans together as one people and defend their rights and freedoms. The Defiance Campaign against Unjust Laws in 1952 was the first large-scale, multiracial political mobilization against apartheid laws. Throughout the 1950s, Black South Africans organized massive protests, despite the ever more rigorous application of repressive laws. In 1955, the ANC sent out fifty thousand volunteers into townships and the countryside to collect "freedom demands" from the people of South Africa. The ANC had started to work together with the South African Indian Congress and the Coloured People's Congress and published that year the Freedom Charter. Nonracialism attained a central place in the document, the movement's principal statement against apartheid.

During apartheid, the NP saw a need to intensify its suppression of the Black population. After a decade of mass protests, it responded with more violence. On March 21, 1960, the South African police, in an area called Sharpeville, opened fire on a mass protest of thousands of Black South Africans protesting the pass laws introduced in the 1950s to control their movement and employment, particularly inside cities. The police killed 69 people and injured 180 others. Despite the outcry in the international media, the South African government after Sharpeville quelled Black resistance through a mix of force, arrests, legislative restrictions, and police infiltration of the resistance movement. They also imprisoned many Black leaders, although some managed to go in exile, and the ANC was banned and its leadership arrested.[102] In 1962, Nelson Mandela was captured. At the Rivonia Trial that same year, he argued for a nonracial democracy in South Africa that included the deracialization of both state and citizens. He demanded the undoing of South Africa's explicitly racial definition as the state of the White nation and the opening up of citizenship to all South Africans without regard to race.[103]

In the late 1960s, tensions grew inside the White nationalist government between hard-liners, who advocated for "exclusive" Afrikaner White supremacy, and the Afrikaners, who supported "inclusive" White supremacy, which incorporated the White English-speaking community. In 1969, the Afrikaner-first hard-liners split from the NP to form the Herstigte Nasionale Party, which advocated for an even stricter enforcement of apartheid. The resistance of Black and Coloured people, migrant workers, and White liberal democrats took its toll. As a political rallying cry, apartheid and its vision of separate and parallel development had reached its limits. Outside South Africa, Prime Minister John Vorster tried to recast the White Afrikaans-speaking South African minority as an "African *Volk*" to other African countries in an attempt to hijack the norms and values of the new postcolonial era and relegitimize South Africa's White supremacist regime.[104] Inside the country, the government's repressive strategy of counterinsurgency, the militarization of the police, and an ever-growing security apparatus could not bring back stable economic growth. Reform was needed.

By the 1970s, the growth and stability that had characterized the postwar economy was replaced by stagnation and inflation. The interests of the White elite and White workers started to diverge. The White business elite had long profited from apartheid, but the exploitation of the Black population and labor unrest started to inhibit the development of a stronger domestic market. The apartheid system obstructed the effective utilization of labor. The White elite were also concerned about their global stigma as racists. They pushed for the loosening of the "colour bar," which would allow Black Africans to compete with White workers. In response, White workers defended their privileged employment opportunities, collective bargaining power, and wages.[105] Throughout the apartheid period, almost 40 percent of White Afrikaans-speaking South Africans remained in blue-collar occupations.[106] The White working class had long benefited from the apartheid system, and they continued to demand state protection. They decried capitalist exploitation and warned about the threat of White poverty. The state, they demanded, must continue to make a distinction between White workers, as citizens of South Africa entitled to state protection and privileges, and Black workers, Africans whom they depicted as *gasarbeiders*, or guest workers, in South Africa and without any claim to rights or residence.[107] White workers said they feared becoming "*gasarbeiders* in our own country" and slipping from a position of precarious White privilege to being equal to Black South Africans. Nevertheless, the apartheid government decided to ease the "colour bar," which permitted Black Africans specifically to compete with working-class Whites.

The rising cost of living and growing unemployment as a consequence of the economic crisis in the 1970s hit the disenfranchised African population hardest. A new generation of Black resistance fighters emerged in response. The Black Consciousness Movement (BCM)—initially a small, intellectual, and elitist movement—argued that race was central to the struggle in South Africa, and its message resonated with a new generation.[108] The Soweto uprising in 1976 was inspired by the BCM. High school students led the protests, which were initially about the introduction of Afrikaans in their schools but resulted in a massive uprising of young Black Africans in the townships. In response to these protests, the South African government clamped down on the BCM leadership. They imprisoned Biko, who was killed in 1977 under suspicious conditions. The BCM's ideas about Black people who had to organize independently from White liberals were central to creating the climate that gave students the confidence to strike out.[109] Nevertheless, the ANC as an organizing body was better able to channel and organize students seeking the end of apartheid.[110] It was the ANC's nonracialism that came to dominate the discourse of the anti-apartheid movement.[111]

A reinvigorated ANC in the 1980s transformed the uprising into a broad-based protest movement against apartheid. Partly from their bases outside of South Africa, partly through their large networks in the Black township, the ANC was able to stitch together an anti-apartheid movement supported by trade unions, youth movements, and new nonracial movements such as the United Democratic Front.[112] The NP increasingly relied on calling a state of emergency and using military rule to reign in protests in the townships. Internationally, the anti-apartheid movement also made apartheid a worldwide symbol of racism.[113] Until the end, however, the NP remained divided about Afrikaner survival and conflicted about the best strategy to maintain White power. By the late 1980s, South Africa had become the pariah of the international community and synonymous with a racist system, just as the American South had been during the civil rights movement fighting Jim Crow.

In 1989, the new president, F. W. de Klerk, had concluded that apartheid had become unsustainable, and he wanted to legalize the ANC and free Mandela. On February 11, 1990, Mandela was released from prison, and the NP began negotiating with the ANC. The negotiations paved the way to democratic elections in 1994 and Mandela's presidency, as well as a new constitution in 1996.

With his charisma and charm, President Mandela in a short time captivated and won over many White South Africans. Early in his life, Mandela had stated that to achieve victory over the Afrikaner nationalists, he had to know what they knew; he had to understand what "made them tick."[114] As president, he continued to use his deep understanding of Afrikaners to promote the "rainbow nation," a concept introduced by Bishop Desmond Tutu to describe post-apartheid South Africa.[115] A year after the first democratic elections, South Africa hosted the Rugby World Cup, which traditionally was a White sport and Black people often cheered for the opposition. However, when South Africa won the final match of the tournament held in Johannesburg, before a crowd of seventy thousand,

Mandela appeared on the field in the Springbok jersey to hand Francois Pienaar, a White Afrikaans-speaking South African and captain of the South African rugby team, the 1995 Rugby World Cup.[116] It became one of the country's defining images of racial reconciliation and bolstered this idea as the new civil religion of Mandela's South Africa.

As part of the political compromise, the NP and ANC established the Truth and Reconciliation Committee in 1996 to expose the apartheid regime's gross, systematic human rights violations and encourage nation-building and healing in South African society.[117] The premise of the TRC was that truth could heal a divided nation; its work was seen as a necessary counterpart to political negotiations and settlement. The media coverage of the hearings made it difficult for anyone thereafter to deny apartheid's atrocities. Nevertheless, survey research showed that the White South African reaction to the TRC, in particular the White Afrikaans-speaking community, was more negative than for any other group in South Africa.[118] Four years after the TRC, two researchers characterized Afrikaners' attitudes as a "state of denial."[119]

South Africa's TRC was consciously modeled as an alternative to the justice-by-trial in post–Second World War Germany. A Nuremberg-style trial, some believed, would focus too much on the perpetrators.[120] The planners of the TRC agreed that the victims of apartheid must be central to the process. They differed when it came to the question of whether perpetrators had to be punished and the question of individual responsibility of perpetrators versus state responsibility. However, despite these differences, the TRC, as in Germany, narrowed questions of racial justice through its reliance on the terminology of "perpetrators" and "victims." The TRC avoided using explicit racial language, which prevented the committee from focusing more on South Africa's racial inequalities and the questions of if and how Whites had benefited from apartheid. Its failure to sufficiently address race, reparations, and racial inequality made the return of these topics inevitable.

Where We Go from Here

By 2000, White South Africans' status had permanently changed, but the process of adjustment had only just begun. My research is organized as a multi-sited ethnography focused on the institutions of work, home, and school. I analyze how people give racial meaning to the world inside these institutions through their talk and actions. As a method, ethnography makes people's cultural and ideological work legible and tangible, but it also clearly locates this work. It is a research approach that helps me to emphasize the importance of place, social interactions, and institutional support for maintaining White identities. It highlights White people's meaning-making processes within, around, and through different institutions. My institutional approach focuses on how people's Whiteness is maintained not just discursively but also materially through White privilege and White identity politics. A multi-sited and institutional approach provides a nuanced understanding of racism, for racism is not an ideology that White South Africans apply everywhere in the same way.

South Africa's public debate about racism between 2000 and 2010 is the focus of the first part of the book, which situates the ethnographic chapters about everyday life at work, home, and school. In Chapter 2, I analyze how the White minority has adjusted and responded to South Africa's shifting racial hierarchy after 1994. I introduce the notions of public and "counterpublic" spheres to explain how unlearning racism happens differently and simultaneously in the public sphere and the counterpublic sphere, the Afrikaans-speaking media. In the public eye, White South Africans practice an identity politics focused on respectability and attempt to destigmatize their White identities by demonstrating that they are not racist and want to be part of South Africa. In the counterpublic, or within their own White communal spaces and the Afrikaans-speaking media, though, they confront the apartheid past and debate which generation bears the blame for apartheid. Counterpublic debates about accountability for the past also become sites for White identity politics, where White people re-empower themselves as victims who deserve mercy. Unlearning racism, I conclude, must involve more than coming to terms with the past. However, the real problem is that White South Africans come to terms with Whiteness through White identity politics.

The rise of White identity politics is the topic of the second part of the book, which looks at unlearning racism in the work sphere. Both the White business elite and White working-class populists practice White identity politics to maintain legitimacy and defend White privilege, but they do so in different ways. In Chapter 3, I explore how the formerly Whites-only chamber of commerce successfully pursued a strategy of public repentance and cooperation with Black and Coloured elites, which suggests that the White business elite have partly unlearned racism. However, these changes also made White privilege less visible—as the overwhelming majority of the organization is still White—and enabled the organization to whitewash its White supremacist roots. In Chapter 4, I analyze the politics of the Solidarity Movement, which represents the White working class and practices populism. Unlearning racism must be reimagined in a context where White populists use the language of multiculturalism and minority rights to practice White identity politics.

Why does White identity politics resonate? In Chapter 5, I explore why White working-class men use such dramatic emotional terms to talk about their place in society. Similar to White men in the public debate, these men's Whiteness and masculinity have become visible, but their markedness is an everyday experience; racial integration has made them a White minority at work. It is this group that is truly forced to unlearn racism. This is a challenge because Whiteness is embodied; White working-class men carry their experiences with them. New norms and relationships in the workplace force them to confront how their embodied experiences might feel natural but need to be changed. Unlearning racism for them is not simply about doing away with racial prejudices but about the difficulty of becoming self-aware about their embodiment. Unable to connect Whiteness to embodiment, they feel affirmative action devalues them as White men. White identity politics resonates because they feel unfairly punished for apartheid, as they imagine themselves to be only minor figures in the grand scheme of apartheid.

Unlearning racism is different at work than it is at home. In the third part of this book, I contrast and connect how White South Africans confront racism in different institutional spheres. In Chapter 6, I analyze how the South African city and home have changed in the eyes of lower-middle-class Whites living in an open neighborhood, as contrasted with the experiences of upper-class Whites living in a gated community. Lower-middle-class Whites limit unlearning racism to work and see the home as a place of personal freedom. They talk about the city in a racialized narrative organized around the tropes of urban disorder and decay that mix fears of crime, poverty, and filth with fears of Black Africans. By contrast, White upper-class residents of the gated community have unlearned the overt racism of apartheid days. They never pretend to be color-blind, and their Whiteness remains anchored in the nostalgic memory of apartheid. Implausibly, they imagine their gated community to represent the apartheid past—for its safety and homeliness—and the multicultural future of South Africa—for its diversity and order—at the same time.

White identity politics has succeeded color blindness as the dominant racist ideology in South Africa, but what does the first explain that the second cannot? In the final part of the book, Chapter 7, I examine this question in the context of the socialization of racism: how children learn racism and how they unlearn it. As I compare White students at two schools—one with an upper-class student body and another with a lower-middle-class student body—I find two different stories of White identity change. White youth do not magically change their views because they are a new generation, but they do not passively reproduce what they receive from teachers and parents either. Even their stories about who they are do not reliably indicate they are unlearning racism. As White identity change is a necessary but not sufficient condition for unlearning racism, we cannot answer the question of what it means to be White without addressing what it feels like to be White. White youth use White identity politics to normalize their White identities in a multicultural South Africa and to justify their feelings and claims to victimhood.

If we step back and think about how we understand racism in today's world, we have the reproduction of racism, on the one hand, through institutional racism that reproduces racial inequality over time, legitimized by shifting racial ideologies. On the other hand, we have calls for critical Whiteness studies; scholars emphasize that people should recognize White privilege, overcome White fragility, and abolish Whiteness. What we do not have is a theory about how people move from racism to antiracism that combines insights from racism and Whiteness studies. For most theorists of racism, the process of unlearning racism has been an afterthought; they have devoted their energy and time to questions of reproduction, proving the overwhelming impact and power of White racism around the world and continued racial exploitation and racial inequality. Unlearning racism has been left to psychologists and educators, which has produced an individual therapeutic model of the process that prescribes individual reflection. My sociological exploration will not offer such uncomplicated answers or straightforward lessons. But what we lose individually in easy emotional rewards ("Now we know how to unlearn racism!"), we will gain collectively with a deeper understanding of the challenges of unlearning racism.

CHAPTER 2

Coming to Terms with Whiteness

A German Idea

The idea that South Africa's White minority would change through a process of "coming to terms" with the human rights abuses of the past underlies the creation of the Truth and Reconciliation Committee (TRC), South Africa's approach to transitional justice. This idea has its origins in the work of sociologist Theodor Adorno, who concluded after the Second World War that Germans were unable to "come to terms" and move forward because they had not confronted past crimes. The German origins of this concept indicate the important role that the Holocaust played in shaping South Africans' ideas about unlearning racism. Despite the fact that the TRC was consciously modeled as an alternative to the justice-by-trial in Nuremberg, South Africans still understood the challenge for White South Africans after apartheid as similar to that for Germans after the Second World War. Germany, however, provides a poor model for understanding South Africa and how the politics of collective memory shapes the process of unlearning racism.

Originally, the African National Congress (ANC) leadership support-ed a Nuremberg-style trial for South Africa. In 1987, South African hu-man rights scholar Kader Asmal, who later became an ANC minister in the cabinets of Presidents Mandela and Mbeki, called for prosecution of apartheid's leaders for crimes against humanity.[1] Eventually, however, the ANC set up the TRC because it could legitimize the new South African legal order and reiterate the morality of the apartheid resistance.[2] South Africa followed in the footsteps of such countries as Argentina, Chile, and Bolivia, where TRCs had been instrumental in consolidating a ne-gotiated democratic transition and installing a new government.[3] In *No*

Future without Forgiveness, South African archbishop and chairman of the TRC, Desmond Tutu, presented the TRC as a "third way" between a Nuremberg-style trial and national amnesia.

Despite the rejection of a Nuremberg-style trial, the TRC leadership continued to view White South Africans as similar to the Germans after the war. In his book, Tutu draws this comparison: "The Germans claimed they had not known what the Nazis were up to. White South Africans have also tried to find refuge in claims of ignorance."[4] Ultimately, South Africans saw Germany as a successful model of change when it came to dealing with their racist past. In *Reconciliation through Truth: A Reckoning of Apartheid's Criminal Governance,* Kader Asmal and his co-editors use Germany to frame how White South Africans must confront their collective responsibility and contribute to "undoing the Apartheid culture."[5] Published before the creation of the TRC, the writers stress the Germans' ability to overcome racism and deal with their past, while conceding that it took more than fifty years to do so.

Yet the case of Germany is actually unhelpful for understanding the process of unlearning racism in South Africa, because the perpetrators were in the majority in Germany, while Whites are a small minority in South Africa. In Germany after 1945, the majority debated in the public sphere whether ordinary citizens were collectively accountable for state crimes and how they should respond to past wrongs.[6] They did so among themselves in a self-critical way and kept the question of collective guilt central to the public debate. In a majority-minority context, such as South Africa, the politics of collective memory in the public sphere is fundamentally different. In South Africa's national conversation, concerns about how to come to terms with the past are intertwined with debates on how to come to terms with the present regarding issues of racism and racial inequality.

The process of coming to terms with the past is always related to how to come to terms with the present. The way this "racial temporality"—how connections are made among racial categories, relations, and processes across time—plays out in societies varies from country to country.[7] In this sense, South Africa is very different from Germany. As the national debate over the crimes of the past unfolds, the White Afrikaans-speaking minority is often stigmatized—sometimes justifiably so—by the majority, not just for what was done in in the past in the name of Afrikaner nationalism but also for racism in the present. White Afrikaans-speaking South Africans—Afrikaners, in short—often respond to such debates emotionally, and it is not always evident whether their emotional turmoil is related to the past or present.

South Africans, however, have followed Germany in overemphasizing the process of coming to terms with the past. A close reading of Adorno's text suggests that he already thought the challenge of unlearning racism—in Germany or South Africa—was never exclusively about "coming to terms" with the past but also about coming to terms with the present. South Africa, moreover, is a postcolonial society for which it is imperative to rethink the history and agency of people subordinated under White supremacy. We need to reexamine the questions that are been asked about the past and to reconsider the stories that are told about its relation to the present.[8] If he were living, Adorno would have told South Africans they were asking the wrong question. He might have suggested it was better for South Africa to focus on how to come to terms with Whiteness.

In his 1959 address "Was bedeutet die Aufarbeitung der Vergangenheit?," Adorno confessed that he remained troubled by how the spell of the past lingered in the present.[9] He was particularly preoccupied by German guilt and Germans' justifications for the Holocaust, as well as the outburst of public emotions at inappropriate times and the lack of emotion at seemingly appropriate opportunities. Contrary to popular belief, Adorno was pessimistic about the usefulness of the terminology of "coming to terms" with the past. Specifically, he found its double meaning of reconciliation and receiving articulation misleading in regard to perpetrator groups. He did not believe that exposing the truth about past crimes pushed perpetrator groups to admissions of guilt. He warned that an obsessive focus on past crimes could prevent a clear view of how racist ideologies such as National Socialism continued to cause harm in the present.

To face the challenge of unlearning racism, I argue that South Africans must be equally concerned with the question of whether White South Africans have come to terms with the past and with how they can come to terms with the present. In actuality, the White minority faces two challenges. First, like the Germans or the Japanese in the Second World War, the White minority is a perpetrator group. They must confront their responsibility for the past, in which apartheid figures prominently. But so far, there is no consensus among the White minority or in South African society about an appropriate response to the White minority's culpability. The second challenge for the White minority is to unlearn their racism. This challenge not only concerns the collective memory of an egregious past but also racism, racial inequality, and how to move beyond White privilege. Moreover, coming to terms with the past is only one possible way—but an important one—to address racism and racial inequality. The question is how these two challenges play out in the majority-minority context of South Africa, as opposed to most other historical contexts, where a majority persecuted a minority.

In this chapter, I employ Nancy Fraser's idea of the counterpublic, a discursive arena that develops in parallel to the official public sphere, to analyze how White South Africans come to terms with the past and the present.[10] Applying the notion of counterpublic to a formerly dominant White minority is counterintuitive: after all, White male South Africans controlled the public sphere during apartheid. Indeed, the National Party tightly regulated the media by owning several newspapers and magazines (*Nasionale Pers* or *Naspers*) and regularly banned foreign media, books, and writers. However, the dominance of the White minority in the public sphere declined after 1994. Now the counterpublic functions as a safe space to reconfigure the collective identity of the White Afrikaans-speaking minority—in particular, to fill a void, as old meanings of Afrikaner culture have become delegitimized and new meanings have to be culturally invented. The concept of the counterpublic helps to reveal how the White minority is coming to terms with the past at the same time as the present—how they are confronting the stigma of their perpetrator past at the same time as their racism.

This chapter begins where most studies on the democratic transition in South Africa end. Starting with 1998, I move beyond the TRC and the Mandela era to analyze what happened after the transitional justice process of the TRC. Mandela's presidency from 1994 to 1998 and the TRC from 1996 to 1998 achieved remarkable things, most notably the transition to democracy and a historic process of accountability and public acknowledgment. Together, they set the stage for the political developments in South Africa in the new millennium. Indeed, despite Mandela's rhetoric of reconciliation and the TRC process, the White Afrikaans-speaking minority was framed as a perpetrator group. This framing caused a split between the debates in the public and the counterpublic sphere. In the public sphere, ANC politicians from Mbeki onwards stigmatized the White minority, who in response started to practice reputation management through various destigmatization strategies. In the counterpublic, however, the White minority more directly confronted their collective legacy of racism. But what emerged out of the process of coming to terms with Whiteness was not what many expected: a White identity politics that depicted the White minority as traumatized and victimized, and demanded the normalization of Whiteness.

Race and the Truth and Reconciliation Committee

The Truth and Reconciliation Committee was established in 1996 to adjudicate the crimes of apartheid and to reconcile the nation. The TRC's mission was to address "the deeper meaning" of reconciliation: reconciliation as a process of confession, repentance, cleansing, regeneration, reparation, and restoration.[11] Archbishop Desmond Tutu, the chairman of the TRC, argued that the TRC provided the framework for the cultural and moral restructuring of South African society.[12] The premise of the TRC's work was that truth could heal a divided nation; its work was seen as complementary to political negotiations and settlement. To forestall the impression of victors' justice, even though the ANC had not defeated the NP, no side was exempt from appearing before the commission. "Its designers hoped the TRC would prevent cycles of revenge by giving public acknowledgment to past wrongs and investigating violations of human dignity both by the prior government and by those who fought against it."[13] The mandate of the commission was to bear witness to, record, and in some cases offer reparation and rehabilitation to the victims. It was also to bear witness to the perpetrators of crimes (they were explicitly invited to tell their stories) and in some cases grant amnesty for crimes relating to human rights violation. Many South Africans hoped and expected that by reckoning with the past the truth would be revealed and a human rights culture would be established.

The planners of the TRC agreed that the victims of apartheid must be central to the process. Not only did the past have to be confronted, but the dignity of the victims had to be restored. A Nuremberg-style trial, they concluded, would focus too much on the perpetrators. The planners differed over whether perpetrators had to be punished and how much responsibility for the crimes was attributable to individuals versus the state.[14] Some people also argued that the process would be meaningless without retribution. Ultimately, the victor's justice of Nuremberg was also given up in favor of the ideals of nation-building and reconciliation because there was no victor in South Africa's political struggle—only a negotiated settlement.

Nevertheless, the TRC's use of the dichotomy of "perpetrators" and "victims" remained remarkably similar to the way Germany's Nuremberg trials deployed these categories. This choice of words had repercussions for how the TRC could address questions of racial justice. From the beginning, the designers of the TRC had been concerned with the tension between individual and structural approaches to justice. Asmal had argued that a Nuremberg-style trial in South Africa would individualize the horrors of apartheid and provide only a piecemeal picture of the past at the expense of attention to its systemic abuses.[15] The Nuremberg trials, he insisted, had only involved a few perpetrators, while ordinary Germans remained wholly outside the trial process. However, the TRC's solution to this conundrum, which focused on victims rather than perpetrators, overlooked the more general problem with this terminology. While it facilitated the uncovering of the truth of the systemic abuses of the past, the individualistic terminology prevented a deeper interrogation of the structural consequences of apartheid in the form of racial inequality and White privilege.

There were three more problems with the way the TRC addressed its task of delivering reconciliation and racial justice. First, the TRC used the categories of perpetrators and victims inconsistently to achieve the goal of reconciliation. The TRC often blurred the boundaries between perpetrators and victims, in particular through the use of the language of trauma.

President Mandela and Archbishop Tutu argued that all South Africans were traumatized and victims of apartheid. As Mandela observed during the inauguration of the commission, "Looking at the guilt and suffering of the past, one cannot but conclude: In a certain sense all of us are victims of apartheid, all of us are victims of our past."[16] Similarly, in the opening speech before the victim hearings at the TRC, Tutu said, "We are charged to unearth the truth about our dark past, to lay the ghosts of that past to rest so that they will not return to haunt us. And that we will thereby contribute to the healing of the traumatized and wounded people—for all of us in South Africa are wounded people—and in this manner to promote national unity and reconciliation."[17]

The TRC's language purposefully mystified how White South Africans stood in a very different relationship to apartheid than the victim groups. The TRC's use of a mix of religious and psychological language—including the concepts of reconciliation, forgiveness, healing, and trauma—obfuscated how the perpetrator and victim communities relate differently to the past. Confusion resulted as well from the way in which the TRC conceptualized cultural change, generalizing from the individual to the national and mixing the social with the psychological. Researchers emphasized the limitations of the TRC as national therapy.[18] American law scholar Martha Minow argues that we do not know how to apply psychological theories to the collective that have only been proven to work for individuals. She also argues that academia knows very little about the process of "societal healing" and that further research is necessary.[19]

The second problem with the TRC was that, although it framed apartheid as a national trauma that required acknowledgment and demanded repair, the actual execution of the process undermined these goals. The TRC had three different subcommittees: the Human Rights Violations Committee, which investigated human rights abuses that occurred between 1960 and 1994; the Reparation and Rehabilitation Committee, which was charged with restoring victims' dignity and formulating proposals to assist with rehabilitation; and the Amnesty Committee, which considered applications from individuals who applied for amnesty. Organizationally, the TRC had disconnected the issue of justice from that of solidarity. In the end, the Human Rights Violations Committee was generally seen as a success; it restored dignity to victims through public testimony and held individual perpetrators to account for their actions. By contrast, the Reparation and Rehabilitation Committee was seen as a failure. Some contributed this failure to the lackluster endorsement of this committee by the ANC government. Others, however, argued that the perpetrators of apartheid—the White minority—should have taken responsibility to initiate reparations.

The third problem was that, in the eyes of the TRC, the White minority was always the perpetrator but never qualified as the White supremacist. The TRC's reliance on the management of justice through the juridical categories of "perpetrator" and "victim" narrowed questions of racial justice to the White minority's culpability as individual perpetrators, predominantly as state agents. Moreover, this narrow framing reinforced Afrikaners' image as the sole perpetrator group (versus the whole White minority). White Afrikaans-speaking South Africans had dominated the state apparatus. The perpetrator frame was influential among journalists too. In Antjie Krog's *Country of My Skull*, her account of the TRC, she centers her narrative on victims' testimonies. However, another main theme in the book is her Afrikaner roots and her culpability as Afrikaner, a narrative in which Afrikaners are consistently framed as perpetrators, not White supremacists.[20] Ugandan political scientist Mahmood Mamdani argues that the TRC was unable to address how apartheid had benefited the whole White minority. He concludes that the TRC was "interested only in violations outside the law, in benefits which are corruptions, but not in the systematic benefits that were conferred on beneficiaries at the expense of the vast majority of people in this country."[21] Apartheid had few perpetrators, he said, but a lot of White beneficiaries.

The TRC's avoidance of explicit racial language prevented it from a clear-headed focus on contemporary racial inequalities and their causes. The TRC did provide a broad overview of the systematic abuses in the past—just as Kader Asmal and others had hoped—but it failed to address Whites' collective responsibility and their White privilege. Even Archbishop Tutu became frustrated at the end of the process with the TRC's inability to address Whites as a collective. On February 18, 1998, Tutu called on "all Whites, especially the Afrikaners" to acknowledge that "dastardly things" had happened in the past. "You White people—if you reject the TRC you will carry the burden of guilt into your graves," he said.[22] Tutu later apologized, but his angry remarks show how the TRC's focus on the White minority as perpetrators frustrated broader questions of racial responsibility and privilege.

Ultimately, the White community's response to the TRC was more negative than that of any other group in South Africa. Despite the convincing claim from American political scientist James Gibson that a majority of South Africans accepted the truth of the TRC's hearings, survey research also suggests that the White minority's response to the TRC was more negative than that of other communities.[23] A poll taken in late 2000 by the Institute of Justice and Reconciliation found that only 29 percent of Whites felt that the TRC had fostered the building of a united nation, as opposed to 77 percent of Black people.[24] In their memoirs, the TRC commissioners stressed the different responses of groups to the final TRC report.[25] During and after the TRC, Afrikaans newspapers regularly referred to the committee as the "Lieg en Bieg Komissie" (Lie and Confess Committee). The South African journalist Max Du Preez pointed also to the failure of the political leadership of former president Botha, who refused to testify for the TRC or seek forgiveness on behalf of the collectivity.[26]

The TRC's failure to sufficiently address race, reparations, and racial inequality made the return of these topics unavoidable. Few people dispute the TRC's important therapeutic role in providing victims with the opportunity to tell their story and help acknowledge their suffering. The hearings exposed the brutality of the apartheid regime and the official web of government lies and deception. The extensive media coverage of the hearings made it much harder for anyone thereafter to deny the atrocities for which the apartheid regime was responsible. Nevertheless, American anthropologist Richard Wilson concluded that the TRC had little impact on the sense of racial justice among Black South Africans. The TRC performance, he maintained, was mainly about legitimizing the new ANC regime.[27]

The consequences of the TRC for the White minority were manifold. The TRC's success as well as its failings set the stage for the developments that followed. Despite the initial surprise of many White South Africans, the return of race and racial inequality as important topics of public debate are understandable in light of the shortcomings of the TRC. Furthermore, the TRC's narrow focus on Afrikaners as perpetrators shaped the post-TRC debate in the public and counterpublic spheres. In the public sphere, debates about racial inequality would soon dominate and force the White minority into reputation management. In the safety of the counterpublic, however, the White Afrikaans-speaking minority started to debate the apartheid past.

The Public and the Counterpublic Spheres

Since the TRC, the national conversation has been dominated by themes of racial inequality and racism, which is a polarized discussion predominantly between the ANC's leadership and White South Africans. The debate narrowly revolves around reputation management, as the ANC stigmatizes White South Africans (including Afrikaners), who in return deploy various destigmatization strategies. Reputation management is about the way groups (nations or individuals) destigmatize their difficult pasts. However, among White Afrikaans-speaking South Africans themselves, there is another conversation developing. In Afrikaans newspapers, as well as in books, music, and art, there is an introspective debate about identity and responsibility. White Afrikaans-speaking South Africans are attempting to redefine what it means to be White and an Afrikaner, and what their future will be as a White minority in South Africa.

Debates about negative historical events and their representation take place in the public sphere. Public sphere theorists Jürgen Habermas and Craig Calhoun argue that the public sphere is fundamentally a communicative space—empirically separated from economic, religious, and family life—with a set of socially established semiotic rules. Originally, the concept of the counterpublic was introduced by Nancy Fraser to supplement the Habermasian notion of the public sphere.[28] In the public sphere, Habermas suggested, people come together to freely discuss and identify societal problems; the national conversation takes place in the arena between the state and the economy.[29] Building on feminist critiques, Fraser argued that the public sphere was often built on a number of exclusions, denying access to women and minorities in particular. Women and Blacks often organized their own public spheres, or counterpublics: "parallel discursive arenas where members of subordinated social groups invent and circulate counter discourses to formulate oppositional interpretations of their identities, interests, and needs."[30] Groups discuss their interests in these separate spaces without the interference of the dominant group. It is a safe space.

Reputation management, stigmatization, and destigmatization strategies occur primarily in the public sphere. White Afrikaans-speaking South Africans use their own media outlets and cultural industry to express their feelings. Together with traditional Afrikaner media outlets, the newly established platforms of the counterpublic create a safe space for White Afrikaans-speaking South Africans, a space that isolates them from criticism, to address what it means to be part of a perpetrator collective, to soul-search in music and writing, and to address questions of shame and White identity. After apartheid, those in the Afrikaans publishing, music, and theatre industries had unprecedented levels of creative production and success.[31] From 1994 on, the industry initiated, organized, and sponsored a network of music and literary festivals to promote the arts in Afrikaans.[32] These platforms continue to be supported by new media, such as the cable music channel Kyknet, which promotes Afrikaans music. The network provided the necessary institutional support for the Afrikaans counterpublic.[33] It is in safe spaces such as exclusive Afrikaans media, music, literature, and ethnic festivals that a new collective identity takes shape and is reinvented.

President Mbeki and the Return of Racism

Although the TRC had not yet published its final report in 1998, Thabo Mbeki changed the conversation from national reconciliation to racial inequality and racism. The debate that ensued in the run-up to his election—mostly between the ANC's leadership and White South Africans—narrowly revolved around reputation management. Mbeki castigated White South Africans as privileged and racist colonizers from Europe. Afrikaners deployed three destigmatization strategies: they emphasized White poverty, claimed indigenous status, and accused Mbeki of being racist. The debate lasted through Mbeki's decade in power but was never resolved.

On May 29, 1998, Mbeki chose the first parliamentary debate on "reconciliation and nation building" in the national assembly to make a statement that was carefully designed to shatter the country's "rainbow nation" dream that had been popularized by the TRC. South Africa's deputy president argued that South Africa is a country of two nations—a rich White nation and a poor Black nation:

> A major component of the issue of reconciliation and nation building is defined by and derives from the material conditions in our society, which have divided our country into two nations, the one Black and the other White. We therefore make bold to say that South Africa is a country of two nations. One of these nations is White, relatively prosperous, regardless of gender or geographic dispersal. It has ready access to a developed economic, physical, educational, communication and other infrastructure. . . . The second and larger nation of South Africa is Black and poor, with the worst affected being women in the rural areas, the Black rural population in general and the disabled.[34]

Mbeki's now-famous "two nations" speech generated controversy in and beyond the parliament as critics and supporters clashed over whether or not he was "raking up the past" or "playing the race card."

The speech seemed to mark a turning point in South Africa's discourse on nation-building. Reconciliation no longer meant absolution but transformation. Commentators argued that Mbeki had made a radical departure from President Mandela. For years, Mbeki had written Mandela's speeches, including his historic inauguration speech in May 1994. Mandela's aim had been racial reconciliation, which included assuaging Whites' fear of change and building bonds of solidarity. After Mandela had cast his vote in the country's first fully democratic election, he addressed the media and outlined the many major developmental challenges the new government would face. He also expressed his concerns "about the minorities in the country—especially the White minority. We are concerned about giving confidence and security to those who are worried that by these changes they are now going to be in a disadvantaged position."[35]

In his public speeches during the early years of his presidency, Mandela kept on differentiating between the politics of the heart and the politics of reason. The ANC had not won the military struggle, Mandela knew, and it had to find ways to neutralize White opposition.

However, if we examine Mandela's actions and rhetoric in the later years of his presidency, it is clear that Mbeki's "two nations" speech completed a change in direction started by Mandela. Over the course of his term in office, Mandela shifted toward a more critical view of Whites and began labeling them as defenders of White privilege. In a speech to the ANC Congress in 1997, Mandela derided Whites for their limited cooperation and reciprocity in nation-building and economic transformation.[36] He branded his opponents as "the architects and beneficiaries of apartheid." He argued that Whites continued to cling to apartheid privileges while the White opposition parties competed for the title of "most reliable and best defender of White privilege." Afrikaner politicians responded strongly; Marthinus van Schalkwyk, the opposition and NP leader, denounced the speech as "unstatesmanlike and paranoid," and said he hoped it was not indicative of future ANC policies. Both inside and outside South Africa, newspapers characterized Mandela's speech as an attack against the White elite.

Mbeki argued that the defining issue of South Africa's struggle for national unity and reconciliation was the question of race. He wanted to lift Blacks out of poverty by acknowledging its cause: centuries of White domination. Less concerned with appeasing Whites, he shifted the country's focus from reconciliation toward transformation and spoke of an "African renaissance." In September 1998, Mbeki presided over a conference about this idea, which he borrowed from Senegalese historian, anthropologist, physicist, and politician Cheick Anta Diop. The concept of an African renaissance stood for more social cohesion among African countries, more economic growth in the African continent, and more geopolitical power for African nations. Nevertheless, ANC intellectuals quickly co-opted the term to sometimes imply as well that Whites were foreign to Africa. Mbeki abandoned the ideals of nonracialism and a diverse but united nation—the "rainbow nation" myth—for an Africanist approach that asserted African hegemony in a diverse nation. It was not so much a reversal of earlier policies but rather a shift to emphasize the Africanist nationalist tendencies that were always present in the ANC.[37]

Mbeki made racism a prominent theme during his presidency. In 2001, South Africa hosted the United Nations Conference against Racism, in preparation for which South Africa's leading Black thinkers and ANC politicians debated the problem of racism at a national conference. Mbeki called on Whites to be part of the movement because "despite our collective intentions, racism continues to be our bedfellow." To that, ANC politician Pallo Jordan said, "Most white people say they are not responsible for apartheid. But they put the [Whites only] Nationalist Party into government in 1948 and returned it to power again and again with a bigger majority until the late 1980s."[38] Some prominent White anti-apartheid activists, aligned with the ANC, started the "Home to All" campaign, whose manifesto stated that they acknowledged the benefits they had derived from apartheid; but they failed to draw significant support from among the White minority. White ANC politicians such as Carl Niehaus also continued to address racism. In 2002, Niehaus called for humility from White South Africans and demanded they admit to their racist past: "As long as the deep and unmitigated racism that was the heart and essence of apartheid is denied by a substantial part of the white community, it will become impossible for them to become part of the new South Africa."[39] Unlearning racism continued to be defined as coming to terms with the past.

Mbeki was inconsistent in how he formulated the problem of racism and its solution. During his state of the nation address to parliament in 2001, he called for "unity in action for change" in the struggle against racism. He praised White South Africans who had reached out to Black communities and connected White privilege to responsibility for the poor. However, a year later, Mbeki singled out a White South African who had used the word *kaffir* to describe a Black South African.[40] Based on this example, he claimed that the country's "success in the struggle to move our country from apartheid to democracy has led many in our country to reach the premature conclusion that racism in South Africa is dead. This is despite the obvious and naked fact that to this day and unavoidably, the racial divisions, inequalities and prejudices of the past continue to characterize our society."[41] The White opposition criticized the president for generalizing about the state of racism in South Africa based on a single incident.

The White minority employed three destigmatization strategies in response to Mbeki's portrayals of Whites as wealthy and foreign to Africa, the first of which was emphasizing that minorities—including the White minority—were being excluded in the new democracy. The 1999 election saw the emergence of the Democratic Party (DP) as the main opposition to the ANC, as the NP lost support for its association with apartheid. Democratic Party leader Tony Leon led an uncompromising "fight back campaign" that presented Whites as a minority that was now being excluded. Leon talked about the *gatvol*, or the fed-up factor, among the so-called excluded minorities. Leon represented the policy of affirmative action as a new form of apartheid. The DP offered what the NP could not: release for Whites who felt guilty about apartheid. Whites did not feel that casting a ballot for the DP was supporting the old apartheid party. During the campaign, Leon told Whites they had nothing to feel guilty about. "You weren't part of a conspiracy of apartheid just because you happen to be white," he said during one campaign rally. "You have got to go out there and assert yourself as an equal. That's what you are."[42]

The second destigmatization strategy of the White minority, which was popular among the White Afrikaans-speaking minority, was to claim Indigenous status—formally and informally. Members of the right-wing group Afrikaner Volksfront argued that the Afrikaner identity and language had developed uniquely and distinctively in Africa away from its origins in Europe. In the late 1990s, they intensified their efforts to claim an Indigenous identity by presenting their issue to the United Nations Working Group on Indigenous Peoples (UNWIP).[43] In 2008, they were admitted to the Unrepresented Nations and Peoples Organization (UNPO). Although right-wing groups pioneered this strategy, well-known Afrikaner anti-apartheid fighters such as Frederik van Zyl Slabbert and Max du Preez have used similar strategies, claiming—perhaps contrary to expectations—to be a "Pale Native" or an "Afrikaner Afrikaan."[44]

The third destigmatization strategy was to accuse Mbeki of the same racism ("reverse racism") that he had so vehemently fought against as a member of the ANC. In December 1998, during the debate in the South African parliament on the TRC's report, Mbeki put the TRC squarely within the context of the long history of White racism. He quoted early European travelers to Africa who painted Blacks as "creatures" and "beast-like people" to argue that the TRC's final report was wrong to "criminalize the struggle." He argued the ANC had fought a just war against centuries of European racial oppression. Again, Mbeki departed from the unifying mission of past politics and pitted Whites and Blacks against each other, adding that Whites in the present time are racists too. White politicians replied to this accusation with equal force. One after another, White politicians in parliament stressed that the White minority voted for the new dispensation. They argued that Whites should not be humiliated or depicted unfairly. When the debate was almost over, NP politician Jacko Maree dropped his prepared speech and spoke frankly: "I first want to say that I have the wrong credentials—I am middle aged, I am White, I am Afrikaans, and I am a man. . . . You made a speech that shocked me. . . . It gave me shivers down my spine. . . . And I thought . . . for a terrible moment I saw in this chamber the ghost of Mugabe."[45]

President Zuma and Black Populism

During the elections of 2009, the White minority continued reputation management, even as the political landscape shifted. In December 2007, Jacob Zuma was elected ANC president, thus beating Thabo Mbeki. In early 2008, the ANC Youth League (ANCYL) also elected a new president, Julius Malema, who had a reputation as a firebrand with a confrontational politics toward White South Africans.[46] In the election debates that followed, Malema supported Zuma overall, but the men took opposing positions regarding White South Africans. Zuma tried to appease Afrikaners by labeling them "the White tribe of Africa." This approach affirmed Afrikaners' destigmatization strategy of claiming indigenous status. Afrikaners successful convinced Zuma of the severity of White poverty. They had the future president visit poor White communities, to great effect in the national and international media. However, Malema presented a populist version of Mbeki's approach of stigmatizing White

South Africans as rich colonizers foreign to South Africa. In return, the White minority focused their destigmatization campaign on Malema and accused him of being racist (much as they had done with Mbeki). They even went to court for Malema's hate speech—and won.

Zuma changed the ANC's approach to the Afrikaner community. Even though Afrikaners were a small minority in South Africa, the ANC needed their vote in the election to obtain a two-thirds supermajority, which allowed them to change the constitution. The Afrikaner community turnout was traditionally large. In contrast to Mbeki, Zuma actively engaged with Afrikaner community leaders. He tried to obtain Afrikaner votes by responding to their destigmatization strategies and aiding them in reputation management, through connecting his own tribal male identity to Afrikaners' culture of patriarchy and claim to native status. As part of his preelection tour in 2008, he visited a small township community of poor Whites who were mostly Afrikaners. Unlike Mbeki, he wanted to recognize White poverty, and he was invited by the traditionally White-dominated trade union Solidarity. Zuma told hundreds of poor Whites he was determined to see them and others in their community get more government grants, subsidies, and basic services. Whereas Mbeki branded White South Africans and Afrikaners as racist, colonizers of South Africa, Zuma flattered Afrikaners by stressing their importance to the country.

Just months before his election, in April 2009, Zuma organized a meeting with several heads of Afrikaner organizations in Sandton, Johannesburg. His speech drew headlines the next day. "Of all the white groups that are in South Africa," he said, "it is only the Afrikaners that are truly South Africans in the true sense of the word. Up to this day, they don't carry two passports, they carry one. They are here to stay."[47] In this single statement, he branded Afrikaners as authentically African and denounced the English South Africans as European settlers. "Afrikaners are the only white tribe," Zuma continued, "in a black continent or outside of Europe which is truly African, the Afrikaner." He welcomed Afrikaners into the fold at the expense of White English-speaking South Africans, many of whom carry a passport from both South Africa and the United Kingdom. "The blame of apartheid is no longer squarely on them," the presidential contender concluded. "Afrikaners should now participate in the new democracy as an African tribe."

Conservative Afrikaner groups responded positively to Zuma's new message. Dan Roodt, one of the attendees and the head of the small right-wing action group PRAAG (the Pro-Afrikaans Action Group), said: "I feel very positive about the outcome of the meeting. . . . It is almost as if Zuma has some pangs of nostalgia for the old, Afrikaner-run South Africa, with its discipline, sense of patriotism, successful agriculture, frugal public salaries and respect for law and order. I think Zuma's interest in Afrikaans culture is genuine."[48] Zuma did not speak of nostalgia for apartheid, but Roodt correctly sensed the implications of Zuma's speech. The presidential candidate was appealing to an anachronistic Afrikaner masculinity with his tribal theme. Zuma encouraged Afrikaners to be seen not as colonizers but as a mirror image of his own isiZulu male identity: patriarchal, chauvinistic, and predicated on the notion of male superiority. During his presidency, he would continue to meet with conservative Afrikaners, and he visited two more small townships of poor Whites. On the occasion of the 2009 visit, Dirk Hermann, spokesman for the trade union Solidarity, said that Zuma "doesn't always take up your concerns and [offer to] be a Mr. Fix-It, but he does listen, and that's hugely important for us. He's like a Zulu king, sitting under his tree, listening to his tribe." Some White politicians were also critical of Zuma's words. The new leader of the Democratic Alliance (DA) (the former Democratic Party), Helen Zille, said that Zuma was "pressing the ethnic button," which should not distract DA voters from the ANC's abuse of power.

The rise of Zuma symbolized a populist resurgence in South Africa. Zuma himself was a populist and supported Zulu ethnic nationalism, but he also gave expression to a more general discontent and a sense of betrayal shared by a diverse group of South Africans. He represented himself as left-wing, traditionalist, and anti-elitist. He depicted himself as a hero of the national liberation struggle. Popular among millions of poor Black South African men and women, Zuma was seen as a respectable patriarch, with his many wives, despite charges of rape. He spoke directly to the poor and connected with their daily struggles, which were not just about being poor but also about trying to hold on to steady relationships, building a home, and so on.[49] His popular song at political rallies, "Awaleth Unshini Wami" (Bring me my machine gun), spoke of his militancy, masculinity, and nationalism but also transported his followers back to the pre-1994 days, with their feeling of togetherness during large political gatherings and mass funerals, when their aspirations and vision of the future were clear and possibly more easily articulated.[50] Zuma appealed to the masses more than to the intellectuals,[51] and his populism included an open attitude toward conservative White minority groups, particular Afrikaners.

The climate of aggressive, radical, and racial populism continued to fester as Julius Malema, who stigmatized White South Africans as racists, was elected ANCYL president in 2008. His charisma and bold strokes commanded the media's attention, and as a central backer of ANC president Zuma, Malema stated that the ANCYL would "kill for Zuma." The media outcry was strong and only subsided after the ANCYL apologized and said the remark was "just a metaphor."[52] A year into his presidency, Malema launched a campaign to expropriate "White land" without compensation and nationalize the mines. The South African and international media from the beginning decried Malema's persona and political style and predicted a quick demise.[53] The South African media used words such as "boorish," "bigoted," and "racist." The American magazine *Time* called Malema a "moron" on its front page.[54] This media outrage obscured how Malema's populism was marked by stylistic continuity, a stigmatizing but substantive racial politics, and policy substance.

Historically, the ANCYL had always presented a more radical politics, particularly concerning race. Nelson Mandela in the 1940s had himself founded the youth league to present a more radical political alternative to the ANC leadership of that time. During the early 1990s, the first president of the unbanned youth league, Peter Mokaba, encouraged Black militancy among the ANC youth, while the ANC leadership negotiated with the NP.[55] He sparked a controversy in 1993 by singing the struggle song "Ayesaba Amagwala" (The Cowards Are Scared), which included the call to "dubula ibhunu" (shoot the Boer) at the memorial rally for ANC leader Chris Hani, after right-wing Afrikaner nationalists had murdered the former deputy commander of Umkhotonto we Sizwe, the armed wing of the ANC in exile. Hani had always been popular among militant Black youth. Mokaba's singing was a strong response to the violence of the White right wing but seen by many in the White minority as racial stigmatization. Malema adopted the style and the struggle song from Mokaba for his own brand of politics.

For Malema's racial populism, the stigmatization of Whites was central. On May 1, 2009, Malema called DA leader Zille a "racist little girl" and warned her that, as the new Western Cape premier, she would report to "President Zuma."[56] On January 11, 2010, Malema argued that former president F. W. de Klerk was a "product of apartheid" who had been "forced to release Nelson Mandela from prison." While celebrating the twentieth anniversary of Mandela's release from prison, Malema said in a speech at Drakenstein Prison in front of several thousand ANCYL supporters that de Klerk left a legacy of racism, unemployment, and housing problems and "must never be celebrated."[57] During another press conference that year, Malema scolded and removed a BBC reporter from the room after he called him a "bloody agent" and accused his questioning of having a "white tendency."[58]

Malema's public attacks on White politicians were connected to a strategic repositioning of himself against Mandela's politics of racial reconciliation. If Mandela championed racial reconciliation and performed nonracialism through calm forgiveness, Malema campaigned on the limits of this vision and acted out the anger of continued racial injustice. Malema popularized a critique of Mandela's racial politics that was rooted in a sophisticated understanding of racial inequality and the rejuvenation of an old left-wing tradition within the ANC. Indeed, the durability of Malema on the national stage—despite his many setbacks and critics—cannot be explained by a superficial reading of his populist style but must be rooted in how the story he told connected his race and class politics. Malema argued that the moment Black people started to govern, Whites began to hide power in invisible places such as multinational corporations, the media, and the judiciary. He said his mission was "to go and find power where it hides, and retrieve it."[59] The story that he told about the transformation from apartheid to post-apartheid became so popular among his poor Black supporters because it rang true.

The White minority continued its reputation management during the elections of 2009 but adapted its strategies in response to the populism of Zuma and Malema. The DA was able to co-opt nonracialism from the ANC to reinterpret it as an ideology of color blindness. Since 2004, the DA had started to use "nonracialism" in their political documents. Together with the positive idea of diversity, the party defined it as a new principle of its politics.[60] The party acknowledged the consequences of the racism and exploitation of apartheid, but the party leadership argued that the answer to racism was not "more racism." The DA political leader, Tony Leon, had critiqued Mbeki for "playing the race card," which for him undermined the true principle of nonracialism: "not seeing race."[61] The DA argued that they did not want to put "colour above all else."

The DA intensified its role as defenders of the ideology of nonracialism in response to Malema's successful racial populism. In 2011, the new leader, Helen Zille, defined nonracialism as each person being "a unique individual and not merely . . . some kind of representative of the category. . . . In a free society people don't have an identity imposed upon them by virtue of [a] racial category prescribed by others."[62] In 2013, the DA argued against the use of apartheid's racial taxonomy as the imposition of racial categories for political purposes; instead, it promoted the concept of "disadvantage" (mostly historical) rather than race. It represented the ANC's political use of racial quotas as the "re-racialisation of South Africa." The DA thus increasingly represented nonracialism as an ideology that promoted "color blindness."

White Afrikaner organizations turned to a radicalized destigmatization strategy in response to Malema's racial populism: legal challenges in the court system that claimed what Malema was saying was hate speech and racism. AfriForum pioneered this strategy, which was established in 2006 by the trade union Solidarity and defined itself as a "civil-rights organization." During a rally at a university campus in March 2010, Malema again sang the song "Ayesaba Amagwala," with its provocative call to "kill the Boer." When Malema continued singing the song at rallies, AfriForum took their hate-speech complaint against Malema to an Equality Court, one of South Africa's specialized courts designated to hear matters relating to unfair discrimination, hate speech, and harassment.

The song, according to them, "made many Afrikaners feel degraded" and was meant "to incite actions that would harm" Whites.[63] The court case continued for a year, but in 2011, Judge Collin Lamont ruled in the South Gauteng High Court in Johannesburg that singing the song "undermined the dignity of Afrikaners and was discriminatory and harmful."[64] AfriForum's destigmatization strategy had the court declare that "reverse racism" by Black South Africans actually existed.

Counterpublic Debates: Marked White Men

The end of Afrikaner nationalism made White Afrikaans-speaking South Africans visible in a new way. They could no longer hide behind nationalism; their bodies have become visible to others. Instead of a stable collective ethnic identity, their Whiteness and gender have become marked. In contrast to the debates in the public sphere, which revolved around racism and reputation management, discussions in the White Afrikaans counterpublic have been more introspective. The White Afrikaans-speaking minority, preoccupied with the stigma that apartheid has left on them, feel their collective identity has been fractured; for many, being White and Afrikaans has become a problem. Their difficulty also goes beyond stigmatization: Afrikaner nationalism no longer offers identification or protection. Specifically, Afrikaner men can no longer wrap their interests in nationalism. No longer powerful enough to racialize, categorize, and label others, their White masculinity has become racialized and embodied. After apartheid, their bodies have become conspicuous to others. They manage this crisis of embodiment in strategic but surprising ways.

In the counterpublic debate, Afrikaner men are visible but remain dominant. Their new visibility forces them to reckon with the apartheid past, but it also enables a symbolic reconfiguration as they make themselves visible as victims, managing their newfound visibility by presenting an injured White masculinity. In part inspired by the language of the TRC—who used the language of trauma and the label of victim liberally—they present themselves as victims. They use the language of pain and trauma, thus echoing the identity politics they once decried. What is emerging is a White identity politics that co-opts the language of identity politics used by marginalized groups to recuperate power.

An analysis of three debates between 2000 and 2010 will show how White Afrikaans-speaking men of different generations claim victimhood through dramatic emotional language that enables them to appeal for clemency. The different generations of Afrikaner men all make themselves visible by laying claim to the troubled and traumatized condition of the victim. Rather than coming to terms with Whiteness in the way Adorno imagined, these White men collectively decry their visibility and battle over who is guilty and should be held accountable for the past and their current predicament.

"We Are Sick"

In 2000, Professor Emeritus Willem de Klerk published *Afrikaners: Kroes, Kras, Kordaat* (Afrikaners: Sickly, drastic, bold), in which he predicted that the end of Afrikaner culture was near.[65] As brother of former president F. W. de Klerk and an important newspaper editor, de Klerk was a powerful figure during apartheid. Among other things, he wrote a book on the history of Afrikanerdom in the 1970s, which was assigned to students at Afrikaans universities. In his new book, de Klerk addressed the future of Afrikanerdom after 1994. His diagnosis was dire: "Afrikanerdom has been sick the last few years. Literally curled up, sick, unwell."[66] He observed that Afrikaners had endured many losses since apartheid ended, but he was most critical of the younger generation's response. Young Afrikaners, he argued, were denying the existence of the *Volk* and their Afrikaner identity; he wrote that they had begun thinking that "survival forces you to shake off your Afrikanerdom at school and in your social group, even in your language use." De Klerk predicted the end of "Afrikaner consciousness" unless the youth started to fight the "disease" immediately.[67]

De Klerk's manifesto was the first time a prominent Afrikaner nationalist articulated the group's pain. However, his patronizing diagnosis of a "sick" younger generation provoked a furious response, and an emotional debate ensued. In an open letter in the Afrikaans newspaper *Beeld*, journalist Chris Louw accused de Klerk—and by extension the entire older generation—of traumatizing their children in order to defend apartheid.[68] De Klerk and Louw differed in age by thirty years.

De Klerk's generation designed apartheid in the 1960s and 1970s, while Louw's generation was conscripted and sent to the South African border to defend it in the 1980s. The letter "Boetman is die bliksem in" (Young chap is hellish) focused on the conspicuous absence of any "I" in de Klerk's manifesto: nowhere did the former apartheid ideologue reflect on his own role. It also accused the older generation of never going to war, yet making their children fight the South African border wars in Namibia, Zambia, and Angola.[69] Furthermore, Louw argued, de Klerk's generation handed over power to the Black majority but never considered the future of Afrikaners. He asked de Klerk what to do next: "Should I quit my job, should I continue being angry and hating, should I go overseas, should I invest all my money abroad, should I just give up?" The older generation, Louw wrote, refused to take responsibility. On behalf of his generation, he argued that de Klerk's generation denied the pain it caused to younger White men and faulted them for not proudly confronting post-apartheid South Africa.

It was also the first time Afrikaners debated how to overcome their troubled condition. Actually, the generations agreed on their distressed condition—they used a similar terminology of pain and trauma—but disagreed about who was responsible and how to cope with it. De Klerk suggested that Afrikaners should readily accept the new situation, while Louw first wanted the older generation to take responsibility. De Klerk remained dismissive of the debate. He never took responsibility, and his stoicism signified the old authoritarian Afrikaner masculinity. In his response to Louw, which was published a few weeks after the open letter, he wrote: "I hope we move away from hidden agendas, self-pitying victim complexes, and the search for a scapegoat."[70] Nevertheless, the newspaper received hundreds of letters, most of which supported Louw's position. Many commenters were former soldiers from the South African Defence Force, who said they felt "misled, intimidated, indoctrinated, silenced and eventually betrayed by their people."[71] Personally, Louw also received many letters saying that finally someone dared to say what many felt but could not put into words. Louw's open letter had captured their experience in the language of pain and trauma, but it had not shown how to confront it.

Afrikaners' "Screws Are Loose"

In 2003, a younger generation joined the counterpublic debate. A group consisting of five former members of a suburban gospel band, Fokofpolisiekar (Fuck-off-police-car), suddenly rose to popularity with loud punk-rock songs in Afrikaans.[72] The members, barely in their twenties, wrote songs about well-worn teenage themes like boredom in the suburbs and rebellion against their parents' Christian faith, but also about specifically Afrikaner topics. Their songs said they felt like ticking "time bombs" caused by "gaping holes" in their upbringing. Their first music video, *Hemel op die Platteland* (Heaven in the countryside), contrasts idealistic images of growing up in the suburbs with lyrics about their troubled state of mind. The song diagnoses the young Afrikaner as suffering from a psychotic condition— "a screw is loose"—and says they feel total apathy. Snapshots in the music video include the old South African Defence Forces and the former all-White South African rugby team, traditional masculine disciplining forces of Afrikaner nationalism. Together with images of Afrikaner nationalism such as the Afrikaner language monument they hint at the nationalist origins of their crisis. The singer taunts: "Can you regulate me?" Sarcastic and ironic, the lyrics address an unnamed other—presumably the older generation—to help them overcome their troubled condition.

Something was wrong with young Afrikaners, the band affirmed, but what? The band seemed to have captured widespread frustration among Afrikaner youth. Yet there was no agreement as to what their success and the outburst of emotions in their songs and concerts meant. The lead singer of the band, Francois van Coke, said they were just rebellious: "The Afrikaner has always been told exactly what to do. . . . We rebelled against that and tried to forge a new direction."[73] The Afrikaans media hailed the band both as victorious ("Afrikaans punk is sweeping everything flat") and dangerous ("Controversial Afrikaans band suffers Christians' wrath"). The rise of Fokofpolisiekar provided a new turn in the debate: the post-apartheid Afrikaner generation was now the center of attention, not those who designed apartheid or fought to defend it. Artist and music critic Andries Bezuidenhout found the band's lyrics angry and nihilistic.[74] Others emphasized their uncertainty and questioning. Youth culture critic Ann

Klopper asked: "Does Fokofpolisiekar advocate regeneration by means of destruction as the songs 'Destroy Yourself' (*Vernietig jouself*) and 'Burn South Africa' (*Brand Suid-Afrika*) suggest?"[75] For all her youth, Klopper remained skeptical that the band's idea of renewal was going to work.

The popularity of Fokofpolisiekar signified the rise of a new kind of identity politics, which responded to the visibility of White men after Afrikaner nationalism. It positioned young White men as a generation of suffering victims. The compilation album *Forgive Them for They Know Not What They Do* features the song "Antibiotics" (*Antibiotika*), which best reflects this politics. In its opening verse, it tells us that Afrikaans survived because of a stroke of luck: "genocide prevented." Van Coke describes feeling like a tourist in his own country. He is "a helpless animal in a cage, taking antibiotics." He continues: "It's the truth that does violence to me! I'm living in disbelief. My suffering is endless." Whether the lyrics of this popular song are ironic or serious, it is the imagery that is striking: it depicts middle-class young White men as helpless and traumatized. However, this language is not unfamiliar to South Africans. Rather, the vocabulary of genocide, violence, and suffering has long been associated with the victims of apartheid—not the sons of the perpetrators. Fokofpolisiekar draws on the language of identity politics to describe their own feelings and situation.

Fokofpolisiekar was the first commercially successful Afrikaans punk-rock band. The band itself was optimistic about having a positive influence on the younger generation. They believed the music gave the youth a new sense of pride. According to lead singer van Coke:

> There is fear and anxiety that our identity will be lost. My point of view: we've never been pro-Afrikaner or pro the Afrikaans language—we just are who we are, like it or not. The most important thing is for people to give it space to breath, to grow, to allow change—change is good. . . . Trying to hold on to what went before, to keep it the same is never going to work. There are a lot of people who are proud of being Afrikaans, and I get a lot of emails saying that because of our music they're proud of being Afrikaner again or that they think Afrikaans is cool.[76]

The band's success opened the door for other Afrikaans bands, which, with similar energy and purpose, tried to define the state of their generation and endow it with pride.

De la Rey Debate

In the summer of 2007, small groups of fans began bringing the old apartheid flag of South Africa to Bok van Blerk's concerts. Young Afrikaners would wrap the orange, blue, and white flag around themselves as they sang along to van Blerk's song "De la Rey." It was a typical rock song with a military march and catchy melody, but it was the lyrics that made it a hit. The song narrated the story of the Afrikaner general Koos de la Rey, who had battled British forces a century ago during the Boer Wars.[77] In the Second Boer War, from 1899 to 1902, the much larger British force overwhelmed the Boers, or Afrikaners, in a scramble for gold and land, but not before General de la Rey inflicted punishing defeats on them. "De la Rey, de la Rey," van Blerk's refrain pleads, "will you come and lead the Boers?" This call for leadership of the Afrikaners, as well as the provocative display of old apartheid symbols, provoked a debate in the counterpublic.

The Afrikaans media raised questions of identity but never captured the song's politics. Did it promote Afrikaner nationalism among young Afrikaners? Were White Afrikaans-speaking South Africans really looking for a heroic figure like de la Rey to lead the threatened Afrikaners? If so, to what end? Or was the song a cynical but commercially successful ploy on the part of a cultural industry tapping into cultural nostalgia? Did young White Afrikaans-speaking South Africans indeed long for the apartheid past, as shown by their wearing the flag? Or was it simply enjoyable to sing along to a catchy song in their native tongue?[78] These were some of the questions the media raised. Koos Kombuis, an Afrikaner musician twenty years older than Bok van Blerk, acknowledged that the song made him long for his Afrikaner upbringing during apartheid.[79] Kombuis's response was peculiar, not only because he was a popular anti-apartheid singer but also because he had symbolically renounced his Afrikanerness in a statement in 2006. This public rejection of Afrikanerness had caused a fierce debate in the media. Kombuis had stated that he wanted to no longer deal with the "psychological baggage" of being of Afrikaner descent. However, as much as he had forsaken his ethnic identity, he said he remained Afrikaner nevertheless; the song pulled him back in, even though he could not politically identify with the message of the song. "It created an incredible tension in my body," he wrote, like a puppet; he worried which heartstring had been tugged. Kombuis articulated what many men felt: they wanted to get away from feeling marked and visible, a new condition that came with being a White man after apartheid.

Bok van Blerk's concerts were an unparalleled ritual of the brotherhood of White Afrikaner men after 1994. His concerts drew fathers and sons in equally massive numbers. Just as Afrikaner nationalism had drawn on a mythological representation of the Voortrekkers, the new White identity politics drew on the dead General de la Rey to stage its post-apartheid trauma and victimhood. What is striking is how progressives such as Antjie Krog did not challenge this performance but reaffirmed it. Krog, the influential South African public intellectual, connected the emotional response to various moral challenges young Afrikaners face.[80] She argued that the apartheid past confronts the younger generation with a set of uncomfortable questions: What is their relationship to the apartheid past? How does apartheid play into the bond with their parents? And how does it relate to their experiences in the present with affirmative action? She said that few young Afrikaners can ignore these moral questions. Krog argued that young Afrikaners suffer from "trauma," which she defined simply as a "nonordinary human experience." In a familiar South African move, she likened the younger generation of Afrikaners to the children of Nazis, who similarly could not share their stories after the war because of the social stigma. According to Krog, the younger generation has to reach back to the "de la Rey generation" because their parents' generation makes them feel too guilty and ashamed to talk about their Afrikaner history. "De la Rey" helps to break the silence about being Afrikaans.

At concerts Bok van Blerk asked the crowd: "I'm proud of my language and culture. Are you?" In the Afrikaans-language daily newspaper *Beeld*, Louis Pepler (Bok van Blerk's real name) represented the lyrics as a claim to belong and a testament to Afrikaner pride. "I'm part of this rainbow country of ours," he said. "But I'm one of the colors, and I'm sticking up for who I am. I'm proud of who I am."[81] His wish to be just like other groups in South Africa and be proud of who he was captures the goal of White identity politics: to normalize Whiteness and thereby disconnect being visibly White from the history of apartheid and White racism.

The German way of coming to terms with the past shaped many South Africans' views about the process of unlearning racism. This fact is often obscured because South Africa's TRC provided a successful alternative model of transitional justice in contrast to the victor's justice of the Nuremberg trials. However, the case of Germany is very different from that of South Africa, where the White perpetrators of apartheid were only a small minority. In South Africa, therefore, there has been a debate in the public sphere as well as a starkly different debate in the counterpublic sphere. In the public sphere, the White minority practice White identity politics with the goal of destigmatizing their identity, while hardly confronting their racism. In the counterpublic sphere, the White Afrikaans-speaking minority address apartheid through an intergenerational debate, in which the younger generation position themselves as victims of apartheid, a move that various South African commentators have legitimized by likening this new generation and their "traumatic" condition to the children of Nazis.

The idea of young White South Africans as victims of apartheid and a racist culture became central to the 2007 "Reitz Four" racism case at the University of the Free State in Bloemfontein. As part of an initiation ritual for their university residence hall (Reitz), four White students shot a video that included five Black Reitz employees who were (seemingly) being forced to reenact initiating rituals for students, including the eating of (what seemed to be) food that had been urinated upon by the students. When the South African media broadcast the video, various ANC politicians called for the students to be expelled from the university. The Reitz case posed a challenge for the rector and vice-chancellor of the University of the Free State, Jonathan Jansen, who had just been appointed.

Jansen was a prolific academic and public intellectual who had often spoken up about racism and Whiteness in South Africa. He had just published *Knowledge in the Blood: Confronting Race and the Apartheid Past*, a study in which he likened young White South Africans to the children of German perpetrators. In the book he paints a portrait of White youth as rather hapless victims indoctrinated with apartheid ideology at home, school, and church. In his role as vice-chancellor, he suddenly found himself in a position to act—how would he judge these boys' racists acts? He answered this question in his official address as he accepted his university post. According to Jansen, the university as an institution had failed the young White perpetrators. In an admirable indictment of South Africa's institutional racism, he argued that the university as an institution had allowed for the racist incident to happen. He decided that "out of a gesture of racial reconciliation and the need for healing," the university would withdraw its charges. Jansen seemed to believe that White youth had no obligation to come to terms with their Whiteness.

However, Jansen's forgiveness of the young White South Africans and his call for racial reconciliation sounded hollow in a country where the magnitude of racial inequality remained staggering. In 2011, Archbishop Emeritus Desmond Tutu, chairman of the TRC, proposed a "wealth tax" on White South Africans for the benefits they received from apartheid. He presented his proposal as a practical way for Whites to make compensation and resolve their guilt. Tutu argued that South Africa's White citizens needed to accept that they all "benefited from apartheid." "Your children could go to good schools," he said. "You lived in smart neighborhoods. Yet so many of my fellow citizens become upset when you mention this. Why? Some are crippled by shame and guilt, and respond with self-justification or indifference. Both attitudes make that we are less than we can be." Tutu acknowledged that this call for a "wealth tax" would have been more appropriate at the end of the TRC in 1998, but that the government at the time "didn't like the TRC, so they didn't do it." Anton Alberts, the spokesperson of the mainly White political party Freedom Front Plus, responded that Tutu's proposal bordered on "the emotional statements" of the Black populist Malema.

Zuma's presidency fanned the flames of Black and White populism. For Malema, the central enemy in South Africa's story of racial inequality was "White capital"—not just "capital" or "economic elites." White capital, he claimed, owned South Africa's land and mines—and he was not wrong. Malema demanded the nationalization of the mines, an idea that had been widely popular among the ANC leadership before the end of apartheid. Malema argued that "White capital" needed to accept "the failures of capitalism" and that the state should be prepared to "own the mines and other means of production." The media and business elite tried to pressure Zuma to publicly condemn Malema's public utterances as "unacceptable" and his conduct as "alien to the ANC." The ANC ultimately suspended Malema from the party in 2011. In 2013, however, Malema founded a new political party, the Economic Freedom Fighters (EFF), which won twenty-four seats (out of four hundred) in the National Assembly in the 2014 general election. In the speech that celebrated the first-year anniversary of the party, the EFF's commander-in-chief attacked ANC politician and deputy president Cyril Ramaphosa, accusing him of being an "economic security guard" for White capital. According to Malema, "There is no real black economic empowerment policy in the country. It was just a system designed by white men to protect their capital."

In the following chapters, I will turn from the analysis of the national debates in the public and counterpublic sphere to the everyday reality of White South Africans. However, in the next two chapters I will first address further the rise of White identity politics: how the White capitalist elite were successful after the democratic transition in enticing the Black business elite to join their project of whitewashing history, and why the rise of Black populism was met by White populism in post-apartheid South Africa.

Elites and White Identity Politics

The New Master's Tools

On August 1, 2003, the Afrikaanse Handelsinstituut (AHI) bestowed President Thabo Mbeki with its highest award of honor at a gala dinner in Pretoria. In his acceptance speech, Mbeki said that South Africa's economic history held many lessons for the country's future growth.[1] He especially singled out the poor Whites of the 1920s and how the White Afrikaner elite tackled this problem.[2] The wealthier White Afrikaner community pooled their resources with the poorer White Afrikaners to uplift the poor. State policies also helped. "This history tells us," he continued, "that without strong economic development of a people, political emancipation may lose its meaning." Today, the country is faced with the challenge of uplifting poor black South Africa. We must "broaden economic participation to all South Africans," Mbeki said, "so that together we can strive to reproduce the economic prosperity that marked the era of Afrikaner development in our country."

President Mbeki's depiction of White supremacy as a model for the ANC's fight against Black poverty is a surprising historical analogy. Even if we consider that he was trying to win over his audience of White Afrikaans-speaking businessmen, this message is in marked contrast to his previous public statements chastising the White South African community for the results of this White-centric economic growth. In his "two nations" speech in 1998, then–Deputy President Mbeki stated that South Africa was composed not of one but two nations: a Black and poor country and a White and rich country.[3] Unlike the case in Germany, Mbeki said, where the West paid to help the East when the Berlin Wall came down, Whites were not doing the same in South Africa. He accused White-owned corporations of dodging their taxes while blaming the government for not delivering services. He explicitly questioned whether South Africa had made progress toward "transforming" into a "nonracial society." Quoting the African American poet Langston Hughes, Mbeki warned that a "dream deferred" would explode.

Mbeki's open threat to the White business elite focused on the structural issues left unaddressed by the TRC. Many saw his statement as a break with the period of racial reconciliation of the mid-1990s. It seemed as well to end a period of "economic reconciliation," to use the words of the South African political economist Patrick Bond, during which the White elite had wielded great influence in making economic policy.[4] The ANC leadership had long been ambivalent toward the development of a Black capitalist class.[5] Officially, the party was committed to socialism and radical socioeconomic transformation. The White business elite used the ANC's ambivalence and their strong insider position to their advantage during the Convention for a Democratic South Africa (CODESA), where they ensured that private property and other capitalistic principles were central to the foundation of a new South Africa.[6] After 1994, international financial institutions together with White capital further pushed the ANC to abandon its ambitious pro-poor program in the face of rising unemployment and the devaluing of the rand. In 1996, the ANC adopted Growth, Employment, and Redistribution (GEAR), an economic program focused more on reducing the fiscal deficit and lowering inflation than fighting poverty and improving livelihoods.[7] The strong popular opposition to this neoliberal program, from within the ANC and its supporting labor unions, raised questions about the ANC leadership's commitment to nonracialism, the South African ideology with its double meaning of rejecting racism and racialism.

At the beginning of his presidency, in 1999, Mbeki painted South Africa's problem as fundamentally one of racism and racial inequality—which Black economic empowerment had to address. His resolve was to connect a new program of Black Economic Empowerment (BEE) with nonracialism, by creating a new Black "patriotic bourgeoisie," a Black capitalist class, who would contribute to the poor Black majority through racial solidarity.[8] In the first year of his presidency, in a speech for the

Black Management Forum, Mbeki unapologetically endorsed this idea of creating a Black bourgeoisie.[9] He framed BEE as essential to the struggle against racism, which he saw as a problem related to the present day and to the legacy of apartheid. Mbeki rebuked those who emphasized class inequality over racial inequality and explicitly warned against following those who failed to focus on racial inequality. However, he confessed at the end of his speech that he still did not know what BEE would entail. For Mbeki, racism was the problem and a nonracial society the solution, but how to get from one to the other remained an open question.

Mbeki got to answer this question at the AHI gala dinner in 2003 by arguing that BEE was to be modeled after the "economic empowerment" of the Afrikaners in the 1930s. On the surface, Mbeki seems merely to be charming his audience and utilizing White history for his own goals. By invoking White poverty in the past, he solicits sympathy for Black poverty today. But this normalization of White supremacy is indicative of a deeper transformation: it signifies the success of a new White identity politics through which the White business elite would co-opt the ANC's anti-apartheid language to neutralize policies against racial inequality. Black Economic Empowerment is a unique South African experiment to fight racism and racial inequality. Its threat to White dominance in the economy was significant in the late 1990s when the ANC gained control of the state and White political parties lost political power. I will focus on the role of the AHI—the only remaining formerly Whites-only chamber of commerce in post-apartheid South Africa—using it as a lens to analyze the White business elite and its cultural narratives intended to maintain legitimacy, destigmatize its apartheid legacy, and project a nonracial image. We shall see how the AHI turned the challenge of unlearning racism and fighting racial inequality to its own advantage. Ultimately, the AHI made President Mbeki proclaim the "master's tools [are able to] dismantle the master's house," to paraphrase another African American poet, the Black feminist Audre Lorde.[10]

South Africa's "Elite Transition"

Political economists depict South Africa's democratic transition of 1994 as an elite transition from apartheid to neoliberalism, during which Whites continued their economic dominance. In the standard narrative, international financial capital and White capital are said to have forced the ANC government to give up its communist and socialist leanings and adopt neoliberal economic policies that largely benefited the affluent White minority. The brokered economic agreements between the ANC and NP firmly ingrained a set of capitalist principles in the constitution, such as private property rights. Furthermore, shortly after the democratic transition, the ANC adopted the pro-growth strategy GEAR, which included policies to achieve stable interest rates, tight control of government expenses, an independent national reserve bank, and the privatization of various public companies. Consequently, the transition to democracy is dubbed an "elite transition," which denotes that the White elite, in politics and business, struck a class compromise with ANC's political elite.

However, there is no consensus on why precisely this elite transition happened and what exactly the role was of the White elite.[11] Theorists of the "elite transition" too easily assume that the ANC's leadership gave up on its goals of Black liberation and that class replaced race as the dividing line in South Africa—a viewpoint Mbeki explicitly rejected. The theory also sits uneasily with the prevalent view that Mbeki racialized the political debate after Mandela and focused explicitly on racism and racial inequality, renewing the ANC's commitment to a nonracial society and the fight against racism and racial inequality. One reason these questions have remained unanswered is because the story of the elite transition has been told in an impersonal and abstract way: a story in which the main protagonists are faceless forces of "capital accumulation," "globalization," and "international markets."[12] This is only half of the story of the transition.

The other half is about the identity politics of the White business elite. This part of the story is about the racial project of the White elite, who have used their access and privilege to seize upon rhetorical opportunities to manipulate the cultural narrative to their own advantage. My analysis builds on but also moves beyond the structural analysis of the elite transition to examine the cultural processes at work at the elite level and how they shape the politics of race. American sociologists Omi and Winant employ the concept of "racial project" to analyze the link between representations of race with social-structural manifestations of racial hierarchy.[13] Different actors try to politically reorganize the state through racial projects to advocate for or resist racial policies and practices. To understand how the White business elite have responded to and accommodated the ANC's racial project and antiracism policies, we must take an in-depth look at organized business: where White and Black business elites meet and cultural narratives are made.

The Sociology of Elites

Sociologists who study elites have long been interested in how power and inequality are distributed in the form of economic, social, cultural, and political capital.[14] More recently, they have emphasized the role of culture in the study of elites—who are concerned about their interests but also their identities—and the ability of elites to accommodate cultural challenges and use them for their own empowerment.[15] American elites, for example, adapted to democratic pressures to be more open and meritocratic by embracing the rhetoric of rights movements, such as the civil rights movement. Elites adapt to change by changing identities and rewriting cultural narratives. Sociologists of elites focus specifically on institutions—such as schools, families, and clubs—as sites for the cultural reproduction of elites.[16] This provides a good starting point for my analysis of the White business elite: inside business organizations, such as the AHI, the elite use culture to help constitute their identities and construct themselves as a class. What has been less clear, in these accounts, is the role of race.[17] In particular, the racial views of the White elite, because of their power and privilege, do not receive the scrutiny they deserve.[18]

The White elite use culture in three different ways to defend their interests and identity: first, they use storytelling to shape the dominant cultural narratives in a society; second, they value cultural capital in the process of the racial integration of elite organizations like the AHI, as the White business elite carefully selects new nonwhite members for their cultural competence and compatibility; and third, they adopt the political strategies and language of marginalized communities to neutralize their effect in undoing White power and privilege.

It is a mistake to place the elite, just because they are elite, outside South Africa's experiment with unlearning racism. Globalization and economic privilege have loosened the ties of the White elite with their country but not completely undone them. Even before the end of apartheid, the White business elite were concerned about their stigma as racists and status as Whites, as well as their need for recognition from the ANC. South African economist Sampie Terreblanche argues that after apartheid the White elite adapted "like a chameleon," a metaphor that captures the success of their change, though not its substance.[19] In fact, we know very little about how the White business elite have adapted and how they think about themselves: how White businessmen—together with Black and Coloured businessmen—exercised agency and created new meanings; how they adapted to the challenge of unlearning racism and Black empowerment by practicing White identity politics.

White elite identity politics succeeded Afrikaner nationalism and its secretive and undemocratic elite politics.[20] White identity politics involves the strategic politicization of a collective White identity. As a racial project, it masquerades as a process of unlearning racism because it co-opts the ideas of nonwhite people and sometimes nonwhite people themselves. However, its goal is to promote White racial self-interest while masking racial inequality and White privilege. By examining the case of the AHI, I tell the story of the White business elite who rewrote history to reclaim legitimacy, influence policy, and project a nonracial identity, a story in which the new Coloured and Black leadership of the organization plays a complicated role. However, it is ultimately the AHI as an organization that has enabled its White members to cloak their interests in cultural narratives that manipulate the discourses of Black economic empowerment and nonracialism to their own advantage.

Black Economic Empowerment and Nonracialism

Black Economic Empowerment (BEE) is a bold South African experiment to address the economic inequality resulting from the history of South Africa's White supremacy rule. By American standards, the ANC government's ambition to foster a Black capitalist class through BEE as a nonracial nation-building strategy is radical: the creation of a new Black middle class that was to become the vanguard of Black integration into the economic mainstream. Through a series of legal acts, the ANC government promoted BEE.[21] The report of the Black Economic Empowerment Commission in 2001 recommended greater government involvement to further support BEE, which the ANC pursued from then onwards.[22] The government proposed in most sectors of the economy that 25 percent of equity ownership be transferred over a ten-year period to Black investors, though it never sought a complete transfer of business ownership to Black people.[23] It used its various powers as legislator, owner of state assets, and large-scale consumer to force industries to cooperate.[24] Yet despite the ANC government's bold BEE program, the deracialization of the economy in terms of ownership, management, and procurement has been slow.[25]

The ANC started using the language of Black empowerment in the early 1990s to emphasize the need to deracialize the economy and achieve a nonracial society. However, it took considerable time to specify a particular policy.[26] In 1994, Mbeki wrote, "Non-racialism in politics has to be accompanied by non-racialism in the economy," which was "a battle for all of us to wage."[27] However, during the transition to democracy, the ANC's challenge was to balance the demands of democracy with those of the international financial markets.[28] President Mandela's politics of racial reconciliation, which resulted in a united government comprising the ANC and the NP, helped win the trust of the international business community. When the ANC took over from the government of national unity in 1996, it was in a position to install more sweeping forms of racial redress to achieve a nonracial society, which took the form of affirmative action and BEE. President Mbeki's move to equate BEE with nonracialism was the logical extension of a long ANC tradition to repurpose the concept of nonracialism for a new political and economic context.[29] The goal was to create a Black middle class, who, hypothetically, would use their new wealth to ensure that benefits would trickle down to the poor. As he committed himself to the creation by the state of a Black capitalist class, he presented it as an essential step toward achieving a nonracial society and winning the fight against racism. Yet in 1999, the president and the ANC still had no policy by which to accomplish their new project of empowerment.

To analyze the role of the White business elite in the emergence of Black economic empowerment, I focus on their manipulation of the ANC's transformative discourse of BEE. I am not the first to point to these manipulative efforts: in 2003, Moeletsi Mbeki, the president's brother, declared BEE a sham, dreamed up by White capital to seduce the ANC away from nationalizing the economy and produce a predatory Black elite.[30] Similarly, the anti-apartheid activist and sociologist Neville Alexander wrote that the ANC government only "serves the interests of the capitalist class." According to Alexander, this class now has a different racial composition but is also "the very same capitalist class who profited from the system of overt and systematic racism which the world called apartheid and which now allegedly is a thing of the past."[31] The problem with these accusations is that they do not explain *how* the ANC was manipulated or *what* the White business elite did to achieve this goal. Furthermore, they present a one-dimensional view of the elite, with the White business elite as perpetrators and Black politicians as victims, without showing how these elite groups exercised agency or interacted.

The White business elite played an important role in the development of the idea of BEE. This idea can be traced back to the response of the NP government to the Soweto uprising of 1976, when the "government cautiously enacted measures to promote African business as a buffer between the White minority and the black masses."[32] In the mid-1980s, the White business elite stopped relying on the NP, in order to avert Black liberation and a democratic revolution.[33] They organized a number of meetings with the ANC, led by Thabo Mbeki, and developed strong ties with the movement.[34] The business elite needed to accommodate the ANC, who in return gave up its goal of the revolutionary seizure of power for a negotiated peace. The ANC, who had been fighting "racist capitalism," became the architects of "capitalist nonracialism." In the early 1990s, specifically White Afrikaans companies, such as the insurance company Sanlam, experimented with BEE.[35] On a voluntary basis, White corporate boards appointed Black nonexecutive directors; businesses were being sold to Black empowerment groups. The White business elite were behind the idea of BEE and its first execution.

When Mbeki became president, the White business elite saw an opening to define BEE and nonracialism on their own terms. The ANC's hesitancy under Mandela to formulate their economic policies provided this opportunity. For the White business elite, BEE was potentially a burden, but the policy also provided potential benefits for them. BEE offered the White business elite a chance to detach wealth from its association with Whiteness.[36] BEE could legitimatize South Africa's political economy and acquit Whites of the responsibility for ongoing economic inequality; economic inequality would no longer be perceived as a racial problem. The White business elite could pragmatically give up limited control and resources to preserve the majority of their power and wealth.[37] Ultimately, BEE would limit the deracialization of the economy in comparison to the radical alternative policy of nationalization and redistribution to achieve a nonracial society. Despite the benefits of BEE to the White business elite, however, they do not explain how this elite influenced BEE policymaking.

What the AHI has done is to take an old idea of the ANC and reuse it to promote their own vision of BEE. In the early 1990s, antiapartheid activists argued that apartheid could be understood as a system of affirmative action for the White population, an assertion they made by pointing to the economic ascendance of the Afrikaners. ANC members drew this historical parallel to make the case for affirmative action for Black South Africans. However, the AHI has turned this notion on its head. They argue that the ANC today faces similar challenges as Afrikaners did in the 1930s and that it can learn from this history—that "economic empowerment" of the Afrikaners is similar to Black economic empowerment. This masks, however, how the economic model of Afrikaners was fundamentally rooted in White supremacy. The organization can promote this historical narrative only because it has also started to diversify its leadership. It has created a new, diverse post-apartheid business culture between the White and Black business elites, which cajoles nonwhite AHI members—through persuasion and collaboration—to shape Black economic empowerment and nonracialism after the AHI's own historical image. In this way, White identity politics reframes the history of White supremacy to normalize Whiteness while creating a positive White identity for its White members in post-apartheid South Africa.

The History of the Afrikaanse Handelsinstituut

From its inception, the Afrikaanse Handelsinstituut (AHI) was closely aligned with Afrikaner nationalism. For a long time, the White English dominated the South African economy, particularly mining and other large industries, with White Afrikaners being dominant only in farming and agriculture. In the late 1930s, with the South African economy experiencing new growth after the Great Depression, a coalition emerged of the nationalist Broederbond and Sanlam, the big insurance company from Cape Town, to promote a specific kind of Afrikaner capitalism. After the centenary celebrations of the Great Trek in 1938, the coalition was able to raise capital in the Afrikaner community. Under the slogan "'n Volk help homself" (A people saves itself), their cooperation resulted in the Eerste Ekonomiese Volkskongres, the First Economic Congress of the People, in 1939. The Volkskongres aimed to create three institutions: a finance house; an organization to assist in a "rescue action" for the White poor; and an Afrikaner chamber of commerce, the AHI.

From the 1930s, Afrikaner nationalism promoted the idea of *Volkskapitalisme*, or capitalism of the people. It aimed to make Afrikaners "economically autonomous." The AHI was officially established in 1941 to ideologically unite large- and small-scale businesses and to establish Afrikaner chambers of commerce across the country. During the war years, many Afrikaner businessmen gravitated toward the NP and the AHI, who together were able to translate their business complaints about English companies into ethnic grievances. Together with Afrikaner farmers, the AHI resisted attempts by government and large-scale enterprises to drive down agricultural prices. Instead, the AHI told farmers to invest their money in the "right places," namely, Afrikaner companies.

White supremacy, of which Afrikaner nationalism was a variant, was built on the lie of a group of White people "rescuing" themselves. Despite Afrikaner nationalists' emphasis on liberation and the virtue of autonomy—they described their position in the 1930s as "economic slavery"—their business enterprises relied on racial dominance, Black labor, and violence against Black South Africans. By 1938, Afrikaner farmers owned 87 percent of all marketed agricultural and livestock produce, an agricultural dominance achieved through land appropriation and other ways in which the South African state had clamped down on Black farmers.[38] None of their enterprises, agricultural or otherwise, could exist or operate without the availability, affordability, and control of Black labor. Profitability depended on uninterrupted access to Black labor. The AHI supported the developing apartheid program from the beginning; it demanded that African urban labor continue to be denied labor rights. Apartheid was seen by the AHI as a means of expediting Whites' access to African labor in urban and rural areas alike. The politicization of the poor White problem was equally about racial domination and racial anxiety. The White elite feared the poor mingling and becoming subordinate to Black South Africans. The apartheid government, with the full support of the AHI, simultaneously constrained Black workers in their rights and movements and demonized them as "cheap labor" and "unfair competition" for White workers.

In 1948, the NP came to power, and an age of economic ascendance arrived for the Afrikaners. The Afrikaner private sector grew, and state-owned companies rapidly expanded. From 1948 to 1976, the share of public corporations, which mainly employed White Afrikaners, nearly doubled in the South African economy. It was a time when affirmative action by the state was White and Afrikaans. It was also a time when the private sector had direct access to the government. Organizations such as the AHI relied on the NP to execute what was best for (Afrikaans) business; most cabinet ministers were, as one AHI member told me, "one call away." Through control of the state, Afrikaner nationalists were also able to get into the profitable business of mining.

The business elite's interests, organized in the AHI, were not always aligned with those of the NP. At times, business organizations such as the AHI pushed for political reforms to reduce economic tensions. This first came to the forefront when the police massacred a large number of Black South Africans in Sharpeville in 1960. Businesses proposed to lessen restrictions on the travel of nonwhite people. By the end of the 1970s, the private sector was increasingly worried about the poor management of the state and pressured the government for reform. President Botha managed to appease the Afrikaner business community through incremental political reforms, but economic troubles only increased: Central government expenditure, inflation, and unemployment kept rising throughout the 1980s.

The Transition to Democracy

By the late 1980s, many business leaders felt the cost of apartheid—at least for business—had become too high, and they pushed to open the door to negotiations.[39] It was evident to many of them that if South Africa were to move beyond apartheid, the ANC would be a dominant political force, and so in 1987, the AHI sent twenty-five members on a mission to start talks with the ANC. In the early 1990s, the leadership of the AHI was also involved in the CODESA negotiations that ultimately settled South Africa's transition to democracy and the setup of the new economic forum, which would later evolve into the National Economic Development and Labour Council (NEDLAC), the economic advisory board to the government. Internally, however, the structures of the AHI hardly changed throughout apartheid: in 1994, it had the same structure as during its inception in the late 1930s. Only Afrikaans-speaking White businessmen could be members, and on its board there were only members from Afrikaans businesses.

The transition to democracy presented the AHI with the task to adapt to democracy. This was the challenge facing the new executive head of the AHI, Jacob de Villiers, a popular former minister from the de Klerk government who was appointed by the executive council of the AHI in 1995. The AHI faced a crisis in legitimacy: how to become a trusted partner for the new government while staying independent and not losing its membership base—White Afrikaans-speaking businessmen. De Villiers thought cooperative agreements were the best way to restructure the AHI without drastic changes; these agreements would increase the legitimacy of the organization and make it a trusted government partner. He brokered an agreement with one of the large Black business organizations, the National African Federated Chamber of Commerce

(NAFCOC), to signal that the AHI had changed its attitude toward Black businesses. In my interview with him, de Villiers argued that the AHI had "an historic duty to cooperate" and that he wanted to work together with Black business organizations to offer them "our knowledge and to provide them access."[40]

However, Black businesses did not need the AHI for access to the government. For the White leadership of the AHI, preventing a merger was a matter of self-preservation and maintaining de facto segregation. Potential mergers could undermine the AHI's goal to remain an independent organization. ANC politicians and various Black organizations tried to pressure the AHI to merge with Black organizations, but de Villiers steered away from a merger because he was concerned about alienating some people, such as other AHI board members. Many thought the organization would not survive a transition to a racially integrated organization. Former AHI president Theo van Wyk said that the majority of White businessmen would not have accepted a merger because they would no longer have felt at home: "It would be a monster in which they would not be heard; it would alienate them and create room for other organizations that would not be so liberal as the AHI."[41] If the AHI did not maintain independence and a level of racial segregation, van Wyk implied, White businessmen would abandon it and replace it with a more racist organization.

The AHI performed a balancing act. It wanted to signal a willingness to cooperate but also to defend its existence as an autonomous and White-dominant organization. When it came to cooperating with the government and lobbying, the AHI leadership maintained it had its own "special" strategy for "confronting" the government. This approach, they said, did not include criticizing the government in the media or making noise during public debates. The AHI leadership argued that it no longer worked for the *trots*, or honor and glory, of their own organization but instead to "change the system for the larger lot." The organization's goals were to cooperate and move ahead together. This, they said, made the AHI a "valued partner" of the ANC government. In 1996, the AHI adopted a new slogan: "Saam skep ons welvaart," or "Together we create prosperity."

The Submission to the TRC

The test case for the AHI to claim legitimacy in the new South Africa came in 1997 with the invitation to submit a statement to the TRC. In the letter to the AHI, the TRC wrote that the goal of the "business hearings" was to examine "the role of business and labor with specific reference to the circumstances and context in which human rights violations occurred," and that the three broad themes of the hearings had the goal of revealing the causes and circumstances of the conflict, namely, (1) the relationship between apartheid and the economy; (2) business, government, and the trade unions; (3) the total onslaught, total strategy, and reform. The AHI leadership saw the TRC as an opportunity to play a role in the future and decided as one of the few Afrikaner organizations to make a submission to the committee.

For de Villiers, it was a moral necessity to claim a new legitimacy: "I thought, this is necessary, what happened was wrong. We are going to work together in the new South Africa."[42] The outgoing AHI president, van Wyk, led the team who prepared the submission. As an experienced lawyer, he took the initiative to write a statement: "We were not going to ask for amnesty; we were going to submit because we felt it is right to say certain things, we have to make a statement, and we want to play a constructive role in South Africa."[43]

The submission did not emerge without struggle. Objectors argued that the AHI should not get involved with the TRC because it represented the ANC "only with another hat." They argued that the AHI had done nothing wrong. Most businesses, these critics said, had actually created work in difficult times. They had educated Black South Africans and treated them well. They felt they actually had done good things during apartheid. Several AHI board members resigned in protest before the final draft was submitted to the TRC.

The TRC hearings were focused on the past, but the AHI used their submission to recast its role for the future. The AHI submission to the TRC is a curious document, full of evasive answers and halfhearted admissions, but the argumentation revealed the future-oriented goals of the document. The opening clause of the submission reads: "With this submission we intend to highlight some lessons that may be learnt from our experience in order to contribute to reconciliation and economic growth. . . . The AHI's submission is therefore an effort to assist in the process of understanding and healing."[44] It further stated: "The submission naturally does not deal with incidents involving gross human rights violations but focuses on the institutional part of our recent history." The AHI mimicked the reconciliatory language of the TRC, but it also boldly stated that there were "lessons to be learned" from the AHI experience.

In the document the AHI presented itself as an "inclusive organization" that was "open for everybody." However, as of 1997 none of the AHI leadership had been anything other than White, and almost all of its members were White Afrikaans-speaking South Africans. Under the header "Vision, Mission and Objectives," the AHI prominently stated its brand-new slogan: "Together we create prosperity"—as if to say the organization had already changed. In the section "Membership and Structure," the organization defined itself as "a voluntary association that spans the entire business spectrum and cannot easily be classified in terms of language or cultural groups."

Much of the text is taken up by a summary of the history of the AHI, which they describe as rooted in victimhood. The document starts with the assertion that "Afrikaners among others were impoverished by the Anglo-Boer War and the depression of the thirties" and that in the early days of the AHI, "economic issues consistently received precedence over political questions" and the focus was on "the economic upliftment of the impoverished Afrikaner." In this narrative, the history of the AHI is part and parcel of the efforts toward Afrikaner economic empowerment from the 1930s to the 1980s. In the AHI's telling, the White business elite was part of an ethnic group that lost a war, was powerless, and was largely apolitical—a group of people that needed to be empowered as victims, rather than victors.

When the AHI's history intersects with the implementation of apartheid and separate development (the years 1960–1976), the narrative of victimhood is no longer sustainable. The AHI had to confront their support of apartheid policies. The submission stated:

At the time the AHI focused on economic issues from a market-oriented point of view and on promoting the economic interests of its members. However, the AHI also made pronouncements on the social policies of the time. The AHI specifically endorsed separate development. Without in any way detracting from the AHI's willingness to accept responsibility for such pronouncements, it must be noted that support for separate development was part and parcel of the majority of the white community's thinking at the time. The white Afrikaans churches, newspapers, cultural organizations, and the wider community broadly subscribed to the notion that the separate development of South African population groups was seen as the best guarantee for overall justice and peace in the country. The AHI was part of that collective thinking.

When possible, the AHI presented itself as the exception to the rule ("We had nothing to do with politics"), but when this strategy seemed implausible (for instance, where the AHI had a documented history of endorsing apartheid policies), they hid behind groupthink. The AHI argued that apartheid's social policies had little to do with economic policy. The submission continued:

It should be noted that the main focus of the AHI activities was not concerned with the promotion of a particular social policy; it was the promotion of the business/economic interests of its members. The AHI promoted the principles of free enterprise amongst its members.

This defense exposed the weakness of the TRC's focus on severe human rights transgressions by the state and its limited attention to the violent exploitation of apartheid as an economic system. Ultimately, at the end of the submission, the AHI unapologetically denies that business profited from apartheid:

We are aware of perceptions that business, in particular Afrikaans business, benefited from apartheid. In as much as individual businesses benefited from apartheid, the AHI's structures were not used for this purpose and neither was it AHI policy to promote individual favoring.

This is a lie. The AHI and South Africa's corporations supported the apartheid regime and made massive profits from policies that inflicted great harm on millions of nonwhite South Africans, keeping them powerless and their labor cheap. The ANC politician Kader Asmal once argued that the TRC must include the category of "corporate war crimes"—using the analogy with the complicity of business with the Nazis in Germany during the Second World War—but it never did. The AHI's argument that its economic interests were not connected to apartheid's policies, which facilitated a hugely exploitative economic system, was remarkable for its audacity and falsehood.

The section on the AHI's history concludes with a portrait of the organization as an active agent of change in the political process, committed to the new South Africa. When it comes to bringing democracy, the AHI suddenly portrays itself as a very political organization. In 1984, the AHI stated that it experienced "a change of heart" that led to the amendment of the constitution of the organization. The amendment "effectively drew a line through the previous exclusivity of membership, and members of other language and population groups subsequently joined the AHI." It takes credit for setting up the NEDLEC:

> The AHI helped pave the way for and contributed to the preparations for the eventual transition. The political initiatives of 1990 were greatly facilitated by the AHI who helped to secure support for them countrywide among businesspeople.

One senses, in the language, a sense of pride, an emotion that is at odds with the purpose of the TRC submission. The AHI wrote that, since 1995, it was committed to and involved in "economic growth, which benefits all sectors of the population" and opposed to "emigration in body, mind and attitude," a reference to the criticism of White South Africans that supposedly many wanted to emigrate to another country or withdraw from South African society by living in gated communities.

At the end of the submission, the AHI admitted to the "major mistakes" of endorsing separate development, not lodging moral or economic objections against apartheid, and failing to produce a proper labor relations law. For these acts, the AHI wrote, it accepted moral responsibility, admitted that fellow South Africans were gravely wronged, and wished to express sincere regret and apologies to those affected. The AHI also admitted that apartheid made South Africa much poorer than the country and its people could have been. Again, this partial admission is used to reject the idea that business profited from apartheid. Despite of all this, the AHI argues in the section "Lessons Learnt" that the organization has learned how to be critical of itself and its history.

Finally, the AHI admitted in the submission that apartheid disadvantaged Black businesses. The organization mentions the impediment to Black entrepreneurship over White-owned companies' vast use of Black labor. However, this is contrasted in the document with the economic success and empowerment of the Afrikaner community, whose success is explained exclusively by virtuous saving practices among White South Africans. The AHI thus tries to displace the economic achievement of the Afrikaners away from the oppression of apartheid. Afrikaners had impressive economic success, the AHI boasted, but White supremacy had nothing to do with it.

This strategy foreshadowed how the AHI would approach Black economic empowerment. The organization presented the economic empowerment of Afrikaners as an example to be followed for Black economic empowerment. Socioeconomic development of all South Africans, the AHI argued, is vital, and "pride, self-reliance, and self-motivation are the keys to the future." Black economic empowerment must endeavor to unlock people's full potential and not evolve into a "new form of harmful race discrimination." The AHI peddled the myth that Afrikaners' empowerment was based on self-sufficiency—instead of racial oppression—and at the same time warned against new forms of oppression. The AHI denied the White racism of the past and warned against anti-White racism in the future.

The AHI was one of the few exclusively White organizations that made a submission to the TRC. The TRC challenged the organization to make an apology for apartheid and it did. As a result, its engagement with the TRC became a political statement in its own right. Van Wyk argued that the TRC submission "saved" the organization:

If we had not made a submission, it would have been a great mistake. Look at the legitimacy the AHI still has. How many organizations are there still? The National Party has died. . . . All the other things have just disappeared. But the Afrikaanse Handelsinstituut still exists.[45]

In a critical evaluation of the White business elite's engagement with the TRC, South African economist Nicoli Nattrass mentioned the participation of the AHI approvingly. The content of the AHI's submission seems to have been forgotten. The AHI's cooperation with the TRC was a stamp of approval and essential step toward legitimacy in post-apartheid South Africa.

Diversity Management

The next step for the AHI was to face the challenge of how to make the organization less White. Until 1997, it had White leadership only, and the large majority of members were White as well. The AHI decided to manage diversity from the top: by inviting a nonwhite person to a leadership position. Central to this effort to change the public face of the organization was the president of AHI in 2000, André Lamprecht. As CEO of a subdivision of Barloworld, a very old and large South African conglomerate, he was asked to join the AHI in 1998. Lamprecht had been the head of Business South Africa (BSA) and had been involved in negotiations around the democratic transition. Without strong political opposition to the ANC, he believed the commercial sector would soon be an important arena of conflict. Lamprecht argued that if the AHI wanted to continue its role as mediator after apartheid and transcend its role as an interest vehicle for a racial or ethnic group, it needed new leadership.

The ANC was making plans around the same time to implement BEE. Lamprecht supported BEE. He said, "For me, it was an absolute necessity. You cannot say to people who have been historically and structurally excluded . . . 'Alright, now you have to compete on the basis of equality.' There is no structural equality. You have to create a structure that can produce opportunities for others."[46] However, Lamprecht also thought the AHI must build stronger ties with the ANC. He suggested appointing

Franklin Sonn, the Coloured former ambassador to the United States during the Mandela government, as vice-president in 2000 and making him the first nonwhite AHI president in 2001. It was Sonn who, after making his name as a successful businessman after apartheid, hosted President Mbeki at the AHI gala dinner when he had become the first nonwhite and Coloured president of the organization.

Sonn was the perfect candidate for the AHI to meet the challenge of BEE: he had a background as an anti-apartheid activist; he was a prominent nonwhite businessman who spoke Afrikaans; and above all, he had close connections with ANC politicians. Most important, Sonn was also a man of ideas. In 1993, he published the article "Afrikaner Nationalism and Black Advancement as Two Sides of the Same Coin," in which he argued that racial justice in South Africa was not going to be achieved by the adoption of a new constitution and that practical steps were necessary. He encouraged South Africans to draw lessons from the American experience, where Whites continued to feel threatened by affirmative action. "We must learn from the US experience and not inherit its attitudes, reactions, and codes."[47] However, he had already heard White South Africans adopt the terminology "racism-in-reverse" and "reverse discrimination." South Africa, he argued, was a unique case that required special treatment. The correction he proposed must occur in a South African way and be rooted in that other way in which South Africa was special: Afrikaner history.

Apartheid, Sonn maintained, could be understood as a system of affirmative action for the White population. What was needed after apartheid was a similar program for the Black population of South Africa. He emphasized that in the 1930s, after the colonial war against the British Empire, Afrikaners found themselves economically dispossessed but empowered with the vote. "It must be remembered that during the depression the rural Afrikaner was a destitute group." Sonn recalled, "Poor whites lived in my grandparents' backyard in Carnarvon in the early thirties and my grandfather often had to chastise his indolent and alcoholic tenant with his large family for beating up his wife."[48] As the NP won elections, gaining political power and taking over the government, it introduced laws against Black labor and for affirmative action for the Afrikaner in industry and trades. Sonn quoted sociologist and former South African prime minister Hendrik Verwoerd, who argued in 1934 that uplifting Afrikaner workers could only occur effectively if they were "protected" against "nonwhite competition."[49] From the 1940s, the Afrikaners also controlled the state and state companies and practiced economic nepotism for Afrikaner business. Soon the White Afrikaner "lived in the main house while my mother's eldest brother died in a mud house in a backyard Karoo location."

Sonn concluded his article in 1993 by underscoring that "affirmative action in its crudest possible form, namely apartheid, can never be repeated no matter what."[50] He quoted Mandela, who said in 1991 that affirmative action must redress the imbalances created by apartheid and be rooted in principles of justice and equity. He was optimistic about the impact of affirmative action. He foresaw that future historians would write about "the renaissance of Black entrepreneurs and of Black people after the installation of a democratic government," just as they had done about the rise of Afrikaner business in the 1930s.[51]

However, almost ten years later, Sonn's ideas had transformed into something quite different. At the AHI conference where Sonn became president, he now argued that nobody understood poverty better than the White Afrikaans-speaking community, and that the economic empowerment of the Afrikaners was a model for the ANC to follow. What had been an innovative critique of apartheid to inspire reparations through affirmative action had turned into its opposite: the idea that the ANC could follow the Afrikaners' example. Sonn even peddled the myth that Afrikaners had not used the government to empower themselves.

For the AHI conference, Sonn had invited the anti-apartheid activist-turned-businessman Jakes Gerwel, former right-hand man of President Mandela. He had also invited a social worker from a township near Pretoria to explain about the poverty there. Sonn told the people in the room, "Nobody in South Africa understands poverty better than the Afrikaner community and knows how to fight it." Referencing the poor White problem in the 1930s, he argued that the Afrikaners had mobilized their whole community to fight poverty. "Afrikaners proved that poverty could be eliminated." Sonn connected this historic reference with currently popular neoliberal ideas among the White business elite that the state couldn't solve all problems. He noted, "The government is largely powerless. There is the expectation, at the highest level [of government], that the Afrikaner community will realize that the problem of poverty cannot be solved by the state."[52]

For Sonn, the many problems of South Africa presented as challenges and new possibilities. He thought that through goodwill and practical actions, unity could be created out of diversity. As he saw it, South African companies were conquering the world, that South Africans had always met the challenge and turned roadblocks into building blocks. He connected this upbeat message with the AHI. Although the "uncomfortable past" was still important, the "South Africans are future-people, like all good businessmen," and AHI members are "today- and tomorrow-people." This made him proud to be part of the AHI: "[The AHI members are] part of a people who were once poor too, but who had lifted themselves up out of the ashes of imperialism, freedom wars, economic depression and concentration camps. We can do this again." The AHI was truly worried about poverty. He quoted the Afrikaner businessman and philanthropist Anton Rupert's warning that "a person will sleep restless next to a hungry person" and said that what was needed was a "total onslaught on poverty."[53]

During his AHI presidency, Sonn was outspoken about nonracialism in the AHI. In an interview in the Afrikaans-language daily newspaper *Beeld*, he emphasized that he was not White and that there was a racial boundary in South Africa: "I see and feel that every day." However, he said, he had "an obsession to bring about a new nonracialism. I see myself as a leader without borders. The fact is that the Afrikaner committed himself to nonracialism." Sonn connected the goal of nonracialism with the language of Afrikaans. He explained that he had not always been a friend of White capitalists; indeed, in the early 1990s, he had been critical of White capitalism. He emphasized that he had brought up his children in the 1980s speaking English. However, he argued that his election as AHI president in principle redefined Afrikaans as nonracial: "It is a language with black roots that was accepted by white people." But he maintained that White Afrikaans-speaking people still had to reinvent, re-create, and transform themselves "to take [their] place among the larger community in South Africa."

Sonn provided the White business elite something their power and money could not buy: pride. Not just pride in their history but pride in their ability to change and become nonracial. Sonn defined the transition of the AHI as his task. Lamprecht shared with me an anecdote from his presidency of the AHI in 2000. He had taken the initiative during his presidency, together with Sonn, to honor former president Mandela and the ANC minister of finance, Trevor Manuel, a former anti-apartheid activist. It was one of Sonn's first official occasions as vice-president of the AHI. Lamprecht said in an interview, "When Franklin Sonn, Trevor Manuel, and I were walking off stage, Sonn said, 'I never thought I would be part of this organization, I certainly never thought I would be president, and I never thought I would do so with pride!' Trevor Manuel answered, 'I never, ever thought I would get an honoree award from the AHI, and I never, ever thought I would accept it with pride!'"[54]

Three years later, in 2003, Anton Botha, a White Afrikaans-speaking president of AHI, argued that BEE was "politically and socially necessary" to get people involved in profitable economic activity who were previously excluded through racial discrimination. The AHI had accepted the cost and necessity of BEE, he said, because it contributed to "social stability" and "hope" for the previously disadvantaged. Botha defended BEE for "its possibilities and challenges" and the necessity to create a Black middle class in South Africa. Botha also wanted to create new inclusive collective business bodies based on "cooperation, effective representation, and functionality." Business unity, he argued, was necessary for the AHI to maintain access to the government and influence policy. He admitted that the AHI must not lead such organizations, given the historical realities; instead, it should strengthen its own organization. The power of the organization, Botha felt, was its members. "We come together to improve and extend our network and to spend time together. As a voluntary organization, we do so because we feel at home in AHI. Within the organization, we can practice our language and our culture and do business with like-minded people. South Africa would be a poorer country if we did not do this job well."[55] For White businessmen, AHI's continuation as a dominant White organization remained important for them to feel at home.

The AHI provided the White elite a moral narrative—a sense of collective pride—about their role in the history of South Africa. In this narrative, the business elite belonged to the first White South Africans who understood that apartheid was wrong and who worked together with other South Africans to end it. The White business elite were the first who had unlearned racism. Japie Steenkamp, AHI president in 2005, argued:

> The chamber of commerce was one of the transition agents. In a way, they realized that the system of apartheid did not work. The exclusion of the blacks from the economy could not work. Our members, the AHI people, were one of the first from the side of business who negotiated with the ANC. The chamber of commerce is not a political organization; we are a business organization that looks at the business side of things. But if along the way we encounter something that obstructs the growth and prosperity of the country, we act. The AHI was strongly criticized by its members for doing so, when they initially said they would get involved in the transformation process. But the AHI switched gears without any trauma because they saw the problem of apartheid, they saw the problem of excluding people from the economy. Of course there were people who said "You are selling us out" and "This is not going to work." But the AHI has seen the bigger picture.[56]

Steenkamp, who was president two years after Botha, was upbeat about the prospects of the new South Africa. He was excited about the future and thought that the country has a lot of potential, and that with the "right policy decisions" it had a bright future. He was proud that South Africa had devised a democratic system when war had been a real possibility. "If we could make that work," he said, "we can make everything work. Businesspeople are not emotional creatures but pragmatic people; we want to solve the problem. If during apartheid I am excluded from the world market because of all the boycotts, then I have a problem. I have to solve it. So what is the solution?"[57] According to Steenkamp, the AHI was a key player in the transition from apartheid to democracy. The AHI recognized that apartheid and the exclusion of Black people were wrong and understood that they needed to change—and they did. Change for the organization was a "smooth process" and "nothing dramatic." It had all happened "without any trauma."

The First Black President

In 2006, the AHI asked ANC stalwart Nakedi Mathews Phosa to become its president. Phosa was an ANC politician who had been in exile during the struggle and after 1994 had become the first Black premier of Mpumalanga. After this first stint in politics ended in 1999, he had become a successful businessman and sat on the board of various South African corporations, often together with AHI board members. Phosa consulted with former president Mandela before accepting the invitation from the AHI, and Mandela told him that the position offered a great opportunity for him to promote BEE to the White business community. So when Phosa became president of the AHI in 2006, he went on tour throughout South Africa to sell the benefits of BEE to the local AHI chambers.

Phosa did not only promote BEE to the White business community, however. He also continued to cultivate the myth of Afrikaner "economic empowerment" and the idea that the ANC could learn from the Afrikaners' past. The AHI pursued three aims with disseminating this myth: to use the historical parallel to build rapport between the White and Black elites, to promote it as a model for the ANC to follow, and to make the past usable for a neoliberal critique of the ANC. The AHI hired the historian Hermann Giliomee and the economist Pieter Haasbroek to write a report, which they titled *The Economic Empowerment of the Afrikaners, a Modern Interpretation*. In this study the researchers present a revisionist economic history of the growth of Afrikaner business. They discuss racial discrimination and inequality but downplay White supremacy's role in making White economic growth possible. For example, they stress that Afrikaner empowerment was not dependent on "forced transfers" of English speakers' assets to Afrikaners. However, they ignore the structural transfer of Black labor value to White businesses during White supremacy and apartheid. They critique the ANC government's intervention in the economy after apartheid and the role of welfare in poverty relief, but they do not mention how the White government in the 1930s and later the NP used their state power to provide poverty relief. Instead, they emphasize the importance of cultural virtues of the Afrikaner community, such as thrift and industriousness, for realizing economic empowerment.

In October 2006, AHI president Phosa praised the revisionist report in his presidential speech, which demonstrated to him that "culture, values and the attitude of people and groups" lead to economic development. In his address, he argued that this is a "time of transformation," but he warned against the unintended consequences of ANC's leveling of the playing field, particularly the slow implementation of programs and the underutilization and layoffs of experienced (White) employees. For him, transformation and forgiveness went hand in hand. He said, "We should not punish ourselves for the past, but we should use our expertise to create possibilities for other people. We live in a place of forgiveness and, more importantly, of possibilities. It is our role as the AHI to responsibly open up these opportunities for our members."[58]

In 2008, Eltie Links, a former ambassador for the old NP government, became president of the AHI. Links, who is Coloured, knew the White elite at the AHI well. He served under the apartheid government as a representative to the World Bank from 1986 until 1990 during Botha's presidency. He was the first nonwhite man to serve as a representative in Washington. Links is sensitive to the critique that he was co-opted by the AHI.

> Look, in my life I have already done many things for which people here in South Africa can accuse me, what we call here, in South Africa, being a "sellout." Someone who is too early, too quick to accept change and who is not sure that it is genuine. I am used to jumping early. My philosophy is, there must be someone who stands on both sides and says: enough is enough. If I would just be a professor . . . you can't do anything, you have no voice. If you have such a post, and you have the IMF and World Bank to support you, you say to your government: The World Bank wants A, B, C, and D. And you have said to the World Bank what they should say, because you

know your country. From the inside, you have an incredible strong position to prescribe what change should take place.[59]

According to Links, as an insider in organizations such as the World Bank, but also the AHI, one is in a much stronger position to change things than being outside of them. He was weary of accusations that he moved too quickly or sold out. Sonn had asked Links, who is outspoken about their position in the organization, to join the AHI.

> We have a role to play. Sonn recognized that here [AHI] is a place where I can influence people's "mindset" for the positive. That he as a brown person can help the organization to include more brown people. He felt he could reconcile himself with the boundaries of the acceptable within the organization. He gives the organization credibility, he makes the organization more useful and he gets himself his own reward. . . . The fact that Franklin Sonn, Mathews Phosa, and I have been heads of the organization has helped many companies decide to become a member of the AHI. They would not have been members otherwise. The usefulness of opposition and the "perceptual payoff" for the organization, if you appoint leaders that represent an inclusive approach that is what makes it for everybody better. . . . I was the third president [of color]. I am just a perpetuation, a changing mindset in philosophy in the way the Afrikaners thinks about the future.[60]

Links liked to think of himself as an ambassador of change and saw himself as representing the "changing mindset" of Afrikaners and the White business elite.

In 2009, the AHI appointed its first female president, a Coloured woman by the name of Venete Klein, a director at the Absa bank. The bank had long-standing ties with the AHI and asked Klein to represent it on the board. Klein was honored by the AHI's appointment, which she attributed to her experience in the "management of transformation." She saw for herself a transformative task for which she was happily co-opted. During Klein's tenure, the AHI welcomed three more women to its board of directors. In her presidential address, Klein spoke of the "further transformation" of the AHI, specifically in terms of "brand." Nevertheless, she also vowed—as the first female and Coloured president—to continue "to protect at all costs the image of the organization with her rich history and that its flawless reputation will be carried into the future."[61]

The White business elite facilitated the elite transition in South Africa by the AHI's public but costless participation in the TRC. However, the AHI's act of repentance functioned doubly as a strategic document that laid out their White identity politics for the future. Their politics co-opts an anti-apartheid narrative to create a false equivalence between the fight against White poverty in the early twentieth century and the fight against Black poverty today. The narrative helped the AHI to incorporate, if not co-opt, a small group of Black and Coloured businessmen and -women in the organization. By 2008, the AHI's public image as an integrated business organization—despite still being a largely White and White-dominated organization—embodied the success of South Africa's elite transition. President Mbeki's early resignation from the presidency in 2008 ushered in a period of Black populism under President Zuma and ANCYL leader Julius Malema. Black populism was a logical response to South Africa's elite transition and the impression that Mbeki had acquiesced to the White business elite and given up on the promise of Black liberation. However, Mbeki's elite transition also saw the emergence of a successful White populist movement, the formerly Whites-only labor union Solidarity. This once extreme right-wing union successfully adopted the style and language of White populism to reinvent racism as White identity politics.

Populism and White Minoritization

A Populist Defense of Multiculturalism

On February 2, 2016, Flip Buys, chairman of the Solidarity Movement, spoke at the F. W. de Klerk Foundation conference on "The Future of Multiculturalism in South Africa."[1] Buys declared that multiculturalism could and should become the ideology of the twenty-first century. Many Western states, he said, including the members of the European Union, had already officially adopted multiculturalism and incorporated it in public policy. He argued that multiculturalism presupposes a positive acceptance of diversity based on "the right to recognition" and respect for different cultural groups, and warned against monoculturalism in South Africa. There is a big risk, he said, that minorities experience democracy not as freedom but as domination because they cannot democratically safeguard their interests. He emphasized that multiculturalism protects cultural minorities from "forced incorporation" into the majority, protecting them from "alienation, isolation, and political impotence" and "guaranteeing participation in public life." He referred to the 2004 Human Development Report of the United Nations that "advocated the right to cultural liberty," which it defines as the freedom to choose your own identity and pursue it without prejudice. South Africa is a multicultural country, Buys concluded, and to make it work, it needs to have a multicultural system of government.

To outside observers, Buys's passionate plea for multiculturalism as the ideology for the twenty-first century might seem counterintuitive. Flip Buys was at the time the chairman of the Solidarity Movement, a White populist movement built around a previously Whites-only, right-wing labor union. Scholars of European politics would be surprised to hear his characterization of Europe as having officially adopted multiculturalism and incorporated it in public policy. A global populist wave has been building since the 1980s in Europe, with right-wing populist parties such as the National Front in France, the League Party in Italy, the Fidesz Party in Hungary, and the Freedom Parties in Austria and The Netherlands, and has spread to the Republican Party in the United States with Donald Trump's rise to power. What unites this diverse group of parties is their dislike of multiculturalism and their advocacy for the kind of monoculturalism that Buys was critiquing. However, the key difference between South Africa and these other countries is that Whites in South Africa are a small minority group and not the majority.

How do we understand unlearning racism in a context where a White populist movement promotes multiculturalism and diversity, yet defines itself explicitly as a White minority? The White elite in the previous chapter adopted multiculturalism through racial tokenism and the appearance of racial integration. White populists in this chapter, however, use the language of multiculturalism, minority cultural groups, and demography to justify their position.[2] They argue that White people have an equal right to protect the collective interests of their own group. Their politics is based on a visible Whiteness that has adapted to the new circumstances of a multicultural South African polity, where racial identities remain key. They claim that White people are a normal group and even a threatened group. Demography in South Africa has always been racialized and politicized. White South Africans have been highly aware of being a minority in Africa, but during apartheid Afrikaner nationalists presented themselves as the majority. By contrast, White populists present themselves openly as a vulnerable White minority to suggest they are not the old racist perpetrators of the past but the new victims of today's racism.

Active White populist participation in identity politics changes Whiteness and racism. Scholars of populism have paid little attention to racism because it manifests itself in the West as White nationalism. Now that White nationalism is dead in South Africa and Whiteness has become highly visible, White populists use the vocabulary of multiculturalism and group rights to reclaim legitimacy.

Today, the Solidarity Movement represents predominantly White Afrikaans-speaking South Africans, or "Afrikaners" (the leadership uses these terms interchangeably). Despite representing a minority group, Solidarity uses a populist political style and cultural discourse that are similar to contemporary European and American populism, championing "the people" against the "elite."[3] However, the surprising combination of a plea for multiculturalism within a populist discourse suggests that there are also important differences between South Africa and countries with other populist movements, differences owing to South Africa's specific demography and political system. Take Buys's description of the threat of monoculturalism in his speech—a remarkable claim for a country with eleven official languages. When he uses the term "minority," he implies Whiteness, and correspondingly, "monoculturalism" is a thinly veiled synonym for Blackness. The different context highlights the salience of race in populist discourse. Solidarity's populist politics in the context of South Africa's demographics provides a unique lens for analyzing the connections between populism and racism: how the populist movement unlearns the old racism and introduces something new.

To understand how the Solidarity Movement has transformed the character of racism, I dissect the deployment of a new populist multiculturalism that uses the idea of rights to frame the concerns of the (White) minority in South Africa's liberal democracy. In his speech, Buys uses the word "rights" thirty-five times. He speaks about individual, human, social, cultural, economic, democratic, civil, and constitutional rights. His is a language that regularly conflates different kinds of rights: he claims that cultural rights are human rights, equal to political, civil, economic, and social rights. Furthermore, the rights that Buys talks about are always threatened; for example, he argues that monoculturalism in South Africa was a system in which the "freedom of majorities" prevailed over the "rights of minorities." By using the language of rights, Buys paints the White minority as vulnerable in the new democracy and hides the fact that Whites hold a disproportionate amount of wealth and power.

Minority rights are always in tension with individual rights. Buys knows that cultural rights are limited by the extent to which they infringe on other human rights. However, his aim is to make a larger argument: that the White minority has a right to protection because it is a cultural community. White South Africans, he concludes, "thought it was essential for black people to get full rights, but now they are concerned that the 'revolution' has been going beyond rights and their own rights are now being prejudiced."[4] Buys projects vulnerability, the threat of loss, and the need for protection of the White minority. By co-opting the language of rights, Solidarity aims to subvert the idea that South Africa's White minority is powerful and privileged.

Solidarity reimagines White South Africans as a minority: not simply as a demographic fact—which they always were—but as a cultural construction, an idea that the populist movement creates, performs, and strategically puts to use as a discourse to reinvent racism. This strategy of White minoritization—a process that I define as the cultural and discursive refashioning of the White population as a minority that is vulnerable, threatened, and entitled to protection—effectively masks White racial interests. Post-apartheid South Africa presents an extreme example of this process. However, in less stark demographic circumstances such as those in the United States and Europe, minoritization is also used to mask, defend, and expand White privilege and power.[5] Populists in the West even use South Africa as a dystopian example of this process.[6] The country does indeed hold important lessons for the West: namely, a warning about how racism is being refashioned through populism.

Populism and Racism

European and American media have questioned just how central racism is to the global resurgence of populism. Nowhere was this more evident than after the presidential election of 2016 in the United States.[7] President Donald Trump ran a populist campaign with unmistakable racist elements. He also spoke to the economic anxieties of the American White working class and styled himself as a blue-collar billionaire.[8] In Europe, the ongoing populist backlash against multiculturalism and immigration has raised similar questions about the extent to which racism is the driving force of populism.[9]

Most academic scholarship on populism devotes little attention to the role of racism.[10] Scholars of populism have spent more energy studying the anger directed at elites than the equally pervasive populist resentment toward people at the bottom, such as migrants and minorities.[11] Racism is part of the populist agenda in the United States and Europe, they will acknowledge, but they do not see it as essential to the phenomenon.[12] The few scholars who do focus on the relationship between populism and racism have pointed to nationalism, which has long been associated with racism, as the main culprit.[13] Racial ideologies, they argue, are not part of populism but of ethnonationalism. It is nationalism as a phenomenon that independently fuels the radical right in the United States and Europe.[14] This argument falls short, however, because it does not consider how populism, as a political style and discourse, might have changed racism as it evolved after nationalism.

Populism has reinvented racism after nationalism. The question is no longer whether populism is racist but how populism contributes to the remaking of racism. The South African case allows for exactly that: a close analysis of how racism transitions from nationalism to populism. The current global wave of populism is too often analyzed as a new phenomenon or as something exceptional, without understanding how this trend is historically connected to colonial legacies and White supremacy.[15] South Africa's recent history of White supremacy allows us to trace the connections between the previous racist regime and the current populist moment.

Racism is as much a part of White populism as it is of nationalism. The starting point of my analysis is an insight from the French sociologist Pierre-André Taguieff, who has suggested that populism in France had been a productive political style and cultural discourse employed to reinvent racism.[16] American historians have made a similar argument when it comes to the origins of the American conservative movement.[17] Contrary to contemporary scholars of populism, they have emphasized how this "countermovement" was a grassroots, populist, White working-class crusade rooted in racial backlash.[18] The reactionary populism of this movement "borrowed" its oppositional language of rights from the very civil rights movement it opposed in order to reformulate its racism.[19]

What is new in South Africa is how Solidarity has integrated the late twentieth-century language of human rights, minority rights, and cultural rights. In his speech, Buys argues that cultural rights are human rights in order to suggest that the ANC is taking away (White people's) rights by promoting ("forcing," in his language) racial integration. Buys presents himself as a victim, but what he has actually lost is the "right" to exclude Black people. American historian Thomas Sugrue remarks that the language of rights derives "its power from its imprecision."[20] It is often vague in nature but rich in association. Solidarity regularly conflates minority and cultural rights with human rights and human rights with "White rights." But Solidarity's use of the language of rights is much more pernicious, not only confusing but specifically disguising White privilege, which I define as the advantages that Whites derive from institutional arrangements that have kept—or still keep—the Black population in a subordinate position. The denial of White privilege is central to Solidarity's populism, language of rights, and their new racism.

From Right-Wing Union to Populist Movement

In 2001, the formerly Whites-only Mine Workers' Union (MWU) adopted a new name, Solidarity, in a grand orchestrated show at the State Theatre in Pretoria. The name was derived from the famous Polish labor movement led by the late president of Poland, Lech Wałęsa. The new name symbolized the transformation from a small, right-wing, and reactionary union to a populist movement that is now a prominent voice in South Africa's public debates. According to 2015 figures, the union represents 320,000 members, more than three times the number of workers it did in 1994.[21] It is also one of South Africa's wealthiest NGOs (nongovernmental organizations).[22] Indeed, Solidarity's name change was the culmination of a long process of reinvention.

After 1994, the MWU had become politically isolated because of its racist rhetoric and pro-apartheid position. In the run-up to the democratic election, right-wing parties had been unable to sustain a cohesive front because of discord and strife over tactics and strategies, in particular about how to secure a separate future homeland for conservative Whites.[23] The MWU had split with General Constand Viljoen's Freedom Front (FF), a new right-wing party established in 1994. The MWU's general secretary at the time, Peet Ungerer, saw both the NP and the FF as too willing to comprise with Mandela's ANC government. In those years, the MWU still warned about the coming "national disaster" and the need for "operation self-defense." Racial integration was presented as a "health risk" and the desegregation of schools was protested as the *infiltrasie van kultuurvreemdes*, the "infiltration of cultural strangers." In 1992, the union took a firm stand against affirmative action. And until 1994, the MWU insisted on job-protection for the White workers in the corporate industry. Even in 1997, the union still demanded special group rights for the White minority. However, all these political positions proved untenable. Most dramatically, while the MWU was supposedly creating a "White superunion" in the early 1990s, actual union membership was declining rapidly.

In 1997, Flip Buys was appointed as general secretary, and he initiated a process of restructuring and rebranding to make the MWU relevant. As Dirk Hermann told me, the new strategy required a "new idiom," together with an "aggressive media-strategy":

> You can see it in the language that we use. It is different. The concepts that we use are not the old right-wing concepts. These are not concepts from the old National Party. We use new concepts such as "self-reliance." These are positive concepts. We developed a language ourselves through which we rebranded the new Solidarity, with new words, and new ideas.[24]

Driving this developing language was the introduction of mandatory affirmative action programs. In 1998, the ANC government introduced the Wet op Gelyke Indiensneming, or Employment Equity Act, which included *regstellende aksie* (which in Afrikaans means "making right" action), or affirmative action programs, among its policies. Some companies and organizations had pursued affirmative action on a voluntarily basis since the early 1990s, but its enactment became mandatory in 1998. That same year, the union adopted its own official position on affirmative action: instead of directly opposing affirmative action, as it had done in the past, the union supported it as a "necessary" policy. However, the union declared that affirmative action should not "hurt" Whites and should not lead to "new inequalities."

With a new name came a new slogan: "Ons beskerm ons mense," or "We protect our people." The motto resonated with the threat that affirmative action posed to White employees. The emphasis on protection and threat became central to Solidarity's populist stance. Contrary to populist scholars, who suggest that the centrality of threat is unique to populism, racial anxieties posing as threats were a common and persistent feature in Afrikaner nationalism.[25] For example, in the 1940s, the National Party (NP) warned against the *swart gevaar*, or Black peril, and "racial contamination."[26] Black peril was a flexible term in the early twentieth century, used by politicians in their political rhetoric to warn White people of the common threat they faced from Black people and the need for White unity.[27] Politicians would invoke the threat of White women being raped by Black men or runaway growth of the Black population.[28]

In the context of the early 1990s, Solidarity repackaged the racist propaganda of Black peril into threatened minority rights. Initially, the union objected to racial integration by claiming White rights. *Die Mynwerker*, the official magazine of the MWU, wrote in 1990 that Whites had a right to have "their own (White) identity" and the right to live a "White man's existence."[29] In 1991, the MWU published a *Manifes van die blanke werker* (Manifesto of the White worker), in which the union stressed the threat that a Black majority government posed to *blankedom* (Whiteness) and the Afrikanervolk (Afrikaner people).[30] In the manifesto, the MWU argues that "discrimination against 'conservative Whites' at work is a failure to recognize their right to their own opinion." The integration of White amenities, such as public pools, is presented as a "health risk." The desegregation of neighborhoods is objected to because Whites have a right to their own "distinctive lifestyle." The MWU says they are tired of "White rights" being trampled upon and that they are the ones being discriminated against as a White labor union. After 1994, however, the union increasingly begins presenting itself as representing "the new disadvantaged minority in South Africa." And in a new manifesto, written in 1997, the union no longer claimed "White rights" but referenced international law and declarations of minority rights for cultural self-determination.

One facet of this repackaged propaganda was a new tactic on how to fight affirmative action. Solidarity transformed the reality of Black advancement into a threat to minority rights, specifically to fight affirmative action. Solidarity's chief executive, Dirk Hermann, has written two books that paint a dark and threatening picture of South Africa's affirmative action program. In his first book, *The Naked Emperor: Why Affirmative Action Failed*, published in 2007, Hermann presents affirmative action as part of the ANC's broader racial ideology that aims for representativity (which he defines as the goal of all institutions in South Africa's society to reflect South Africa's racial demography) and majority democracy. "Democracy" writes Hermann, "is therefore not defined in terms of how it protects the minority, but in terms of how it serves the will of the majority."[31]

What is striking, however, is how loosely Solidarity's leadership uses the concept of minority rights. In his second book, *Affirmative Tears: Why Representivity Does Not Equal Equality*, published in 2013, Hermann focuses on the story of Renate Barnard, a White employee of the South African Police Service (SAPS), who claimed to have been denied a promotion on account of being White.[32] The SAPS management argued that White employees were already overrepresented in top management. Solidarity initiated a lawsuit on behalf of Barnard, but the Constitutional Court upheld SAPS's decision, because it was based on their employment equity plan.[33] In the media, Hermann attacked other police unions for not protecting "the rights of minority groups within the SAPS" and argued that Solidarity was "not going to sit back and meekly accept the racial discrimination against its members." "Solidarity," he said, "is the only union in the police prepared to fight for the rights of minorities."[34]

During my fieldwork, I participated in *Solidariteitkunde*, or Solidarity-ness, a regular seminar that introduced new staff to the history of the Solidarity Movement. In the introduction to the course reader, Hermann writes that the union represents "a tiny minority amongst an overwhelming majority" and that many Whites "feel alienated" and "withdraw from society" or "emigrate abroad."[35] Solidarity must provide an answer and that answer is: "We protect our people." Solidarity's employees, it continues, "aren't just employees, you protect your people. If someone asks you what you do at Solidarity, your answer isn't 'I'm a secretary,' but 'I protect my people by oiling the machinery through excellent administration.'" "At Solidarity," the introduction concludes, "you always work in the context of the bigger dream of Solidarity." During the workshop, Dirk Hermann deftly wove the themes of being a White minority and feeling threatened together to argue for the need of protection:

> Today we are a minority in a majority situation and we do not know yet how to handle this. How to survive in Africa? We want to be here, we want to be from Africa. But we are in a powerless situation, because we have no political influence. All over the world minorities are protected but we are a discriminated minority. This is a moment in which you and I must fight. What is the answer? . . . One time, I was at the congress of the South African Communist Party (SACP), when Blade Nzimande, the leader of the SACP, said in his speech, "But White workers, you are on your own." And we are "on our own." . . . We are alone; we should not have any illusions. But every one of you who sits here today is a part of the answer. The word is "protection"; I protect my people.[36]

Underlying the oblique call to arms was the warning that the White minority cannot and must not depend on Black South Africans. There is little reason to disbelieve that Nzimande actually stated that White workers were on their own.[37] However, Hermann interprets the statement through the lens of Black peril, where everything and everybody is interpreted as a racial threat.

"The People"

Despite debates about the definition of populism, scholars agree that populism has a specific political logic that "pits a virtuous and homogenous people against a set of elites and dangerous 'others' who are together depicted as depriving (or attempting to deprive) the sovereign people of their rights, values, prosperity, identity and voice."[38] In other words, populists divide the world in two opposing camps: the good people versus the elites and dangerous outsiders. In the West, populist movements often claim to represent the White working class, but Solidarity has transformed into something more extreme. The union used to represent the White working class exclusively; nowadays, it claims to represent all White people and not just its working class.

The Solidarity Movement declares that it speaks on behalf of the "Afrikaner people" and uses "the people" in its historical narrative. It rewrites the union's history by borrowing terminology from the ANC and the anti-apartheid movement. Solidarity presents itself as South Africa's first "freedom fighters," who at the dawn of the twentieth century resisted the "injustices" done to Afrikaners. In an interview, Buys told me that he felt very proud of the Afrikaner anticolonial war: "We were the first freedom fighters in Africa, and we fought for Afrikaner freedom. . . . The Afrikaner has a rightful place in South Africa and he must be able to be free." In a video on its website, Solidarity claims to have been founded in 1902 in the aftermath of the Second Boer War, a time of hardship when Afrikaners "lost their freedom" and were "displaced" from the countryside to the minefields by the British. During the union's "struggle history," the MWU supported its members, who are depicted as politically disadvantaged and economically marginalized. Ultimately, Solidarity presents the "Afrikaner people" as a group whose rights were threatened in a very similar way as today.

Thus, while Solidarity reinvented itself as a civil rights organization in the present, it also began projecting this "civil rights struggle" into the past. In the same video, Solidarity describes itself as having always been a "civil rights organization." Not only does the video mask the union's working-class roots, it claims that the MWU was founded to protect "the rights" of the Afrikaners. Switching to the present, the video's male voice-over claims that Solidarity today "is the oldest civil rights organization in South Africa." The video shows headlines of high crime levels and failing services; the voice-over says that Solidarity will continue to secure a "safe, free, and prosperous" future for "our people."

Solidarity also highlights the poverty of Whites in the past and present to obscure White privilege. It claims to have been a central force in addressing the "poor White" problem, poverty among Whites in the 1920s and 1930s. It thereby espouses the myth of Whites lifting themselves out of poverty by their bootstraps, that Whites in South Africa climbed out of poverty through self-help and hard work. Solidarity presents the union as the embodiment of the self-reliance of the Afrikaner people. What is missing in this narrative is how the state, founded on White supremacy, alleviated poverty among White Afrikaners. In fact, in an interview Dirk Hermann claimed that Solidarity was working against the government: "The 1930s were the worst time for the Afrikaners. But that is when they began their empowerment efforts, even when the government worked against them. This was nothing like the Black economic empowerment today, where the government rolls out policies." Implicitly and explicitly, Hermann insinuates that Black people should be able to help themselves. Solidarity's historical revisionism—the White minority's independence from government help and its anti-state stance—lays the groundwork for its contemporary neoliberal critique of the ANC and government-led programs for affirmative action, Black economic empowerment, and poverty alleviation.

During my fieldwork, these talking points were reiterated by the leadership, the staff, and its members, and represented in the union's magazine, on their website, and in their press releases. During *Solidariteitkunde*, Hermann described the union as "the gold thread running through the development of the Afrikaner" and as central to the successful history of "self-help" that lifted up the people. Solidarity has rewritten the history of White South Africa to centralize its role, while simultaneously hiding its historic support for the NP and apartheid, as well as the role that the NP and apartheid played in advancing Afrikaners. Solidarity obscures its roots as a White working-class union and masks class with race in a new narrative that broadens its membership to Whites of all classes while continuing to advance its White supremacist goals.

"The Elite"

For Solidarity, "the elite" consists of a White elite and a Black elite, but its ultimate strategy is to connect the two and represent them as against "the people." The White elite, embodied by the NP, is blamed for its democratic compromise, for the new constitutional dispensation, and for failing to defend "Afrikaners' rights" to self-determination. The Black elite, embodied by the ANC, is accused of trying to destroy everything that is Afrikaans. Solidarity specifically blames these elites for their compromise to end White supremacy and the lack of protection for the White minority.

Despite its historical support of the NP, Solidarity portrays the party as being naïve, weak, and a party of traitors. Solidarity distances itself from apartheid by suggesting that the union has a history of being independent from and in frequent opposition to the NP. The movement argues that between 1990 and 1994 the NP sold out the "Afrikaner people" to the ANC. In an interview, Buys said they had felt that "the NP gave the land to the ANC without any form of protection." Solidarity argues that the NP misled the White minority about what life was like in a democracy. Dirk Hermann used a story of two wolves and a sheep in his interview to illustrate what he sees as the problem with democracy: "The two wolves and the sheep have to vote for what they will eat for lunch. And out of principle, the sheep was eaten that afternoon. Because the majority vote of the wolves was successful. The sheep contributed fully to democracy but democracy ate him up. There was no protection for him as a minority and this is the problem we have as a minority: democracy eats you alive if it's a majority-democracy. It offers no protection for minorities."[39]

The NP, Solidarity argues, had a misplaced trust in the new democracy and, in particular, the constitution. In a characteristic passage in his newspaper column, Buys writes that "it is not the constitution that governs and that White South Africans were naïve to think that 'just a document' would protect their rights."[40] "Rights do not realize themselves," Buys likes to say. In his eyes, the NP failed to defend the Afrikaners' right to self-determination, and Solidarity has had to come to the rescue to take up the fight for the White minority.

Solidarity's critique of the ANC is equally harsh. During my fieldwork in 2010, the leadership said that "the Mandela era" was now over and that the hopeful days of the inauguration of democracy, reconciliation, and the birth of the constitution were gone. Buys said that they "had always looked beyond Mandela's beautiful words—which were beautiful words and we appreciated them. But we also looked at what other ANC leaders said. And that is when we realized how we are in many cases excluded." Solidarity claimed that the ANC government aimed to change everything that was connected to White South Africans. Solidarity criticized how the ANC used state power to intervene in the economy and create redistribution policies. In contrast, Solidarity created a history of self-help, bootstrapping, and economic self-sufficiency.

Manufacturing Crisis

On May 5, 2015, the Solidarity Movement organized a *krisisberaad*, or crisis council, to focus on "the growing crisis in the country" and how to respond as a community.[41] For its location, the Solidarity Movement had selected the amphitheater at the Voortrekkers Monument, the massive granite structure built in 1949 to commemorate the departure of the *Voortrekkers* from the Cape between 1835 and 1854. The meeting's agenda was long: increasing crime; deteriorating infrastructure; affirmative action or the "tightening of racial laws"; growing racial intolerance (purportedly against Whites); the threat of majority domination; the state's growing interference in the economy; the threat to property rights; the disadvantaging of Afrikaans language and culture; the criminalization of Afrikaner history; and finally, unemployment. Solidarity's leadership warned its members of "the numerous signs that the government was governing against Afrikaners."

The *krisisberaad* exemplifies how Solidarity has manufactured a permanent feeling of crisis to draw attention to its political concerns and goals. A few days before the meeting, Buys criticized the ANC government in a newspaper article and claimed that the dysfunctional public services, crime, corruption, and violence signaled "the imminent collapse of the state."[42] During my six months of fieldwork at Solidarity, the talk of crisis was ubiquitous among the leadership. It is true that post-apartheid South Africa faces many structural challenges, such as infrastructure maintenance, government corruption, and municipal administration. However, for all of Solidarity's talk of crisis, in the years of my research (from 2000 until 2015) none of the central issues, such as crime, affirmative action policies, or services, have changed in a radical way. Nor have Whites lost more rights. Instead, the Solidarity Movement has used South Africa's structural problems, such as the poor state of the infrastructure and high crime rates, as building blocks for their racialized performance of crisis and their defense of White privilege. By the end of my fieldwork, I saw this crisis talk as the displacement of what was actually in crisis: White power and White privilege.

Solidarity practices a populist style of rhetoric: conjuring "crisis" in order to position themselves as the representatives and protectors of "the people" that fight against "the elite," but also, more broadly, the dangerous other, namely, the Black South African majority. Solidarity carefully performs a series of crises that strategically depict the White minority as threatened and under attack. For the strategy to work—and to do so continuously—the movement has to keep reimagining and staging the crises in order to create a rationale for continually opposing and critiquing the ANC and the Black majority.

Indeed, Solidarity points to South Africa's transition to democracy and the new constitution as the "constitutional crisis." This is the foundational crisis of their crisis narrative; all crises can be traced to this first mistake. Solidarity talks about a "constitutional crisis" despite the fact that it often pursues legal action to oppose government policies and has done so successfully. The leadership argues that South Africa has moved from being a "constitutional state" to a "transformation state." The term "transformation" has long been part of the ANC's social and economic policy agenda and often simply means change. However, Solidarity depicts the ANC as running a "transformation state" that is against all things White and Afrikaans and above the law—specifically, the constitution.

Although the "constitutional crisis" is central, Solidarity uses various other subthemes to reinforce the sense of crisis and threat for the White minority, including crime. South Africa has a high crime rate, particularly when it comes to serious crimes like murder.[43] However, Solidarity racializes this high crime rate by singling out crimes with White victims. In press releases, protests, and national campaigns, they accuse Black criminals of being racially motivated and using excessive violence against White people. In January 2010, Solidarity delivered 23,000 protest letters to President Jacob Zuma's Cape office, Tuynhuys, to protest crime. When Zuma did not respond, Dirk Hermann said to the press (who were present): "This is a slap in the face of every South African who democratically shared their feelings with the president, who has refused to listen to the pain of these South Africans. . . . The question now is whether the president will collect them or ignore them and let the feelings of South Africans blow away in the wind." Solidarity has also worked with popular artists such as Steve Hofmeyer to promote the crises-of-crime narrative in the media. Solidarity has a permanent *veldtog*, or campaign against crime, which the organization has waged for more than a decade.

Solidarity also manufactures crises along another theme: *armblankes*, or poor Whites. The campaign plays on historic fears that without political power and state assistance, the White minority will (again) be targeted and become impoverished. It creates these "poor Whites" to mask the privilege of the White minority. During my fieldwork, Solidarity garnered a lot of media attention, including from international media companies such as the BBC, by arranging for the ANC president Jacob Zuma to visit an informal poor White settlement. On July 23, 2008, he arrived in Pretoria's Bethlehem settlement, where two hundred Whites were living. In his address, Zuma called it a "historic day" and said that he was "shocked and surprised" by the sight of White poverty but that he had come to help. "All this time I did not realize a section (of the White population) that could be referred to as poor Whites." Buys said at the meeting that "it wasn't politically correct to talk about White poverty" but that poverty knew no color. This claim is true in the abstract, but it belies the reality that South Africa's poor are more than 90 percent Black.[44]

The movement has set up its own charity arm, Helpende Hand (Helping Hand), which focuses exclusively on charity work to benefit poor Whites. It continues to be successful at drawing the attention of the ANC leadership. In 2013, President Zuma marked Nelson Mandela Day on July 18th by officially handing over new houses to the poor White community of Danville in Pretoria. Ultimately, Solidarity's campaign tries to undercut the ANC policies that address racial inequality.

Minoritization and the Language of Rights

The manufactured "constitutional crisis" allows Solidarity to deploy and twist constitutional rights to protect White privilege. South Africa's constitution does not refer to the concept of minorities but rather to communities; the idea of minority rights to language and education, however, does have an important place. For example, South Africa has eleven official languages, of which Afrikaans is one, and everyone has the right to receive an education in the official language or languages of their choice in public educational institutions.[45] Solidarity thus shifted tactics and translated their reactionary protest against the end of White supremacy into a protest about "minority rights."

To present the White minority as vulnerable and powerless, the Solidarity leadership often talks about threatened rights, where in actuality, they are referring to historic White privileges. For example, in my interview with Buys, he claimed that White people in post-apartheid South Africa are disillusioned because they have lost their rights, but in fact he conflates rights and privileges. "They thought: only the Blacks received new rights. They didn't think that they in practice would lose their rights. You can have all these rights on paper—administratively you still have your rights. You can vote and such. But in practice it is only the ANC who decides what happens." According to Buys, the majority can only gain its rights at the expense of the minority—as if it is a zero-sum game. "The majority governs the country and its institutions. The majority does so in a way that excludes us." But minorities in the new South Africa have not lost their rights: the White minority has only lost its exclusive White privileges and the ability to deny rights to others. Furthermore, the recognition of rights for Black people does not, as Buys suggests, mean that Whites are now excluded or powerless. It is more likely that the loss of White privilege feels like the loss of status and hierarchy.

In this way, Solidarity refashions the White population culturally as a minority that is threatened and entitled to protection—the process I called White minoritization—by manipulating the language of rights. They do so in five different ways: (1) they have set up the organization AfriForum, which uses minority rights to protect White privilege; (2) they mimic the language of the ANC to make their case; (3) they instigate lawsuits to popularize their cause; (4) they use the international community and minority rights declarations to position the White minority as vulnerable and in need of protection; and (5) they portray democracies as inherently unjust for minorities.

In 2006, Solidarity set up a special organization, AfriForum, to coordinate its campaign around what they called "civic and constitutional rights." Since its foundation, the organization grew to 210,000 members in 2018, according to its own reports.[46] In an interview in 2008, the CEO of AfriForum, Kallie Kriel, said that the organization was "a civil rights initiative to mobilize civil society and specifically minority communities, in order to take part in democratic debate."[47] According to its website, the organization campaigns for "the protection and consolidation of civil rights" and gives the Afrikaner community "a voice in a society where minorities are increasingly being ignored." AfriForum's language of rights and its reinvention as a civil rights organization that confronts racial integration is strikingly similar to the response of the White working class in the United States to the civil rights movement.

Counterintuitively, while AfriForum uses the language of the American civil rights movement, it also mimics the anti-apartheid movement. It has even drawn up a "Civil Rights Charter" that is explicitly modeled after the ANC's 1955 Freedom Charter, although the ANC's Freedom Charter was explicitly nonracial. The Freedom Charter famously starts with the declaration: "We, the People of South Africa, declare for all our country and the world to know: that South Africa belongs to all who live in it, Black and White." Instead, AfriForum's Civil Rights Charter reads: "We, the compilers and supporters of this charter, exercise the deliberate choice to lead a meaningful existence as Afrikaners . . . with our deeply-rooted foundation at the southernmost tip of Africa. We know no other home." The manifesto vows to make every Afrikaner "feel at home as first-class citizens in the country of their birth." AfriForum's strategy to appropriate ANC's political language is driven to its extreme by its use of the terminology of reverse racism to discredit former anti-apartheid struggle songs.

AfriForum actively promotes its own definition of racism. They do not deny racism is a problem but argue that "this phenomenon must be opposed actively by means of the advancement of mutual recognition and respect amongst communities." They emphasize the "mutuality" aspect and decry the "selective morality" of focusing only on "White-on-Black racism," while other forms of racism are tolerated. Their policy document on the definition, causes, and manifestations of racism promotes a definition of racism that argues that "racism occurs when any person (irrespective of his or her origin) harbors negative feelings toward another purely based on skin colour or origin and also when a person treats another differently simply based on skin color or origin."[48] Echoing Mandela's words that nobody is born racist, AfriForum argues that politicians must not be "constantly labeling" one population group as racist, because it provides a "breeding-ground for racism on and against both sides." They define "racism against whites" as "politically driven statements which specifically portray all farmers and whites in general as brutal tormentors," while "racism against blacks" is the result of a "feeling of indignation" because "white lives are valued less." AfriForum does not just endorse reverse racism but argues that today's White racism is the result of Black racism.

Solidarity and AfriForum regularly bring lawsuits against ANC politicians to popularize their cause. In their most famous case, AfriForum took Julius Malema, then president of the ANC Youth League, to court in 2010 for singing "Ayesaba Amagwala," the ANC struggle song with the words "kill the Boer,"[49] which again had become notorious after the murder of the former leader of the Afrikaner Weerstandsbeweging (AWB) at his farm.[50] The South African Human Rights Commission (SAHRC), who in 2007 had already determined that parts of the song were hate speech, received hundreds of complaints about Malema and the song.[51] In their filing, AfriForum argued that the song contained hate speech against White people.[52] It claimed that singing the song "adversely affected the rights and freedoms" of White Afrikaners, undermined their human dignity, and propagated hatred and incited violence based on language, culture, and ethnicity.

In the *AfriForum v Malema* case, the Equality Court ruled in 2011 that the song indeed contained hate speech and was "derogatory, dehumanizing and hurtful."[53] The judge concluded that White South Africans are a minority group who are particularly "vulnerable to discriminatory treatment and who, in a very special sense, must look to the Bill of Rights for protection." He wrote: "All genocide begins with simple exhortations which snowball. . . . Words are powerful weapons which if they are allowed to be used indiscriminately can lead to extreme and unacceptable action." When the constitution and the bill of rights were passed in South Africa in 1996, the international community heralded them as a progressive triumph and an essential safeguard for the rights of the people in the majority who had been discriminated against on the basis of race for centuries. Now, just fifteen years later, the judge portrayed the White minority as threatened by genocide, based on a song's lyrics.

Solidarity demands that South Africa's White Afrikaans-speaking minority be included in international covenants that protect vulnerable minorities. For example, many Solidarity press releases refer to the United Nations' Declaration on the Rights of Persons Belonging to National or Ethnic, Religious and Linguistic Minorities. Solidarity also regularly accuses the ANC of stripping minorities of their rights by politicizing the commission based on section 185 of the constitution, the commission set up for the protection and promotion of cultural, religious, and language communities; for example, in 2012, AfriForum's Kallie Kriel argued at the UN Forum on Minority Issues in Geneva that the "South African government strips its minorities of their minority rights."[54]

Despite these international demands for minority rights and the legal reality that the individual rights of White South Africans are protected by the constitution, Solidarity argues that minority rights mean very little in a "majority democracy," unless you have institutions to actualize them. As Buys says: "Rights do not realize themselves." Solidarity's leadership points to Zimbabwe's "amazing" constitution to ridicule the idea that a constitution by itself would afford any protection to the White minority. In 1999, the government of Zimbabwe pursued a "fast track land reform" that not only transferred four thousand White farms to Black ownership but also involved forcible seizure, often accompanied by violence. However, for all its talk of rights, Solidarity only emphasizes the potential loss of rights and never the importance of shared, universal rights. In their view, when it comes to rights, there are only haves and have-nots.

In an interview in 2008, I spoke with Buys about racial integration and the White minority. Our discussion revealed how Buys performs White minoritization and portrays ANC's majority rule as infringing upon the rights of minorities:

Look, South Africa is integrated. So, the problem we have had is that the majority accepts many things as self-evident, for which the minority has to fight. You accept as self-evident that your child goes to school where he understands the language. The majority accepts as self-evident that the school supports your values. The majority accepts as self-evident that you can turn on the television and see a show in your own language that you understand. A majority accepts as self-evident that you can decide over the taxes you pay. And a majority accepts as self-evident that you have a say in the governing of a country. And a minority does not have those things, those rights.[55]

In post-apartheid South Africa, there is nothing the Black majority finds "self-evident" about having education in their native language or having the right to vote. They didn't have these rights in the past, and they still do not have some of them today. Indeed, many Black South African kids still do not receive education in their mother tongue, as they attend English-only schools.[56] Moreover, it is unimaginable that after apartheid Black South Africans do not have a firm grasp of what it means to be without rights. Yet because it makes them look indifferent to the "vulnerable" White minority, Buys wants people to believe that the Black majority take their contemporary democratic rights and political power for granted. His focus on the "self-evident" nature of these rights and privileges is meant to portray the Black majority as ignorant and privileged. Buys ignores history in order to mask how the White minority enjoyed vastly more rights and privileges than the Black majority and continues to enjoy the legacy of the apartheid era.

The strategy of minoritization is ultimately about White power. Buys endeavors to obscure this, using the words "majority" and "minority" demographically to disconnect races from power relationships. However, the centrality of power becomes evident when he talks about the democratic transition and the referendum of 1992, in which most White South Africans voted for talks with the ANC. According to Buys:

> The Afrikaners, while still in the majority, said: "Come, we give the new South Africa a chance, come we integrate in all areas, we now have a constitution, we have individual rights and this will work out." The Afrikaners have integrated. Solidarity was worried that these easy solutions would not work.[57]

Although Buys begins by claiming that Afrikaners were "in the majority," this was never true. During apartheid, the White minority was in power and oppressing the Black majority. By depicting the White minority as the majority, he attempts to enhance his portrait of a benevolent White population giving racial integration a chance, but what he reveals is that in his mind, minority status is about powerlessness.

Grassroots Neoliberalism

In the media, AfriForum sometimes calls itself a civil rights organization that aims to protect the rights of minorities and property rights. Indeed, Solidarity and AfriForum have become adept at rearticulating questions of socioeconomic inequality and redistribution as issues of rights. Solidarity uses neoliberalism to protect White privilege by critiquing the elite, mocking state-led redistribution, and calling for the end of state-controlled institutions in favor of "self-reliance." Thus, Solidarity's politics aligns neatly with the elite neoliberal project outlined in the previous chapter, while simultaneously projecting a populist message. The White community's economic concerns mix effortlessly with discourses about the ANC's conspiracy to target the White minority. The Solidarity Movement must therefore be understood as a driver of South African neoliberal political and economic order, and not a reaction to it. Solidarity's neoliberal critique of the state is racially motivated and has as its aim the defense of White privilege.

Nowhere do these concerns about the threatened White minority, the crisis of crime, and possible economic marginality become more evident than in the trope of the threatened White farmer, a powerful symbol of White prosperity and vulnerability. In 2016, the ANC decided to increase its efforts toward land reform. Twenty-five years after apartheid, the White minority still owned 72 percent of private farmland in the country.[58] Parliament had passed a bill allowing for "the expropriation of property for a public purpose or in the public interest, subject to just and equitable compensation." The government could now legally force White landowners to give up their land in return for a fair price; the land would then be redistributed to Black South Africans. In response, Solidarity's long-running campaign against the supposedly race-based killings of

White farmers merged with its staunch defense of property rights. Previously, Solidarity and AfriForum called for the recognition of a "national crisis" of farm murders. Now they spoke about the threat "to property rights and human lives in South Africa. This threat is especially real for minority communities in general and for White farmers in particular."[59]

In 2017, Solidarity and AFriForum helped to organize Black Monday, a nationwide protest against crime, specifically against the attacks on White farmers. Two years later, in 2018, the ANC proposed to expedite the land reform process and amend the constitution to make it legal for the government to seize land without providing compensation as long as it didn't undermine the economy, agricultural production, or food security. The ANC was under pressure to deliver policies that would gain traction among the nation's (Black) poor. However, it needed a two-thirds majority of lawmakers in parliament to change the constitution, which currently mandated that farmers need "just and equitable" compensation from the government for seizing land. That same year, the deputy CEO of AfriForum, Ernst Roets, published a book about farm murders, *Kill the Boer*, named after the ANC song, in which he claimed that ANC politicians were complicit in the "proliferation of farm murders," which he believed were racially motivated.[60] At the launch of the book, AfriForum asked the ANC government for an independent commission of inquiry to determine the factors that led to farm murders, despite the fact that farm murders in South Africa were at their lowest point since 1998.[61]

During the international promotional campaign for the book, AfriForum was able to secure a spot on Fox News. On May 15, Roets was interviewed on *Tucker Carlson Tonight* in a segment on White farmers in South Africa. According to the show's host, White farmers were "being targeted in a wave of barbaric and horrifying murders." In the interview, Roets argued that the government was culpable because it ignored the crisis, continued to endorse negative stereotypes about the White farmers, and propagated hate.

On August 22, 2018, President Donald Trump tweeted that he had asked his secretary of state, Mike Pompeo, "to closely study the South Africa land and farm seizures and expropriations and the large scale killing of farmers. South African Government is now seizing land from White farmers." It was the first time Trump had tweeted about Africa—580 days into his term—and he focused on the fate of the White minority in South Africa. Trump had tagged the Fox journalist Tucker Carlson in his tweet, which suggested that it was the *Tucker Carlson Tonight* show that had inspired his tweet. Indeed, on his show that night, Carlson had a second segment on South Africa: under the headline "South Africa Farm Seizures Begin," Carlson suggested that the ANC government had already begun seizing land—it had not—and that current "seizures" were based on skin color.

Trump's tweet exemplifies Solidarity's successful neoliberal strategy to synthesize the protection of Whites' economic interest, the language of minority rights, and the idea of a vulnerable White minority into a single narrative. Although few would have predicted the international spotlight on the Solidarity Movement, populism today has become a global movement. And as Solidarity reaches out to powerful White allies around the world, they stay focused on autonomy from the state at home. A few months after the *krisisberaad*, the large meeting at the Voortrek-kers Monument at which Solidarity members debated the dismal state of the country, three thousand White South Africans assembled again in Centurion, near Pretoria, to attend Solidarity's Toekomsberaad, or future summit. At this meeting, Solidarity launched Helpmekaar 2020 (Mutual Aid 2020), a plan for a free, secure, and prosperous future for the White minority in South Africa, offering them the support and protection they were being denied by the ANC government. Solidarity argued for au-tonomy and declared that it would no longer rely on the state to create a future for White South Africans.[62]

The Solidarity Movement's White populism makes clear how populism has offered a new style and discourse to the former extreme right to go on the political offensive and transform the uses of Whiteness in every-day language. White populism made the reconfiguration of racism pos-sible, from an explicit racism embedded in Afrikaner nationalism to a defense of White privilege through White minoritization. South Africa's White minority must be understood as a demographic fact and a cultural construction. Through White minoritization, Solidarity has reframed the historical image of White South Africans from a powerful, affluent, and privileged group to a small and ostensibly powerless minority without rights in the new South Africa, a White minority that the Black majority threatens and Solidarity needs to protect. White populism is a powerful political style for presenting a distorted picture of the racial balance of power in a highly unequal liberal democracy with many structural challenges. Ultimately, Solidarity's populist discourse also shapes their grassroots neoliberal politics, which is aggressively anti-state and intended to undermine the constitutional order and a multiracial South Africa. In the next chapter, we will see how White embodiment renders Solidarity members susceptible to this populist message.

CHAPTER 5

White Embodiment and the Working Class

The Story of Eric Sommers

Eric Sommers is a fifty-two-year-old human resources manager at Eskom, the South African electricity supply company. For White working-class men such as Sommers, work is central to their identity, and their work has dramatically changed after apartheid. The company has been at the forefront of new affirmative action policies and Black economic empowerment. For Sommers, this means that he now works in a multicultural environment and is part of a new White minority there. The ANC government also opted to privatize Eskom as part of their broader neoliberal strategy. After privatization, however, the company has performed poorly: in 2008, South Africa experienced countrywide electrical "blackouts" caused by government disinvestment, loss of institutional knowledge, and corruption. Sommers embodies his Whiteness, so he struggles to make sense of the situation and his feelings. Unlearning racism is about losing your privileges but also about learning what equality feels like.

After 1994, Sommers told himself he had to change. "You have to tell yourself 'I accept, I submit, I'm going for it.'"[1] He learned to be tolerant. He agreed with affirmative action in principle. "We know we come from the apartheid era; certain rights were withheld from certain groups. A person realizes that affirmative action is there for a reason." He still takes pride in his work. However, Sommers no longer feels valued at work, and this sense of disenfranchisement translates to a general feeling of alienation.

A person has to feel you are still a first-class citizen in this country. And many times I feel this is not my country anymore. I am a mercenary here. Because you feel you are dependent on favors and gifts.

But it is my country. I was born here and I want to die here. I often think back to the times at the farm in South Africa. You had the farmer and the people that stayed in houses on the farm property— *die bywoner* [literally meaning "cohabitant"]. He did not work. He just lived there. Today you are a *bywoner*. It feels like that. We are just *bywoners*. They just tolerate us . . . while I think we have much to offer the country, the Whites, but specifically the Afrikaner.[2]

Sommers uses the term *bywoner*, an Afrikaans word used for tenants or sharecroppers that has strong ideological resonance. In the 1930s, Afrikaner nationalists made the figure of the *bywoner* a central target in their fight against the so-called poor White problem.[3] They understood poverty and farm life through a moral lens. White poverty was defined as a moral disease against which farmer families could protect themselves by strengthening their nationalist ideology and character. The Boer, or farmer, was positioned as a man whose work and productivity was vital to the White nation. The *bywoner* was positioned as the Boer's ideological opposite—a pathological individual who lived in poverty because of his character flaws and physical and social proximity to Black South Africans. In *The Poor White Problem in South Africa: Report of the Carnegie Commission*, published in 1932, South African sociologist J. R. Albertyn argued that the *bywoner* had a moral responsibility to uphold White society.[4] He blamed commercial farmers for treating them as if they were Black laborers. He feared that without state intervention, the *bywoner* would be lost to the White race.

For Sommers, the figure of the *bywoner* captures his feelings about his current position in South Africa. This is not because his working conditions are similar to those of the *bywoner*. He is a stable employee at a privatized public company; they are nothing alike. Nor is it because the White elite paint Sommers as a pathological figure. It is because he feels he no longer embodies Whiteness. He does not feel White enough to meet his own standard of Whiteness. In the past, the White working class were stigmatized by the White elite, but nowadays, White working-class men themselves find their own Whiteness wanting as they slip back to feeling like *bywoners*. After apartheid, affirmative action made Whiteness a liability. Because the men held on to the notion that being White is both physically and socially far from being a Black South African, work has become misery. They insist on feeling differently—and labor emotionally to do so—but overlook the possibility of letting go of Whiteness.

Maybe Sommers does not yet feel "lost to the White race," but he is anxious about losing his Whiteness. At the human resources department, he is one of only two employees who are White and Afrikaans-speaking. He worries about how his proximity to Black people is affecting him. His work environment is stressful; a few years ago, he began taking pills for high blood pressure. He struggles with the different cultures at work. "One speaks Xhosa, the other Zulu," he said. "In the evening, I am happy to go back to my own culture, but the next day, I have to return to the mixed culture."[5] Sometimes the anxiety keeps him up at night. The closer he works with his Black co-workers, the more he worries that he is becoming "just like them." He is afraid to adopt their culture—that he might slowly *verval*, or slip, into a culture of "tomorrow is another day." African culture, for Sommers, is defined by lateness and laziness, and his Whiteness by punctuality and a good work ethic.

Sommers's anxiety suggests that unlearning racism is about more than having good relationships with people of color. He says he gets along fine with his nonwhite co-workers: "There are a lot more conversations between White and Black people than in the past. We all have similar interests, like parenthood, and everybody has the same heart."[6] A few years ago, he also became part of a mentoring program for new Black employees at Eskom, which provides them with support and training. After mentoring them, he has kept in touch with his mentees.

Yet although he emphasizes how the common humanity of Black and White people bridges racial boundaries, this does not make him feel good. Despite his antiracist stance, Sommers resents his current position as a White worker. He blames affirmative action and Black workers for the failure to uphold standards at Eskom, a problem that he sees "everywhere, and this has affected everything."[7] Black workers who underperform, he claims, "do not get fired but promoted." He manages these feelings of racial resentment by drawing a moral boundary between Black workers and himself. Sommers likes to emphasize that he still has *trots*, or pride in his work, and in the same breath he says that Black workers do not take pride in their work. He seems to be asserting his pride in his work for fear of being perceived as the same as his Black colleagues, as well as for fear of no longer being seen as White enough.

Whiteness beyond Words: White Identity Politics and Emotions

For this chapter, in 2008 and 2010 I interviewed members of the Solidarity Movement, working-class and lower-middle-class White workers who in many cases have been employed for many years by former state entities such as Eskom and Telkom. I analyzed these men's cultural talk and feelings to understand the process of unlearning racism. The Solidarity members held complex views about race and racial relationships at work. Many expressed strongly critical judgments about their work and co-workers, but they also described colleagues they appreciated. The men were open about their fears and anxieties in regard to their new status at work and in society. Indeed, despite their steady employment, White working-class men depict themselves as being in a precarious position. To a certain extent, this is simply a fact, certainly in comparison to the privileges they enjoyed as Whites during much of the twentieth century. But it was not their lost privileges that worried them most.

What stuck with me was the dramatic emotional terms these men used to describe their feelings about their place in society: how they felt alienated, cast aside, and like second-class citizens in their own country. These sentiments were remarkably similar to what scholars of populism in the United States and United Kingdom have documented in their studies of the White working class.[8] American sociologist Arlie Hochschild titled her study of White members of the Tea Party *Strangers in Their Own Land*.[9] In her analysis, she emphasizes the importance of emotions for how we see the world, and especially the social norms that dictate what are appropriate feelings. She argues that people follow "feeling rules" that do not describe what people feel but prescribe whether they should or shouldn't feel a certain way. However, scholars such as Hochschild are unclear about the role of Whiteness and racism in this politics of feelings.[10] This leaves them empty-handed in their efforts to explain why their White subjects feel the way they do.

Why does White identity politics resonate? The previous chapters have documented the rise of White identity politics in the public and counter-public spheres and demonstrated how this politics borrowed its language of pain and trauma from previously marginalized groups. This in part explains the use of dramatic emotional rhetoric by working-class men. We have also seen how the White elite and populists actively produce White identity politics. This chapter moves beyond the rhetorical to examine the inner lives of White working-class men at work and the process of un-learning racism, in order to elucidate what it is that these White men feel and how they express it, and then why it is that they feel what they feel.

At first glance, White identity politics and its language of threat and victimhood resonate with these men because of affirmative action. The men feel that their jobs and positions are threatened, and they complain about never being promoted. White identity politics helps them to puzzle through a problematic situation.[11] They feel that they are being punished for apartheid while being only minor figures in the grand schemes of apartheid. White identity politics resonates because it offers a political strategy that justifies the men's feelings, affirming their feelings of victim-hood. The threat posed by affirmative action, however, is not sufficient to explain the feelings of White working-class men after apartheid. To do so, we must understand how Afrikaner nationalism during apartheid both conferred privilege on the White working class and disciplined them ideo-logically, through norms about what it meant to be a man and strict rules about how to feel about Black people. Afrikaner nationalism inscribed Whiteness in the bodies of these working-class men in a way that is still being felt decades after its demise. British sociologist Stuart Hall wrote that race is "the modality in which class is lived," and this is as true for Blackness as it is for Whiteness.[12] White identity politics appeals to White working-class men because they feel its supposed truth in their bones.

White Embodiment

White embodiment is central to the emotional challenge of unlearning rac-ism. Race has always functioned as a property of bodies, one that makes bodies come to be seen as alike. In *Black Skin White Masks*, Franz Fanon writes incisively about racism and the Black body.[13] Racism shapes what it is that bodies can do and are allowed to do. Racism cannot be reduced to talk, nor unlearning racism to cultural change. As South African social psychologist Derek Hooks argues, racism is a phenomenon that is "as psychological as it is political, affective as discursive, subjective as ideological."[14] The same is true for unlearning racism: this process can never be only cognitive but must also be emotional. White embodiment may be defined as the White body's way of being in the world, a type of racial embodiment that has historically, in South Africa, come with confidence, ease, and entitlement. This chapter will explore the emotional response that is produced when White embodiment is challenged, jolted, and changed.

White embodiment means that we carry our racial experiences with us. It is about the deeply ingrained habits, skills, and dispositions that White people possess owing to racialization during their lifetime.[15] Once racial experiences are embodied, they begin to seem natural. Yet things that feel natural to us—that are embodied—are not necessarily natural at all but the result of processes of socialization and racialization. Throughout our lives our bodies come to recognize certain physical sensations. We learn to move our limbs in a specific manner and to know when to feel joy and fear. This often makes the experience of Whiteness invisible to those who consider themselves White. In South Africa, Whiteness has long been experienced as normative and thus as normal and natural to White people. While Whiteness has always been visible to others, White people's awareness of their own Whiteness during apartheid was often obscured, lived as a background to experience. White people did not have to face their Whiteness; they were not oriented toward it. This did not mean, however, that their bodies were not oriented by it; White embodiment always oriented bodies in specific directions. It was only after apartheid that White people were forced to confront their White embodiment and to understand how they carried their racial experiences with them.

While White working-class men—maybe more than White middle-class men—regularly acknowledge that Black South Africans suffered under apartheid, but they do not always recognize the full extent of the injustice. They identify historical wrongs done to Black people but struggle to see how they themselves at the same time benefited from White privilege during apartheid. They develop genuine relationships with their Black co-workers but still find it difficult to fully contextualize the other. They recognize apartheid's history but are not always able to place themselves in that history. Most important, it is their White embodiment that sits in the way of fully adjusting to change.

White embodiment is not an issue that uniquely confronts the White working class. In contrast to South Africa's White middle and upper classes, however, the working class find themselves in a position where this is systematically challenged at work. They can no longer escape de-segregation but must conform to Black expectations and be supervised by Black bosses. New norms and relationships in the workplace force them to confront their old practices, which still feel natural to them, be-ing embodied, but need to be changed. Unlearning racism means they must untie the emotional knot of anger, resentment, and grief and be-come aware of how their Whiteness is embodied. White working-class men struggle to adapt because their need to unlearn racism presents an emotional challenge. They are unable to disentangle Whiteness as an ide-ology from its embodiment. In the end, it seems easier to claim victim-hood through White identity politics than to make progress on the path of emotional growth.

Afrikaner Nationalism, White Masculinity and Racism

Afrikaner nationalism always offered an equivocal bargain to the lower classes.[16] Apartheid provided this group with preferential treatment and exclusive access to employment, from which poor Whites benefited tre-mendously. During apartheid, Afrikaner nationalists lifted hundreds of thousands of poor and White working-class Afrikaans-speaking South Africans out of poverty.[17] Specifically, the apartheid government supplied jobs and security through a growing civil service and the takeover of para-statal companies, state-owned economic institutions such as South African Railways and the South African iron and steel company (Iscor). By the early 1970s, these companies employed a large share of White Afrikaans-speaking lower-middle-class and working-class men.[18] Guaranteed em-ployment provided stability and security to White working-class men. Apartheid also provided them a "psychological wage," to use the words of American sociologist W. E. B. Du Bois.[19] They felt they belonged and had access. Yet White working-class masculinity was never fully secure.

Afrikaner nationalism promoted and enforced ideals about what it meant to be a "real" White man that were hard for poor and White working-class men to achieve. Men assess their self-worth through ideas about manhood, and historically dominant conceptions of masculinity permeate this process. As a consequence, White working-class men during apartheid were always in danger of being—and feeling—not quite White and manly enough. They could never fully embody the hegemonic masculinity of Afrikaner nationalism, which celebrated a particular kind of White man: specifically the Boer, a mythical figure who embodied the values of religious puritanism, austerity, and strictness.[20] The Boer was never just a farmer but a pioneer, a warrior, a family man, and a benevolent patriarch.[21] In the 1930s, during a time of urbanization and social disruption, Afrikaner nationalism promoted a hegemonic masculinity rooted in a romanticized and heroic rural past.[22] The Boer represented the best of the Afrikaner character: its bravery, perseverance, and resourcefulness. His mythical masculinity was used to mobilize people, create order, and ensure solidarity; he symbolized a cultural ideal to which White men should aspire. Nevertheless, the Boer embodied a sense of independence and individuality that was hard to achieve for the average White working-class man because of his class position and employment.

More important, Afrikaner nationalism also vilified another kind of man, the *bywoner*, or sharecropper. Hegemonic masculinity in a culture is always defined against other forms of masculinity.[23] The *bywoner* embodied the opposite of the Boer: unmanliness and unwhiteness. Afrikaner nationalists wanted to unite the *Volk* and create class solidarity, a concern they first problematized and then politicized through their goal to rehabilitate "poor Whites." Ordinary poor Whites were conceptualized as male. Poor Whites, nationalists argued, were mainly a result of rural decline, and their theory of rural decline was based on the ability or inability of men to provide for their families. Specifically, the *bywoner* was singled out for his supposed failure to work hard, earn a living, and support a family.[24] Nationalists maintained that, because of capitalism, the *bywoner* had lost not only his livelihood but also his sense of identity. He was accused of being idle and wandering, a Boer who had lost his values and his manhood.[25] Most significant, the *bywoner* was seen as being on the verge of losing his Whiteness because of his proximity to Black South Africans.[26] According to Afrikaner nationalists, the *bywoner* was no longer quite White. This pathological White embodiment of the *bywoner* was constructed out of nationalist ideals about White men that connected Whiteness, masculinity, and class.

Afrikaner nationalists' racist dreams were violently imposed through social policy backed by social science. International philanthropic organizations used the poor White problem for their civilizing mission to control the bodies of poor Whites. South Africa's government was deeply invested in creating and manipulating the White body—particularly that of poor and working-class Whites—as a problematic signifier of Whiteness, masculinity, and domination.[27] In the name of global Whiteness, social scientists measured the intelligence of poor Whites, photographed them, and documented their everyday habits. In the case of those who fell short, social scientists advised policy makers to forcibly remove their children, force them to move out of integrated neighborhoods, and force the women to undergo mandatory sterilization.

As a consequence, for the White working class during apartheid, Whiteness did not mean only privilege and a psychological wage but also being policed harshly and brutally. The White racism of nationalists prescribed strict separation between the races and enforced feeling rules to prevent White people from feeling equal to Black people and building interracial solidarity. Nationalists consistently argued that the proximity of poor and working-class Whites to Black South Africans was a major problem that needed to be condemned and corrected. South African sociologist Geoffrey Cronjé was especially concerned that poor and White working-class people would enter a "gradual process of feeling equal, or *gelykvoeling*, with non-whites" if they lived and worked together.[28] This had to be prevented. The most important feeling rule for White South Africans was to feel superior to Black South Africans at all times and to understand that this superiority needed to be translated into separation and not solidarity. During apartheid, slowly but surely, Whiteness became embodied for the White working class. Nevertheless, their Whiteness was never fully secured. South African historian Danelle van Zyl-Hermann has shown how South Africa's most prominent White working-class leader and White trade unionist, Arrie Paulus, was haunted in the 1970s by a rumor that he was not actually White.[29]

After apartheid, White working-class men have started to consciously feel White. South African color-conscious policies such as affirmative action address the men's Whiteness, and sometimes fellow South Africans view them through stereotypes. During apartheid, what it meant to be White also meant feeling a certain way, not just superior but also desirable, invulnerable, and respectable. What the men are struggling with after apartheid is not just the loss of White privilege but unlearning feeling superior. South Africa's apartheid granted White working-class men specific White rights and at the same time ingrained a feeling of superiority in them. Unlearning racism is difficult for these men because it is about feeling their way toward racial equality: learning to be part of a White minority without privilege, learning what it feels like to be equal and to no longer need to feel superior based on one's skin color. In many ways these men do not know how to act or feel normal in the new situation; they yearn for the way apartheid felt. Whiteness as embodied knowledge is disrupted and malfunctions; the men's emotional experiences register this fact. During apartheid White embodiment was made, but after apartheid it is unclear how it can be unmade. As a consequence, White working-class men wrestle with what their Whiteness is still worth, but they are afraid to let it go.

The history of Afrikaner nationalism in South Africa shows that in White supremacist societies the moral order has always been shaped by the racial order.[30] American sociologist David Sears has argued that in the United States, in the wake of the civil rights movement, traditional racism anchored in prejudice and hate declined among White Americans and was replaced by racism rooted in the American values of individualism, hard work, and self-reliance.[31] Sears and others trace these moral values to a specific American civil religion.[32] The case of South Africa suggests there is nothing specifically American about these values or the general connection between the moral and the racial order. Furthermore, this relationship is neither new nor specific to the United States. In fact, the history of racism in both countries teaches us that the two are never fully separated.

In post-apartheid South Africa, the relationship between the moral and racial orders changed after democracy. The ANC government's affirmative action policies undercut the White privileges of White working-class men, to the point that their Whiteness became a liability. In the past, Afrikaner nationalism had provided White working-class men with exclusive White citizenship, White rights, and a feeling of national belonging to the White family—including at work; they have lost these rights. The ANC government's neoliberal strategy of privatizing public companies in fact worsens their working conditions. White working-class men need to emotionally manage this challenge to their White embodiment, which they try to do through "pride talk" and an emphasis on individual morality and the work ethic. They feel resentful toward their Black co-workers but also try to manage their feelings through what I call "grassroots neoliberalism": an ideology centered on moralized talk about individual strength, pride in their work, and antigovernment rhetoric. For these men, Whiteness has become a problem, as they can no longer live up to the racial ideals of embodied power, privilege, and paternalism. Their Whiteness is wanting; it has become risk-laden. Whiteness becomes, as Willoughby-Herard has written, a form of diminished selfhood and soul injury.[33]

The End of Apartheid: "The Family Story Has Ended"

White working-class men always anticipated—and feared—the losses they would sustain when the ANC began to govern the country. Men I interviewed recall the scary stories that circulated in the early 1990s, when it became evident that the ANC would take power and Nelson Mandela would become the first Black president. The stories were apocalyptic and hyperbolic: Whites would be "chased into the sea" and be "repressed." Such fear-mongering was familiar to the men; stories about the "Black peril" had been central to the apartheid state for decades. Whiteness had always been embodied in this way. As the democratic transition drew near, however, anxieties about what the new racial order would bring for these White working-class men reached a fever pitch.

These horror stories never materialized, but work did change quickly after 1994. According to the men, the transition from a protected position as a White employee to the introduction of affirmative action was fast, total, and full of conflict. Henk Sadie, an employee of Telkom, recalls:

> Things very rapidly changed. Affirmative action was happening for over ten years. This started very early. The "affirming" was quick. And yes, in the beginning, this caused great conflict. Because the people who were appointed were, of course, incompetent. Useless in comparison to what we were used to. You really had to be good to move up in Telkom. The competition was strong. Then they brought these people in from the street, and they just had to swim. And this caused even more conflicts. This was very traumatic. Like I said, we were used to a good team of directors, people who could make decisions for the benefit of the company. And then you got people who had no knowledge whatsoever and who made decisions that were really poor for the company.[34]

Sadie draws a stark contrast between past and present—and implies that the new Black employees ruined the company. His description of the personnel change as "traumatic" highlights the impact of racial integration on the men. Although Sadie never mentions race directly, the negative trajectory of the business is explained through a racial lens. And his contempt for the new Black workers ("people in from the street") and the process of affirmative action is evident.

When these lower-middle-class men talk about how they experience work today, the past is never far away. In their perception of the present, stories about the past play an important role, as they contrast their positions and experiences then with those now. According to them, Eskom and Telkom during apartheid were like a family. The old companies were organizations where "everybody" worked, everybody "wanted" to work, and, most important, "everything" worked. Flip Meyer, who works at Eskom, recalls:

> It was like you were part of a family, the whole thing felt like a family. It was totally different. Then, you were all from the same culture. That was one of the biggest changes thereafter. . . . We used

to play cricket together, the men. The women used to play netball. The women knew each other, they would arrange social activities, go to concerts. . . . We made friends and we were friends. . . . This has totally changed. That cultures now differ plays a big role. . . . It is not the same anymore. The family story has ended.[35]

For these men, the company was sometimes literally a family, as many had parents or siblings working at the same company. The social spirit and relationships of the past were deeply cherished, and they feel this culture has been lost. Henk Niekerk, another employee of Eskom, straightforwardly admits that he lived a good life during apartheid. Everything has gone downhill since then, he says, particularly at Eskom: during apartheid, everything worked well; Eskom had enough people, the salaries were good, and cooperation between Black and White people was smooth. Rhetorically, he asks, "What has improved since then?"

The men feel that the work pressure has increased but the company is not as good as it was in the past. As Jady Schalkwyk, an employee of Telkom, recalls:

It was good. This was still under the old regime at Telkom. These were the years when people said, "We work great," but this is not so anymore. Then, we had it good at work. You would *braai* on free days, you had social activities. Those things do not happen anymore.[36]

Schalkwyk's image of the past is one of strong bonds with co-workers and a deep commitment to the company. The meaning of work has radically changed for these White Afrikaans-speaking men. In the past, everything was "calm" and you did the work "the way you wanted." The men are nostalgic about the feeling of community at work. In the past, work always meant more to them than earning a living; it was about belonging, being part of a community, and feeling at home at work. What, then, changed for the men after 1994?

Confronting Affirmative Action
Before 1994, the men felt they had job security. This, they know, has permanently changed. Today they must compete with all other workers for

the fewer jobs that are still available. The safety of a job has now been replaced by a fear of possible retrenchment and job loss. Chris Rensburg, who lost his job at Eskom in 2004, says:

> Everybody knows. . . . All White men know . . . still know this can happen to him any time. Like a car accident. You can drive safely, and you should not have an accident. But I think all White men in South Africa experience that they can be fired tomorrow. . . . And yes, of course this hurts a person. This affects you, because you as the breadwinner don't have work anymore. And there is nothing you did at work that got you sacked. It is not like you got fired. You did nobody anything wrong; you did not hurt anybody; you did not drink at your job. So, it is pure this political correctness that is enacted by society. Anybody would experience some consequences if you would lose your job as a consequence of affirmative action. . . . It is like the world around you collapses. What now?[37]

Rensburg uses dramatic emotional terms to describe the situation. He also has deep distrust about what the future holds, expressed by his emphasis on the words "any time" and "tomorrow," and his question, "What now?" Although the other men in this chapter still have their jobs, the fear of being laid off is not exceptional. Becoming unemployed has serious financial consequences in a country with a limited social safety net such as South Africa. But anxiety about employment also increases, because it threatens their masculine identities as "breadwinners." Rensburg feels indignation and a strong sense of injustice about losing his job. He stresses that he did nothing wrong. He feels powerless in his inability to prevent his layoff, as if he had been personally punished, and he feels that he always did his work correctly. Rensburg does not connect his current position with the historic advantages he received because of his White privilege in the past.

Solidarity's talk of the threat to White men and the crisis in South Africa, discussed in Chapter 4, has resonated with White working-class men such as Rensburg. Traditionally, most White workers at Eskom have been union members. At Telkom, however, Solidarity only arrived in 1991. The union took on a new meaning with the introduction of affirmative action programs. As Andre Durandt, who works at Eskom, said, "Dit het 'n ou kwaad gemaak" (This made a man angry). Before affirmative action, the men noted, the unions were "just there" and hardly played a role; nowadays, however, the men describe Solidarity as a movement that protects the rights of the White minority.

Solidarity's language of rights has resonated with the men's experiences in their changing work environment resulting from racial integration. Echoing Solidarity's campaigns, the men say that rights "have to be demanded now." According to Andre Durandt:

> I don't have a problem with [Blacks]. It is just . . . a man has to start with a union. A man has to fight for his rights now. A man sees that Eskom is changing, and a man tries to get back the old Eskom, especially when this comes to safety.[38]

Durandt strings his concerns about the union, racism, and rights together. He argues that Whites have rights too. He does not like how Eskom has changed and wants to fight to get the old Eskom back. His comment about safety made it clear that he doesn't just want to return to a White Eskom but also to a company that upholds its standards.

Solidarity has provided these men with a way to understand their situation in the new populist discourse of White identity politics. For Roche Gerlach, an employee at Telkom:

> They were for me the people who did the best things and the most for us, as Whites, Afrikaners, and South Africans. And the passion they had for the work, and the work they did at that time, that was for me . . . it provided me with a lot of guidance. This was a place where I felt home. This was my movement. . . . I have a right to be who I am as a human being. They can't force principles and concepts onto me. I have a right to be Roche, not someone else. . . . This has been my upbringing from when I was young that made me into who I am. They told me I had to stand up for my rights.[39]

Gerlach uses Solidarity's language of rights not to reaffirm his right to work but his right to be White. He argues that he has a right to be himself (White and South African) and that nobody should tell him to be someone else. The Solidarity Movement's White identity politics, which emphasizes their (White) right to be and love themselves, resonates with the men's feelings of their Whiteness being wanting.

The Solidarity members echo the movement's argument when it comes to affirmative action. None of the workers straight-out denied the justification for affirmative action programs; what they object to primarily is the execution of such programs. In their view, affirmative action programs should benefit everybody, but in their current form, only Black people (men and women) and White women have benefited. The company was losing "skills" when its White workers were laid off, making the company worse and negatively affecting both Black and White workers. The deterioration of companies like Telkom and Eskom was never related to other problems, such as its privatization or poor capacity management. Any hint of a critique of the government's neoliberalism was overshadowed by the focus on affirmative action as the root of all problems.

South Africa's affirmative action policy is based on the assumption that the White working class had enjoyed White privilege in the past, under the apartheid system. The men I interviewed challenged that perception, presenting themselves as victims of the apartheid regime because they had to fight in the army and had suffered the consequences in their personal lives. Now, when they finally have normal work, they feel victimized again.

> I was also disadvantaged. I was two years gone from my family when I tried to protect the country. I have returned, and now they tell me I cannot get a promotion because I am a White man and already have been advantaged. Where was I advantaged? Such things get stuck in your chest—you cannot set this aside in the way you take your clothing off. And this makes a person unhappy, and today still with affirmative action. . . . This is the heartache from affirmative action. First you have the Black woman, then the Black man, then all those people and more, and now the South African government tells me Chinese are also included in that group? Now there are so many people ahead of you, where does the White man go? He has nothing.[40]

According to Faurie, White privilege is a relative term. His army service made him pay a high price for the "privileges of apartheid." He suffered a breakdown and a long period of alcoholism after he returned from military service.

While Faurie shows sympathy for the people who were disadvantaged during apartheid, he denies getting any advantages himself. In his view, therefore, affirmative action is not justified:

> Everything we had, had been for us. We did give them something, but we gave them poorer services. And this was wrong because they are also people. I would say that is wrong and should not have happened. But still I just feel, like I said, that I did not reap the benefits. Here I am, today, I am just an ordinary breadwinner, equal to anybody else. I did not reap the benefits. Why should I be second now?

Faurie is fully aware that Blacks were worse off during apartheid and that White South Africans were mainly to blame. It is an injustice that he attributes to the failure of Whites to acknowledge that Blacks are human beings too, though not necessarily to the political dominance or economic greed of Whites. In his view, he derived no benefit from that history.

White men such as Faurie are unable to see that being an "ordinary breadwinner" (a lower-middle-class White man with job security who can provide for his family) is the privilege in this scenario. As a consequence, his acknowledgment of the culpability of White people for apartheid does not stop him from portraying himself as a victim. For White men such as Faurie, the frustration is that their personal pasts don't logically add up to the present situation. They search in vain for personal reasons why they must pay the price for apartheid.

Shifting Social Norms

Affirmative action has changed the culture at work. It has changed the composition of the workforce but also the relationships of power between employees. This is something the men feel on a daily basis. Specifically, they complain about the change in what they are able to say or talk about at work. New social norms at work challenge the men to unlearn their racism. Black employees do not appreciate their paternalistic thinking. The men's complaints, however, show that the mindset of White superiority—thinking of oneself as above one's Black co-workers—is hard to unlearn or even to reflect upon. Far too often, the White men still see themselves as boss and as the person who determines how interracial relationships must be structured.

Johan Naude, who has been a leader of a Telkom team that fixes telephone cables for twenty years, says, "If he greets me decently, it is fine. If he asks me nicely, it is fine. If he does his work, it is fine. The people I have worked with, I bent them to a certain extent to fit my own rules."[41] Naude seems to assume that Black people aren't normally hard-working or responsible and that his White paternalism was required to make them work to his standards.

The men's attitudes of paternalism and White superiority are now challenged at work, and they complain about how these new race relationships "feel forced." The men highlight what they see as the compulsory character of interracial collaboration and how they are "made" to feel good about it. Chris Rensburg, for instance, says that today there is only "political correctness" and that he cannot even "look at [Blacks] with a smile" because such smiles are interpreted as racism by the management. Jady Schalkwyk, the Telkom employee, says that racial friendships are "forced" and that it is "expected of you" to act socially. But this, he claims, rarely comes "from the heart."

> In the past they had much more respect, and . . . things completely changed. Not that we wanted them to say "boss" to you, but he had respect for you. "Yes boss." He had always seen you higher than he had seen himself. And I am sure, you always treated him with respect, and you were good to him.[42]

Schalkwyk believes that Whites and Blacks were closer during apartheid and collaborated better. He contrasts the "forced" racial relationships of today with a nonexistent idyllic past, when race relationships were still "spontaneous" and Blacks had "respect" for Whites. What Schalkwyk interprets as the respect of Blacks for Whites in the past is actually Blacks knowing their status and acting accordingly. Schalkwyk fails to see that these "good" racial relationships were based on White domination and the clear, unequal roles of master and underling. During apartheid, these supposedly good relationships were dependent on the benevolence of Whites as the dominant race.

White embodiment is a way of being in—and feeling—the world. White working-class men such as Schalkwyk fail to see that they must unlearn their racism and accept racial equality, especially in daily relations at work. Their old position of White superiority is no longer appropriate or legitimate. These men have no choice but to develop a different attitude toward racial relationships and to adjust to the practices and habits of the Black majority in the company. Their career success depends on better interracial relationships and more sensitivity to the new norms. Yet the men seem almost viscerally unable to accept the new reality of racial equality; instead, they prefer to "stick to their own kind" at work, as they already do at home.

White men claim that an "innocent joke" can now result in the loss of their job. They justify the racism of some jokes by arguing that these are "tough men" who do "men's work"; such jokes are seen as a test of masculinity: if you can't take a rough joke, you aren't a real man. The White men believe that Black co-workers use the new regulations to address personal vendettas and retaliate. According to one man, "It feels like we have to put a lock on our mouths." The men also complain that topics such as politics and religion have become perilous conversational territory; some issues are treated with trepidation and reluctance, while others must be completely avoided. They say they have to constantly be careful about what they discuss during work hours.

> I can sit down with these [Black] people, and we can drink a soda, and we will work. The common goal is still to make electricity. But we stay away from topics like politics. You know you don't talk about politics with other people. You don't talk about religion. You know what to talk about and what not to talk about. These men also have a house and children, so that is what you talk about. You have to choose your topics because you know what to talk about.[43]

In Faurie's view, certain topics only create tensions with their Black fellow workers and bring division to the workplace, whereas other topics, such as sports, houses, or cars, are more manageable. The men attribute this "loss" of freedom of speech to the fact that Blacks now have gotten "many rights."

Emotion Management through "Pride Talk"

In South Africa, the racial order has always deeply shaped the moral order. This is still true after apartheid. In *The Dignity of Working Men: Morality and the Boundaries of Race, Class, and Immigration*, Canadian sociologist Michèle Lamont dissects the thinking of the American White working class.[44] She argues that for White workers, keeping the world in order—in moral order—is at the top of their agenda. In her analysis, she separates the men's investment in the moral order from the racial order, even though she recognizes that these orders are intertwined. By contrast, White South African men demonstrate that it is not the moral order that takes preeminence. Rather, the men's emphasis on morality, such as their "work ethic," functions to re-create a racial boundary between new Black employees and themselves. It is the way these men cope with their negative emotions about their Whiteness, their work, and their company.

The White working-class men use "pride talk" to emotionally manage their feelings about their work. Pride talk is the emphasis the men put on their individual morality and work ethic to feel better about their Whiteness. In the past, Afrikaner nationalism provided the White working-class men exclusive rights to work at companies such as Eskom and Telkom and a feeling of familial belonging. The men are aware that their misgivings about affirmative action, their nostalgic picture of the past, and their critique of the companies could give people the impression that White workers are no longer willing to do the work—that they only complain and criticize. They counter this impression through pride talk. After apartheid, Afrikaner nationalism and its national companies no longer provide White pride and positive feelings of belonging. Neoliberalism and privatization have made it an individual challenge of emotional labor.

The White working class must emotionally manage the challenge to their White embodiment at the individual level. They try to feel good about their work—despite their misgivings, particularly about their new Black co-workers—through emphasizing their pride in their work:

You have to remember that still for a White man, it is about that he does the work that he does well, and that he gives his best. So you are still always willing to do your work well. If there is work, you will do it well. Although you might feel uneasy about your supervisor because this is a nonwhite person who is young or a woman, and you know that if he or she will get other work tomorrow, they will go. And they are appointed as superiors to you. There is not a similar option in the company for you, but you have pride in yourself, and a mission to make it happen. This is the thing.[45]

Faurie stresses that even amid all the change and seemingly unfair promotion opportunities, the White worker still does his work "as good as possible," and he always "gives his best." The White worker, although facing adverse conditions, is defined by his pride in his work.

Affirmative action programs challenge the self-image of the men as proud workers. The men feel unrecognized for their senior status and for the expertise and skills that they developed over the years. Many men have worked for more than two decades at Eskom and feel they are entitled to a certain respect for their accumulated knowledge and skills. In the past, they say, knowledge and skills were valued; respect used to increase with age, including across racial lines.

My parents have taught me that if a person is older, say, 10 years, then you call him *oom*, or uncle. If a Black man was older than me, I would have always respected him. I was still willing to learn from him at work. At work I would have respected him, or I still respect him.[46]

The men attribute the lack of respect for elders to a reward system (*meriete stelsel*) that no longer functions properly. They feel workers do not receive the proper recognition for their work. As Henk Sadie says, "Jy soek daai pat op die back" (You're looking for those pats on the back). The men are looking for recognition for their contributions to the company.

The expertise and knowledge a man had, a man easily shared, passed on, and educated new people. I have been at Eskom for 20 years. So I know the company from where the power is made until where the costumers are serviced by our people. I know all of the company. So, a man could easily share these things with others. But the person with whom you shared your knowledge is gone. They have moved up in Eskom. And this man stays where he has always been.[47]

For all the expertise and knowledge Durandt built up over the years and still shares with his new Black co-workers, little recognition is provided in return. Instead, men like him see Black workers moving up in the ranks of Eskom through affirmative action.

Work has changed for the men, and the shifting racial order at work is central to it. The changing racial hierarchy affects not only their experiences or their identities but their White embodiment as well. The men's preoccupation with moral pride and individual dignity is connected to the resentment they feel about their devalued White status. The progress of nonwhite South Africans in the workplace is interpreted as a threat to the value of the White men's work. The men feel left behind. They maintain their identities as dignified men through emotion management and "pride talk," which affirms their White embodiment and assuages their anxiety over losing their Whiteness.

Racial Boundaries

White working-class men draw racial boundaries in different ways: morally, generationally, and through gender. The threat to their Whiteness and White embodiment that they experience motivates them to reconstruct their White identities.

First, the men assert that White working-class men have a different work ethic than their fellow Black workers: whereas White men take pride in their work, the Black man does not. Moreover, they argue that Blacks often cannot do the work, no matter how well educated they are.

> They do well at university and at the training centers. I mean, academically they do well. When he comes back to you in the workplace, then he cannot do the work. This is what we experienced as White technicians. In general, they have often obtained higher scores than the White person, they easily have gotten 80 percent and we got 60 percent for the exam. But then it comes to the practical applica-

tion of technical matters, then we experience they cannot cope. And then you have to carry them, the whole path down.[48]

According to Rensburg, even when Blacks have a better education, the White man has to "carry them." The working-class men draw on these examples to show how cultural differences manifest themselves in the workplace. Pride, one man says, makes the White man finish his work on time; he will finish all his work before lunch, whereas a Black man might more readily go for lunch regardless. The men tell various stories to make a similar point: that it is the pride in the work that separates the White worker from the Black worker.

Second, the men draw a boundary between new and older Black workers. For the men, their dignity is the main concern when they judge the new generation of Blacks coming into the companies. The men say they prefer the older Black workers to the new generation, whom they see as "arrogant." The older generation, they say, has learned to respect Whites—they know how to say *baas* and *meneer*, or boss and sir, whereas the younger generation "wants" everything and is difficult to "get a grip on." Johan Naude argues that young Black men do not lack education; they lack the moral education of paying respect to other people. He says, "[These are] young people who still believe it is better if all White people are pushed out of the country. They still exist. And these are all . . . extremists."[49] The new, young Black employees are seen as snobbish and as holding high opinions of themselves.

This man does not even have a child; he does not know how other people think. He does not have any emotional steadfastness inside him. In other words, this man will jump around from job to job because this is about money. And that is why the turnaround of Blacks in companies at the moment is very high, while at the same time White skills are being lost. Because that Black guy, who is two months in his position, then goes on to another position. . . . He has taken up another White guy's position, and this White man has left the company as a consequence of this. And then the Black guy leaves anyway. So what did the company win? Just nothing. On the contrary, the company has lost.[50]

Faurie sees the young Black employee as undeserving of his new position within the company. Although Faurie's reasoning focuses on the overall loss for the company, it is the negative image of the young Black worker that is striking for its racism. He is depicted as an adolescent, insensitive, and lacking emotional stability. It is the new, young Black employee who does not have the patience to stay on the job for more than a split second longer to get the work done and brings down the company. Some men also suggest that rapid promotions are not beneficial for young Black employees, who suffer from being insufficiently prepared to function in a higher position.

Third, the men say that Black workers are not interested in doing the work but often just pretend to work hard.

> When the boss is there, they say, "We did this and we did that." But if he turns his back again, then they just chitchat and all that kind of stuff. And this also happens in a group—all the show and puff, the glamour, and that kind of stuff. If it comes to the work, then this is done by Whites. . . . You know, for all people of the call center—we are with almost eighty people—if you look at the work, there is always this showing off of clothing they wear and the car they drive. But if it comes down to the work, it is just Whites. . . . It is glamorous for them to be at work . . . they just want the money, but if it comes to getting some work done, they don't want to do anything.[51]

Durandt argues that Black workers work only for the "glamour" and do not actually do the work. He highlights the "show and puff" that Black workers put up when the boss is around. He argues that their sense of glamour, clothing style, and showy behavior masks that they do not do their work, and that they only want to drive a company car to show off. In the end, coming full circle, he asserts that it is only Whites who do the work.

White Masculinity versus Women at Work

The men's concerns about the dignity of work are thus related to their masculinity. Durandt singles out (Black) female workers as being only interested in money and consumption. The focus on Black women reveals that the men feel that not only their White identity is threatened but also their masculine identity. Before 1994, many of the technical positions in the company were reserved for men. This has changed.

> This is another thing that bugs me. It is that they appoint people on technical posts even with the technical service because that is where I saw it. They appoint [Black] women who cannot do the work. It is not suitable for women to do that kind of work because they often do not have the physical strength to do the work. But because we have a gender policy, they are appointed. Never mind the man who has to carry them on the ground—the man who has to do his own work and also her work to make the whole process run smoothly.[52]

According to Durandt, women who are newly appointed cannot do the work, and therefore men have to do double work. What resonates in his comments, however, is how the new gender policies deprive the men of yet another source of pride, namely, their physical strength. For White working-class men who do hard physical labor, this is never just a burden but also a source of pride and distinction. They can no longer bolster their masculine identities with exclusive claims to "tough work."

This suggests that there is something quintessentially masculine about the experience and interpretation of the changes at work: the crisis of belonging is due to male socialization and a failure to be more empathetic with their Black co-workers. Do women's stories about change differ significantly? They also need to adjust to new circumstances—their work surroundings used to be just as White as those of their White male co-workers. Of course, affirmative action does not affect women as much as men, since they are included as a group that was also previously disadvantaged. Nevertheless, their work environment has also changed rapidly and radically. How do they experience change? To what extent are the women concerned with pride and dignity—or very different emotions?

Like the men, the women present a very positive image of the past. They describe a feeling of community and cohesion at work during apartheid. They also had various family members working at Telkom and Eskom, and they viewed their company as one big family. Today, the women feel that things are not the same. In the past, people were "easygoing," and you could "work like you wanted to." People worked together and according to rules and standards. Everyone worked so hard for most of the week that on Friday there was time "to socialize and barbecue." Women are concerned about the deterioration of social relationships at work. Specifically, the women note how the change of language affects socializing in the work environment. They feel forced to speak English, a language they have mastered but not as well as their native tongue, Afrikaans. In the past, they say, the company was "very Afrikaans," and they had many friends at work. They feel that this switch in language impedes social communication.

Lack of Care

Sociologists have demonstrated that the validation of masculinity is an integral part of class identity for working-class men.[53] They show that working-class men desire respectability. What they have not explained is why men demand dignity at work or why they stress this theme so strongly.[54] Is this demand for dignity about being *working-class* men or about being working-class *men*? In listening to White women at work talking about change, I was struck by the difference in the tone and language they use. They also have concerns about people's pride in the workplace, but they formulate their concerns differently. White working-class men's demand for dignity would thus seem to have more to do with masculinity than with class. Psychologists of masculinity have suggested that manhood, in contrast to womanhood, is a precarious state that requires continual social proof and validation.[55] In South Africa, the workplace is no longer set up around the demands, culture, and emotional needs of White working-class men. They experience a deep emotional crisis, as their White manhood is no longer validated every day at work.

While White men are preoccupied with their dignity and pride, the women express their discontent more in a language of care. According to Marie Nell, who works at Eskom:

> The atmosphere at work has changed. It changed, as if people don't care anymore. If in my division, a client for instance would ask me to do something, and I am not in the office, I would do it immediately

when I return. But they don't any longer care about customer service. What I can't do today is a problem for tomorrow. I didn't grow up that way. I am not like that.[56]

Nell says that the new workers do not care about the company and their work, while she still has a "passion" for her work. She attributes their lack of motivation to the absence of care for the company. It has also become more challenging to have pride in the company they once loved. In the words of Rita Schoeman, an employee at Telkom:

> From 1995 till today it has only become worse. Nobody is doing [his or her] part. The people who have worked for Telkom for many years will receive the same salary as the people who have just been appointed. But the people who are newly appointed don't do anything. They see how little they can do and get away with it, and they do get away with it. So, I think the whole Telkom is completely unmotivated; there is no motivation to work for Telkom. And that is bad. There are a few [who] try, but I think the biggest problem is that people lack a sense of pride. You have to force people to work because they don't have pride anymore in what they do. My whole heart tells me they have no pride in what they do. They don't help the clients. If a client calls, they look around and think, "Who can I give it to because I don't want to do it?" There are so few people who just help out a customer, and that is bad, very bad. We are working toward our own downfall in Telkom. That feels terrible for me. That is really the worst situation.[57]

The emphasis for women is thus different. The men emphasize a lack of respect, while the women focus on a lack of care. The men feel they should be shown more respect for their seniority and position, while the women feel that others should engage more. Nevertheless, the underlying concerns of the men and women are very similar. Their different wording cannot hide that both men and women feel that their company, once a source of pride and community, has become a source of embarrassment and shame. Schoeman continues:

> In 1995, I was more proud to work at Telkom than I am now. Now, I feel a little like . . . you are really embarrassed to say you work for

Telkom because the service we provide is horrible. The fact that they want to give the company a new image is pathetic.

Nevertheless, the women report less racial animosity at work. They say that, in general, women of different ethnic and racial groups respect each other and get along. They mention that the various job tasks do not demand any specific cultural traits or qualifications. Sonja Hattingh, an employee of Telkom, says:

I love all of them. I have nothing against any of them. I believe that if you are at work, you forget all the personal stuff. My colleagues at my work, we work together. We have a reasonably good relationship. I think we respect each other for who we are and not because of who you seem to be. . . . Telkom has many processes that you have to do accurately. It does not matter who or what you are but whether you work in a certain way.[58]

There are few hints in assertions such as Hattingh's that only White Afrikaners are doing the work. They distance themselves less from their Black co-workers, and there are few concerns about pride and dignity. This does not mean the women do not feel that social norms about race and racial language have changed, but perhaps it is here that the women most clearly articulate a different view about the experience of change.

Change in a Different Voice

Women describe working in a multicultural surrounding as difficult and stressful; there are always differences and misunderstandings that cause insecurity and uncertainty on how to work with the various groups.

In the past, you weren't scared to say something, or do or look at something, or feel unsure about the way you did things. Today that is totally different. But even when I am the boss, I have to think, "Am I not being offensive?" Because now we have many cultures at our office, so now . . . You can say something wrong and then you are in trouble. So you think all the time, you want to be sure. . . . This is a stressful world, a lot of stress. I wish many times I could go back to that time. But yes, the balance has shifted. . . . Well, the people have different colors and different cultures and certain people will feel—I can't tell you straight how they feel—but they will feel offended. It is fine. But that causes trouble. And they like disciplinary action because now, you were offensive to them. You have to get to know them as people, before you can speak up about it. So, if, at a certain moment, I feel angry, I first have to cool off. And then I can talk to them. So I had to learn that through the years.[59]

Gouws longs for the past, where they "just worked hard" and did not care about being offensive, whereas now she stressfully self-monitors. But note how she describes the emotional upheavals these adjustments cause her, and the consequent need for emotional management. What is most remarkable about the women's stories is their ability to articulate the transformation and its emotional challenges, how the experience of change is shot through with moments of intense despair, insecurity, and self-doubt.

Take Rania Scholtz, who has worked for nineteen years at Eskom. Shortly after 1994, she was moved to a division were there were hardly any Whites working. She now is in the unusual position of working with many Black men.

When I started working with them, I really started to become aware—this is a different world. This is a completely different world to work together with them, then to be together outside. . . . You did not know what to expect because I just worked with a group of White people. . . . It was difficult. It was a tremendous adjustment for me. I did not know how to approach them. I did not know how to talk to them. If they would talk their language, I would think they talk[ed] bad of me. I was terribly uncertain in the beginning until I found something out: There was a Black woman who cleaned the kitchen, and she told me that people could see I was a good woman, a good human being. And stuff like that. And then I thought I first have to prove myself in their world so I could win their respect. Or at least give them the opportunity to talk to me. This is where things started. I had to prove myself for them, and say to them, "Don't worry, I am OK. I do not want to hurt you." I was frightened in the beginning, but in time, it turned out alright. And this made it much easier for me in the future. You are scared as a woman because you do not know what they are going to do. So this opened doors in my life, to work together with them. And this has become easier all the time. People become almost like family at work. Everybody understands everybody. You learn to know each other. You learn their moods, you learn about their needs. And you start to learn their personalities.[60]

Scholtz narrates the path from her initiation in the "new world" from being uncertain, fearful, and suspicious if Blacks talked in another language to being understanding, trusting, and learning their "moods" and "needs." The old family metaphor is applied to the new situation: Working with Black people now means you get to know them like family. This is indeed a narrative of change.

Work has changed for White working-class men, who for the most part now work in racially integrated and multicultural spaces. The ANC government's affirmative action policies have also undercut their White privileges. In the past, Afrikaner nationalism provided these men with exclusive citizenship and labor rights, as well as a feeling of national belonging to the White family, all of which they have lost. The ANC government's neoliberal strategy aimed at the privatization of public companies further worsens their working conditions. Thus they support a grassroots type of neoliberalism—an ideology that centers on individual strength, pride in work, and antigovernment sentiments. As these men must manage this challenge to their White embodiment emotionally, they struggle with this and feel resentful toward their Black co-workers. For them, Whiteness has become a risk-laden liability; they feel they no longer can live up to the White racial ideals of embodied power, privilege, and paternalism. At work, their feelings of Whiteness are often overbearing, and the men hurt themselves by holding on to them. This leads to the question, How do White South Africans experience Whiteness away from work—namely, at home?—which is the topic of the next chapter.

CHAPTER 6

Whiteness at Home

The Story of Sonja Hattingh and Karin Jacobus

Home is a haven for Sonja Hattingh. It is a place where she can relax, where her loved ones gather, and where she can invite her friends. Home is peaceful and free of emotional stress. Married for over ten years, she is happy in her home in the city where she has lived all her life, Pretoria, the capital of South Africa. However, she has seen the city changing since apartheid: crime has increased, and she no longer feels safe in many public spaces. Her home remains her favorite place, where she feels she can be herself.

We met Sonja Hattingh, an employee of Telkom, in the previous chapter. She believes in racial integration at work and the need to accept Black co-workers. She likes her colleagues and the fact that at work it is all about how you do the work. But she has different rules for her life at home:

> At home I have no contact with other cultures. They do not visit my house. I only have to work with them. It is all right to come into contact with other cultures outside of the house. This does not matter to me. At work, your culture cannot have an influence on you. I believe in equal rights, so what they do does not bother me. I don't like it when others unjustly treat someone else. I will stand up and argue with that person. But this does not affect my personal life.[1]

At work, Hattingh accepts and adapts to integration; she even speaks out if someone is treated unjustly. But she draws a sharp line between her professional life and her personal life, where different rules apply.

The South African city has changed since apartheid. How this affects feelings of home and the process of unlearning racism for lower-, middle-, and upper-class White women is the subject of this chapter.

During apartheid, Afrikaner nationalists tried with brute force and violence to make the city a White space. The city was regarded as a home for White people. Afrikaner nationalists bulldozed mixed neighborhoods and destroyed millions of homes. They removed most nonwhite people to special reserves outside the city. South African cities during apartheid became separate and unequal, White and Black, rich and poor. After 1994, the ANC government adopted an ambitious program to make the city a democratic space and undo racial segregation. Spatial apartheid would be done away with thanks to creative and determined urban planning. But they had mixed results.[2] Ambitious plans to provide housing, water, and electricity to the urban poor could not keep up with the influx of new residents into the cities. City centers have become more integrated, but there has also been White flight from the cities. The South African city has changed but remains divided.

One reason for this is that White developers promoted new forms of segregation, such as gated communities, which they justified by the rise in crime after apartheid. Crime is very high in South Africa, especially in cities. Scholars agree that fear of crime is a deeply racialized process, but it remains unclear how important crime is in shaping White people's feelings of home and how this varies between White people living in or outside gated communities.

When we think of home, we tend to think about a physical rather than a sociopsychological place, but feeling at home is as much about safety as it is about the feeling that you can be yourself. As I tried to understand how White people's feelings of home had changed after apartheid, how this was related to race, and how this might be different for different parts of the post-apartheid city, I realized that people judge their home life in reference to their experiences with racial integration at work, in the church, and the broader city. Sonja Hattingh's story makes clear that unlearning racism at home is connected to the challenge of unlearning racism at work, where she defines the home as a retreat from the emotional labor spend at work on unlearning racism. It is, however, also connected to urban developments after apartheid, where the post-apartheid city is increasingly perceived as a Black city. For both the richer and poorer White South Africans, home remains the place where they have the most control.

Women like Sonja Hattingh, who belongs to the lower middle class, travel the newly integrated city on a daily basis. They describe the city in starkly racialized terms: to them, it has become a Black city. But their home experience is barely influenced by the city or by work. Instead, home offers a counterpoint to outside experiences and the emotional work they invest in unlearning racism:

> The moment you leave work you forget everything and everybody. The different cultures do not affect my house. I do not talk to them; I do not hang out with them; I do not have anything to do with them. I do not have a maid at home. I will not allow this to affect my life. I am happy with my life as it is. At home I am totally myself, like I want to be. Emotionally, there isn't that repression.[3]

The contrast Sonja Hattingh draws between home and work highlights how unlearning racism is a process that always depends on context. It underlines how emotionally challenging this process is for lower-middle-class women. At work, these women accept racial integration and equality and work to adapt. At home, they are looking for relief from this process. Home means harmony, while work means worry. Their racially integrated work environments are stressful, a place where they do a lot of emotional labor. At home, White South Africans seek safety from crime but also peace of mind.

Upper-class White women similarly view their home as a haven but in a different way. Karin Jacobus is a resident of Golden Sun, one of the oldest and most prestigious gated communities in Pretoria, with around one thousand households and six thousand inhabitants in 2018. She does not draw a contrast between work and home; her gated community provides a different way of preserving her Whiteness at home:

> Golden Sun is, for me, the closest thing a person can get to an ideal place to live. This is beautiful and peaceful. This is safe. This gives one a feeling of contentment. For me, here, it feels as if all kinds of different people are together. Not just Black but also Indians from Asia. Here, all the people who represent South Africa are together. And because there is respect for each other, this works well.[4]

When I first arrived at Golden Sun and began talking with the people living in the estate, I was struck by the positive tone of their assessments of the community. After reading the literature on gated communities, I had expected the inhabitants of this new urban landscape to be fearful of crime and the racial other. However, many people expressed positive sentiments about race relations in the estate and the possibility for gated communities to re-instill hope for a diverse South African society. Implausibly, they imagined their gated community to embody both the apartheid past and the multicultural future of South Africa. What was going on?

By comparing the process of unlearning racism among White upper-class women in the gated community of Golden Sun to that of lower-middle-class White women living in a traditional neighborhood in North Pretoria, the ways in which race and class intersect in the experience of Whiteness are made clear. Gender plays a role as well. In contrast to previous chapters, the focus here is on women who have had to remake Whiteness at home after the end of Afrikaner nationalism, an ideology that had a strict gender order, a traditional conception of domesticity, and a highly circumscribed set of women's roles.[5] Perhaps because of the demise of White nationalism, I found that women had particularly rich narratives about the home as a racialized space. The two groups of women, as evinced by the stories of Sonja Hattingh and Karin Jacobus, speak very differently about race in the city and in their community. To a much greater extent than during apartheid, when White nationalism united different White groups, there now exists a spectrum of White identities.

Beyond Fear of Crime: Feeling at Home and Aesthetic Politics

Gated communities are a global phenomenon, but post-apartheid South Africa is distinctive in that these communities developed at the same time as efforts to dismantle the apartheid racial order.[6] This country offers a unique opportunity to analyze how new urban forms modify how race is experienced and understood; how the feelings of home of White South Africans are racialized in different ways depending on class and community; and how this matters for the process and challenge of unlearning racism for different groups of White South Africans.

Despite the popular picture of terrified White people holed up in their homes in fear of crime as depicted in the South African media, home remains a haven for women of both classes, although in different ways. The White upper-class South African women I met in the gated community, though wary of crime, appreciated their community for more than the safety it provided. They praised the beauty and spotless appearance of the estate, as well as the sense of order and tranquility. It symbolized to them the moral decency of the community. The estate represented the closest thing to their dream of an ideal South African community and gave them hope that a multicultural South Africa was possible. The White upper-class South African women had unlearned the overt racism of apartheid days, although this did not mean they were White without Whiteness.

The White elite's positive view of their gated community contrasted starkly with the view of the White lower-middle-class women I spoke to, who did not live in a gated community. They loved their home life too but emphasized that Pretoria had become a Black city that they feared, speaking in explicitly racial terms about how the city had changed. In the previous chapter, we saw how these women had unlearned racism at work, but as Sonja Hattingh makes clear, unlearning racism at home was a different matter. My question was how to think about Whiteness at home so I could analyze the outlook of both these groups of women and explain their positive and their negative stories.

What I realized was that the dominant analytical lens of urban scholars in the United States and South Africa has its limitations—they view White people's response to difference only in terms of the fear of crime. Fear of crime is certainly an important mechanism in the creation of the contemporary South African urban landscape, and crime discourses are strongly racialized. In South Africa, crime levels are substantially higher than in the United States, particularly when it comes to murder rates, the most reliable crime indicator.[7] However, the upper-class women's positive outlook on race relationships—exemplified by Karin Jacobus—suggests that gated communities restructure the relationship between race and place in more complex ways than the lens of fear of crime allows for; it is a mistake to equate fear of crime with a general fear of difference.

One reason the complex relationship between race and place has been poorly understood is because researchers have limited their research to the question whether crime drives White residents to gated communities.[8] In fact, crime drives anyone who can afford it to these communities, not just White people. We can only explore the full implications of gated communities if we ask *how* Whites' racial outlook is transformed inside and outside the gates, and not just *why* White people live in gated communities. We need to know what happens to Whiteness at home once White people are living inside the gated community.

Whiteness in this context can be understood as a new aesthetic politics—manifested in the way taste and the appreciation of beauty are related to the distribution of power and resources—that has transformed racism for White upper- and lower-middle-class White South Africans. To fully understand the relationship between race and place, we must realize that racism is not only driven by fear and hate for Black people. Historically, racism has always been expressed by negative, anti-Black narratives and positive, pro-White narratives about Whiteness. In South Africa, fear and racialized discourses about crime strongly shape White South Africans' anti-Black attitudes. Yet hopeful and positive racialized aesthetic discourses about place shape White South Africans' experience of Whiteness at home. The members of the White elite in gated communities are able to avoid talking explicitly about race and anti-Blackness while simultaneously deepening their investment in Whiteness. Meanwhile, White lower-middle-class people talk explicitly about anti-Blackness and the city but define home as a place where they can give their precarious Whiteness a break.

This post-apartheid aesthetic politics is thus deeply shaped by class and race privilege. In the gated community, White upper-class South Africans still find themselves in the White majority, and they continue to have significant control over their environment, aesthetically and politically. Contact with racial others is limited and strictly controlled. Their emotional experience of community is defined by the pleasure in and feeling of control over its appearance. Whiteness at home allows them to feel positive about themselves based on a sense of community and historical continuity; they draw a continuous line between their experience of living in a gated community and that of growing up during apartheid. By contrast, White lower-middle-class South Africans feel that they have lost ownership over the city, although not necessarily over their neighborhood. In their aesthetic narrative about the city, they echo the apartheid imagery of dangerous Black masses infiltrating the city. Meanwhile, their homes remain places of relief; already a White minority at work, they consistently contrast home with work as the place of last emotional resort. For them, it is a space where they can feel free from the emotional labor of unlearning racism at work.

Racism and the New Urban Landscape

Racial and spatial inequalities in cities have proven durable after apartheid. For urban scholars of South Africa, the central theme is explaining this pattern of change and continuity. Some scholars argue that urban apartheid has changed from being race-based to class-based.[9] Others emphasize the spatial implications of fear of crime, leading to a new form of apartheid. The first group of scholars suggest that race has become less relevant, while the second suggest that it remains a problem, mainly owing to fear of crime. Given that place-making in South Africa has always been a deeply racialized process and that racial and spatial inequality has persisted, the claim that race no longer plays a role seems doubtful. Furthermore, we should move beyond the dominant fear-of-crime framework. A third approach, emphasizing the role of Whiteness in explaining the transformation of South Africa's urban landscape and the continuing high level of racial inequality, provides a new way to look at what American studies scholar George Lipsitz has called "the racialization of space and the spatialization of race" after apartheid.[10]

At the heart of the puzzle of change and continuity is the rise of gated communities, new institutions that reorganize urban space and the relationship between race and place. My analysis both expands on and challenges an approach that implies a too direct relationship between fear of crime and fear of difference in gated communities. American studies have found White residents using coded race talk to preserve homogeneity in their gated communities.[11] In an increasingly ethnically diverse United States, Whites want to recapture the close-knit, picket-fenced, homogenous communities of their childhood; emotions—not just fear of crime or difference but also feelings of home and nostalgia—drive Whites to gated communities. South African scholars too easily conclude that White people move to gated communities for racist reasons, that the trend of gating in South Africa "perpetuates the divisions that were inherent in the apartheid state" and that fear of crime is used "as a justification for a predominantly racist fear of difference."[12] In fact, all South Africans want to protect their residential locations against crime.

We cannot analyze White folks in gated communities simply by looking inside the gate. The effects of gating must be understood within the broader context of the post-apartheid city and the experiences of White people who continue to live outside of these communities. Most South Africans—including White South Africans—live outside the gates. We need to understand how the post-apartheid urban landscape is racialized everywhere. Spatially, the difference between apartheid and post-apartheid South Africa is that apartheid provided a comprehensive spatial plan to organize racial relations, rights, and privileges. Racial segregation manifested itself at the national, city, and community levels. After apartheid, White nationalism lost its power to make the nation's landscape after its own image, but White South Africans did not lose the economic power to impose spatial policies at the local level. At this level, gated communities remake the relationship between race, class, and space through new forms of racialized spatial governance, while outside the gates the national government continues to press ahead with racial and spatial integration that, while not fully realized, has changed the urban landscape considerably since apartheid.[13]

The problem is that Whiteness at home is never just about feeling safe, as urban scholars assume, but also about feeling free.[14] Home, as both haven and heaven, taps into the desire for security as well as for a place for self-expression. This is manifested along race, class, and gender lines. White lower-middle-class South Africans no longer feel safe and secure in the city. But more important, as shown in the previous chapter, they also no longer feel free at work. As Sonja Hattingh confirmed, they perform a lot of emotional labor. Their home might not be completely safe, but they imagine it as the last place they can feel free as White South Africans.

The White elite has the power and resources to define the aesthetic experience of their community, unlike lower-middle-class White people, who have lost such power and resources. The White elite use their power and resources to beautify the landscape of their communities, which signifies privilege while offering legitimation for why they choose to live there.[15] The elite prefer aestheticization as a way of managing race and class because it allows them to simultaneously enhance, naturalize, and conceal their privilege. Beautiful landscapes are the most effective mask for economic and racial advantages because they hide the cost of producing them. The burdens of making and maintaining these landscapes, which are imposed on nonwhites, remain unseen by visitors and residents alike. Instead, the elite deploy the politics of aesthetics to promote a progressive and multicultural narrative about race relationships in South Africa.

The rise of White identity politics in South Africa as a new form of racism is certainly fueled by fear of crime, but other, more positive emotions play a role as well. Rising crime rates allow White people to position themselves as victims under a new form of apartheid. White identity politics depends on the claim to victimhood to be politically effective. As discussed in Chapter 4, White populists emphasize the racialized nature of crime—specifically farm attacks—to falsely claim that after apartheid Black criminals are specifically targeting White people. But while White lower-middle-class people talk much more explicitly about race and the city than the White elite, this does not necessarily mean the White elite are less racist. The White elite in gated communities simply do not need to rely on this kind of explicit race talk and hate to defend and mask their White privilege. Instead, they celebrate their Whiteness in more subtle forms: they love and cherish the rural idyll of their community and celebrate the past. Their feelings of home are bound up with Whiteness and the apartheid history. These historical parallels are made possible by the aesthetic beauty of Golden Sun, but their positive feelings toward the community also make them hopeful about a multicultural future for their country.

The White identity politics of the elite in gated communities is thus marked by White people's imagining themselves as taking part in a multicultural South Africa, with their feelings of Whiteness unchanged but normalized. Emotions play an outsized role in shaping White people's "sense of realness," the buttressing of racial ideologies, and the reinforcing of institutional racism. In the United States, the emotional investment of White people in their White identity and racial beliefs explains why they do not change their minds and actions when they are presented with evidence of the systemic injustices of color-blind racism.[16] In South Africa, however, the White elite do not practice color-blind racism; they do not avoid race language or substitute color-blind terms and racially coded language for it. Instead, they practice an aesthetic White identity politics that allows their Whiteness to continue to feel at home in the changing city. As new urban forms, gated communities modify how people experience Whiteness but ultimately sustain and fortify it.

It is interesting to compare racism as manifested in South Africa's post-apartheid urban landscape with urban developments in the United States after the civil rights movement. In America, White flight to suburbia created a conservative political movement and a mass culture that shaped a new suburban White identity.[17] This new mass culture represented American cities, on the one hand, as sites of decay and danger, occupied by dark-skinned criminals, and suburbs, on the other hand, as sites of order and safety inhabited by homogenous groups of White people. American studies scholar George Lipsitz speaks of the "White spatial imaginary," characterized by racial exclusion, privatization, and the deception and self-deception necessary to deny both privileges and problems.[18] In South Africa, the White minority no longer has the political power or the cultural dominance to impose a single White imaginary. Instead, there is a White spatial imaginary that is fragmented along class lines. The lower classes living in normal neighborhoods imagine their home as a refuge wherein to escape the Black city and the pressure to unlearn racism at work. Only the White elite have the power and resources to spatially impose a new White imaginary, which reflects not racial exclusion but a White identity politics that tries to normalize Whiteness as part of a multicultural South Africa.

Ultimately, we need to think more strategically about how the process of unlearning racism manifests itself in different spheres and how these spheres are connected. American sociologist Edward Telles has argued that in Brazil, racism is a bigger problem in the spheres of work, education, and politics than it is among friends, family, and neighbors.[19] South African sociologist Jeremy Seekings claims that the opposite pattern holds for South Africa. Racism, he argues, has more or less been eliminated in some spheres, such as work and education, but remains resilient among White South Africans in the spheres of family, friends, and the neighborhood. My findings confirm Seekings's view but also explain these differences. Racism and Whiteness at home are resilient not only because of the new aesthetic politics of gated communities but also because unlearning racism at work is seen as emotionally demanding.

Race and the City: A Short History

South Africa's landscape has always both mirrored and masked the unequal distribution of power between White and Black people. In 1652, the Dutch settlers of the Dutch East India Company occupied land previously used by nomadic Khoikhoi (called Hottentots by the Dutch) and Bushmen. South Africa's Native Land Act of 1913 evicted and displaced thousands of African families in the South African interior and created the first "reserves" to segregate Black South Africans from Whites. At the start of apartheid in 1948, Afrikaner nationalists set aside merely 13 percent of South Africa's land to create Bantustans for millions of Black South Africans. This was a strategy specifically designed to take away their political rights by declaring these areas their "original homes" and allowing White South Africans to remain in control as the new demographic majority in South Africa. Ideologically, Afrikaner nationalists' love of the land masked their loathing of Black people. Apartheid was the ultimate spatialization of racism—the idea that White and Black people should live completely separated geographically—but it is clear that this history started much earlier.

South African cities were historically imagined as White spaces, but the government did not actively segregate them during the nineteenth century. Towns such as Cape Town and Johannesburg were relatively small, mostly White places but also included racially and ethnically mixed neighborhoods. City governments developed racist spatial plans but lacked the tools to exclude Blacks and coordinate segregation or even to build private developments. In the 1880s, mining companies created segregated, single-sex compounds for the Black African male workforce that would later function as models for urban segregation. Urban planning only emerged at the end of the nineteenth century, to regulate companies that sought speculative opportunities as the economy developed and urban growth began.[20] The colonial government also designed new forms of governance to impose its racist views on the urban order, using urban planning (or as it was originally called, "town-planning") as a tool to deny Black Africans a decent urban life. From the late nineteenth century on, planning policy set out to dictate and restrict the pattern of Black settlement, particularly in urban areas. But urban apartheid was based on a central contradiction: the White government wanted to secure labor power without Black laborers.[21] As a consequence, urban segregation evolved over a long period of time in a rather haphazard and piecemeal way.[22] In 1913, South African provinces were officially awarded the power to establish and administer townships—the term for urban ghetto areas for nonwhites, namely, Indians, Africans, and Coloureds, only.

White politicians saw Black urbanization as a major threat to White South Africa, but the large influx of Black residents into the cities was a phenomenon of their own making, closely connected to capitalist development. Throughout the twentieth century, the White supremacist South African government tried to balance the demands of White agriculture, mining capital, and the manufacturing sector while at the same time ensuring racial privilege for the White population and urban segregation, but these goals often conflicted. White farmers were promised a ready supply of labor; the mines were assured that the system of migrant labor—Black men were contracted to work in mines while leaving their families and rights behind in the "homelands"—on which they had come to depend would remain intact; and White workers were given to believe that segregation would protect them from competition in the job and housing markets.[23] Rural and agricultural policies of the new South African state, founded in 1910, such as the Natives Land Act of 1913, resulted in large-scale migration of the Black population to urban centers. In the countryside, Black peasant families on White-owned land found the terms of tenancy insupportable; intergenerational conflicts among Black people increased; the migration of labor to the mines escalated; and agricultural lands set aside for African farming—the so-called reserves—became over-used and deteriorated rapidly. Increasing poverty in the reserves forced the Black population to urbanize, leading to a severe housing crisis in the cities during the first half of the twentieth century.[24] The majority of the Black population in the cities lived under circumstances that can only be described as wretched.

White South Africans were concerned about Black urban poverty and "slum life" in the early twentieth-century South African city, but pre-dominantly through the racist lens of the threat of infectious diseases.[25] Specifically in response to the influenza outbreak after the First World War, the government started to look into controlling the movement and settlement of Africans. The first legislation was passed to facilitate town planning as well as "slum clearance." In the early 1920s, provincial gov-ernments started to consider Africans as only "temporary residents" of urban areas. In 1923, the Natives (Urban Areas) Act separated the plan-ning of "locations" for nonwhites from the planning of the rest of urban South Africa. In the 1930s, the national government granted provincial and local governments full power over urban planning and made town planning compulsory. Planning became a powerful instrument for achiev-ing more complete racial segregation. Urban segregation was never just an economic strategy to produce cheap labor but the result of broad White fears about urbanization and Black poverty, and concerns about how to control the forces unleashed by industrialization and maintain White hegemony.[26]

What distinguished South African cities like Johannesburg and Preto-ria in the 1920s and 1930s from other colonial towns in Africa was that a large number of its citizens of European descent were poor. In the urban centers, the divide between rich and poor, on the one hand, and White and Black, on the other, did not map neatly onto each other. Among the political elite, racial segregation as an ideal emerged hand in hand with racialized attitudes toward the poor, with "deserving" White poverty and "threatening" Black poverty.[27]

To achieve racial segregation, the government practiced residential restructuring by building public housing for Whites and trying to re-move Black people to remote locations.[28] These processes were often directly related. In 1934, the Slums Act granted local authorities extensive powers to clear existing areas and replan them. Before the Second World War, plans were developed to reconstruct central Cape Town and Johannesburg.[29] By the late 1930s, the social forces that would shape apartheid had taken hold: rural dispossession, rapid urbanization, racial segregation, and poor housing conditions.[30] It was only a small step after the Second World War to push for racial zoning and complete segregation.

What shifted in the late 1930s and 1940s is that conservative Afrikaner nationalists contrasted these White fears about the modern industrial city with romanticized views of the countryside as a source of social order, tradition, and deference. They mixed White fears about racial degeneration with modern anthropological ideas about cultural relativism to promote apartheid as the preservation of the distinct identities of different cultures. Afrikaner nationalists pursued their apartheid vision of racial segregation with rigor and brute force. Spatially, apartheid's policy aimed to remove Black people completely out of sight to create the illusion of South Africa as a White-majority nation living peacefully alongside artificially created "Black nations." Apartheid not only further segregated public spaces and amenities; it removed 3.5 million people off their land and out of the cities. White supremacy was recast as calling for the "separate development" of separate nations inside South Africa. For White South Africans to feel at home in their own country, they had to remove all "nonwhite" people and provide them with separate "homelands," the new name for Bantustans in the 1970s. Apartheid curtailed the movement of nonwhites through a system of pass laws, which in the 1950s provoked the first massive resistance movement. Examples of the ruthless application of apartheid policy in cities are the complete destruction of District Six, a Coloured neighborhood in Cape Town, and Sophia Town, a mixed neighborhood in Johannesburg.[31] On top of the rubble of the latter neighborhood, Afrikaner nationalists built Triompf, a White lower-middle-class neighborhood, symbolizing that White home life during apartheid was literally built on the destruction of Black lives. Thus the South African apartheid city by 1990 reflected and disguised the violent history of White racism.

During apartheid, Pretoria was forcibly made into a White city. Named after the *Voortrekker* leader Andries Pretorius, the city long served as the seat of South Africa's administrative branch of government. By 1936, there were roughly equal numbers of White and Black South Africans living in and around the city. Before apartheid, the city was racially segregated, but Black people lived adjacent to White people and near the city center. The Group Areas Act of 1950 designated separate residential areas for Whites, Indians, Coloureds, and Africans.[32] People were moved to townships and suburbs far from the city center, which made it difficult for them to get to their place of work. In Pretoria's city center, the Separate Amenities Act of 1953 designated almost all of the restaurants and recreational facilities "Whites only," and park facilities were divided so that the better city parks likewise became "Whites only." In 1954, a large statue of Paul Kruger, the president of the South African Republic from 1883 to 1900, was installed in the centrally located Church Square. Thus Pretoria was "successfully" made into a White city, demographically and symbolically. In 2001, White people were still a 67 percent majority in the city.

From White City to Black City

Despite Pretoria's remaining a White-majority city, in the minds of the lower-middle-class women living there now the city after apartheid has become a Black city—a dangerous and disordered one. After apartheid, the city integrated its facilities and amenities. Pretoria became the central part of the Tshwane Metropolitan Municipality in 2001, which brought the city and former townships together in one administrative unit of more than a million people. For the White working-class women I interviewed, the city feels unsafe. Being in the city—driving or walking—is perceived as dangerous, and fear of crime influences their living patterns. They stay at home during the evening and avoid certain areas of the city. When outside their homes, they are continuously on the lookout. Bernadet Blignaut moved three years ago to Pretoria, from a small village in the Free State.

This is not safe. Not safe at all. I am not used to this lack of safety. You will never be used to it. Never. I never carry my jewelry. If you stop at a traffic light, they will steal your wallet, your phone. No, it is unsafe. I look around all the time. I know so many people who had things happen to them. I stay at home in the evening. It isn't safe.[33]

Blignaut describes the constant fear that grips these women when they are outside of their homes. For them, being stress-free in a public space is impossible.

Talk about public safety is strongly racialized. Lower-middle-class women still rely in part on public transportation and frequent the downtown business district, which is where they work and where the African majority is becoming dominant. Its spaces are depicted as dangerous places, much more dangerous than either home or work. The women feel as if they may be assaulted at any time, even if they travel by car. Rosita De Klerk, who lives in Pretoria, says:

> I am OK at work and I am OK at home. I am not totally comfortable in the city anymore. It's getting too crowded. And this has become very Black. This is really, really Black. And robberies and stuff like that have happened. For instance, they cut off the complete hand of a woman, just to get her ring. Then they ran away with her hand. So yes, many of the things that are happening are scary. But you can't do anything about it because it is the same everywhere. . . . I do feel safe in some places. If I am honest, I go to bible school and there I feel safe. At the bible school, the majority is Black; there are only a handful of White people. But at the bible school it is special.[34]

De Klerk's negative perception of public space is explained by race and crime, which come together in her horror story. Such stories emphasize the brutality and cruelty of crime, but they should not necessarily be taken as an accurate representation of South African crime, as there are simply too few statistics on the brutality of criminal violence to say anything useful about it. Apart from the questionable truthfulness of crime stories, however, such narratives express a sense of constant threat. Note the escalating tone ("This is really, really Black") when she acknowledges the increased participation of the Black majority in public life. As another White woman said: "You feel safe nowhere." But De Klerk's testimony also shows that race is not the only fear factor: she attends a bible school that is predominantly Black, and there she's not afraid at all.

What resonates in these women's descriptions of home versus the city (or private space versus public space) is the theme of order versus chaos. The whole city seems to have slid into anarchy. They complain about the deterioration of services and decry the impossibility of getting things such as water and electricity "fixed and done." They complain about street litter, roads in disrepair, and no adherence to traffic rules. The symbol for them of road anarchy is the taxi driver, who is described as ruthless, dangerous, and out of control. Complaints about services are often wrapped in the language of "standards": most are said to be below "the standards" of the past.

All of this may very well be true, but it becomes racialized when the women attribute meaning to this course of events. Their stories of chaos and decay in the city are strongly racialized. What starts with a lament about the state of urban services usually ends with accusations against Black people. One woman asserts that "they" shit everywhere and that "they" never use the bathroom. Another woman complains "they" simply feed their children on the street, showing their breasts in public. Yet another says that "they" never throw trash in the trash cans:

> *Ach* . . . you know, our municipal services. . . . The streets are full of papers. They do not go to the bathroom. When I walk to my parking garage, they will stand against a tree. And they just do what they want to do. Here, right at the corner. It stinks. I park around the corner of my work, where I pay for a spot. But the surroundings have gotten so bad. There are feces all over. You can't walk through without feeling you have to throw up. And this has become unsafe and I was attacked. As a woman alone, I cannot go to my car anymore. I have to kick the trash from the path. And this is dirty: our streets, our parks. The bushes have grown man-high. Our trash cans, which we pay for through municipal taxes, they didn't come to collect them for a whole month. Every weekend we dropped our own trash can. This stuff did not happen twenty or thirty years ago.[35]

Nell stresses dirtiness over danger when it comes to public spaces. Her lament about municipal services is immediately racialized, with "they" referring to Black people. Women like Nell imply that Black people do not care about things such as public morals and public spaces. For lower-class women, the public decay is explained by race. A similar line of reasoning connects loss and race in the account given by Antjie Du Plessis:

> Look, there are things that give me real heartache. These are things that pierce my heart. Look at the train stations for instance. The train stations used to be the pride of the railroad network. Trains used to run on time; the old Trans-Karoo line that used to ride, you know, people used to go on holiday with that line. This was *lekker*. The Blacks used to have their part of the train, Whites used to have their own parts too. The train stations were beautiful. We used to say to each other that the police at the stations were a bunch of "station flower pots." But they served a purpose. They made sure nobody was able to damage the station. But if you look at any station today, you know. A few days ago I took my brother-in-law to the train station in Krugersdorp. The train did not arrive because there was no power on the net to ride the train from Johannesburg to Krugersdorp. They sent a bus to pick people up. The station is a ruin. They used to have a fountain where they had fish. This is still there, but—this really hurts your soul—you think: "When I was still a child, I had a little piece of string and a hook and I would catch the fish with a piece of bread." But all that is left is a wall, and this wall was toppled over. It lies on the ground. It is overgrown with bushes that they planted there. About the building I can't say anything, because it looks like a pig's house. They never paint it anymore. And look at the trains people have to ride to go from one station to another to go to work. Look how people are thrown off the train. In those days, it was a real train. You came in, you sat down, and you could read the newspaper. That is how it was. And this is where I say: it looks like it does not have any value for Blacks.[36]

Du Plessis recalls a time when the public transportation companies instilled a sense of pride in their passengers. Of course, as she acknowledges, this was a time when trains were mainly for White people. In post-apartheid South Africa, the ANC government has struggled to fund the semi-privatized railway system and maintain decent service, at least in part because of the expanded customer base. However, Du Plessis interprets the demise of train stations through the prisms of race and law and order. She claims that Black people do not care about public transportation. The loss associated with a dysfunctional public transportation system thus becomes an additional source of racism.

Ultimately, the image of the public sphere as a place of chaos, crime, and dirt becomes an infectious threat for the women—a threat or disease that will affect White people too. Marie Nell added:

> The sad thing is, the White people are changing also. Crime is also affecting them. Yeah, they also do crime now. . . . They also start not to care anymore. And all those immigrants that come in, the illegal immigrants. They have no respect for my privacy or property. They just live on my doorstep. And the White people are starting to do that too. You know, that bugs you. I help no one anymore. The Whites are in decline. The respect they used to have for themselves. . . . But I say, there are many, many Black people who . . . there are many Indians who are good people. Our country . . . I don't say the Black people are bad. I don't say that. I say particularly the people who come from across the border, those that come to steal our jobs. . . . If things don't change, there will not be a future here.[37]

Echoing themes that once were the justification for apartheid—the idea that bad habits were contagious—Nell underlines the fear she has about the encroaching chaos she experiences and the fear that she can no longer stop what is happening. In a surprising post-apartheid twist, and adhering to the new social norm, however, she argues that Black people are not to blame. Instead, she accuses illegal immigrants of these things, a group that is politically a safer scapegoat in post-apartheid South Africa than Black people.

As the city has become a place of decay and disgust in the eyes of the women, the apartheid past is depicted as positive by contrast: life then was still safe; the roads were still taken care of; everything looked better. The present perception of decay and feeling of loss so dominates that the women cannot help but emphasize the positive images of the past.

Apartheid to them is not a collective crime but a historic period when there was beauty, order, and safety:

> What was good then was that South Africa looked better. It was better taken care of. And these days, the streets are dirty, the parks have become ugly. This is no longer safe. If you are in Europe, you can pass people's homes in the street and you will see their house, and you can see the furniture inside the house. In South Africa you won't see the house. This is behind a high wall and bars in front of the window. That isn't happiness. That isn't safety.[38]

Blignaut's argument about apartheid has an aesthetic focus but also a particular language. She argues that South Africa "was better taken care of" in the past. It is the same language of care the women use to complain about the attitudes of Black people today: they do not "care" anymore about public space and safety. Public space during apartheid was perceived as safe because it looked orderly; public space after apartheid is perceived as dangerous because it looks ugly and chaotic.

The women's memories of apartheid are a mirror image of their current encounters with the city. They recall a past in which streets were safe, beautiful, and orderly. Their loss of feelings of safety and beauty is real, and they long for that bygone time. To call this nostalgia would miss the point—the women draw a contrast between specific issues in the past and the present. They know that apartheid was wrong and benefited them, but in regard to those issues about which they care deeply, such as order, safety, and well-maintained public facilities, apartheid compares favorably in their eyes. The apartheid past, as a system, is not viewed through a hazy nostalgic prism but through the specific, class-colored lenses of lower-middle-class White South Africans.

White Working-Class Neighborhoods: Home as Haven

In contrast to their depictions of the city, these White women describe their homes as havens. They do not have the luxury of hiding behind gates and fences; they live in formerly Whites-only neighborhoods near the city center of Pretoria. But these lower-middle-class neighborhoods have not become racial battlegrounds after the demise of apartheid. Rather, interracial interactions in neighborhoods are limited in comparison to other social spaces. The women say their neighborhoods are relatively stable and peaceful places. The demography, they say, has hardly changed. Most Black people have moved to new developments and not into their neighborhoods, which are the older areas of Pretoria.

> This is a normal suburb. I enjoy living here. This is very centrally located. But I still think it is not safe. They broke into our house twice, one time when I was at home. I don't think this is a safe neighborhood. But this isn't the most dangerous neighborhood of Pretoria either. We have lived here for nine years. I feel at home. This is mainly a White area; there are very few Black people.[39]

De Wet feels at home in her neighborhood, just like most of the women I interviewed. Despite their view that crime has increased, they say that their neighborhood is still fine. Some Black people have moved in, they acknowledge, but they hardly ever see them or have any problem with them.

Crime is indeed a regular occurrence. Most women experienced their homes being burglarized at least once in the last few years, and family members have also been victimized. The women are always aware of the threat to their security. One woman says that she often finds cigarette butts in her garden in the morning—evidence, she says, of criminals who have tried to commit burglary and fell asleep on her lawn. Another woman says that she is regularly woken up by people shining a flashlight into her house. Extensive alarm systems are often unaffordable for the lower middle class, who instead improvise with dogs, barbed wire, and broken glass on walls and keep baseball bats, pepper spray, and sometimes guns ready. Nevertheless, the house is believed to be comparatively safer than other spaces.

At home, the women claim the space for their own culture in order to be stress-free, free from the pressure to change. It is a place of relief and continuity:

> At work there are all these tensions from people. And you always have to keep the peace. At home I can be myself. If I want to be mad, then I am mad. If I want to laugh and be happy, then I am. I can't be like that

at work. At work I am like an actor, like a performer: you constantly have to think about what you say and what you do, and what the right thing is to do. . . . You can't just act if you are angry. At home, you can be angry. Then I am and it is over. At work that is not possible. You have to think: What will happen if I will react like that?[40]

For Giliomee, home is the only place where she can "be herself," a condition she equates with the ability to express and act out her emotions.

What it means for these women to be themselves at home is intimately connected with how they perceive the new racial hierarchy at work. At work, the women labor hard to unlearn racism. Since the workplace has been racially integrated, they have lost their dominance in that space. They accept—and have had to accept—cultural diversity and the need for adjustment. Things have changed since 1994. They emphasize that at work everybody is equal and there are no racial differences; they accept racial equality and racial integration. Nevertheless, they struggle to adjust to the new racial landscape. They feel pressure to be sensitive and act appropriately toward their new Black colleagues and superiors, and this causes emotional stress.

Social life at work has become acting, the women say. The metaphor of acting captures what it means for lower-middle-class White women to play the new social role of a nondominant minority. The social norms at work have changed: racism is no longer tolerated, nor is White dominance. Women like Giliomee have become hyperconscious of what they say and do in the workplace but also of how they feel. They have to learn anew how to behave and speak without the support of privilege and racism. At work, emotion management is an important part of Giliomee's "act" because how she feels often no longer corresponds with how she perceives she has to act. She feels that she cannot show her anger at work because it would have negative repercussions. The women's main emotion-management strategy is not to adjust their feelings at work or to explore the origins of those feelings in racial beliefs but rather to draw a hard line between home and work.

The women say they have good relationships with their co-workers of color, but many admit they don't communicate socially with their colleagues all that much. For example, Marie Nell says:

When I come in at Telkom I am at work. There, we are all the same. We work for the same company. Their blood is just as red as mine. It does not matter who sits next to me. Whether they are Muslim, Indian, . . . All have a heart that beats; all have blood that pumps around. That is my motto.[41]

For Nell, there are no racial differences at work. All workers at Telkom have the same goal. She emphasizes the equality of all workers. That this acceptance of equality at work demands adjustment from the women is a price they are willing to pay.

As a consequence, the women make a strict separation between home and work. They do not extend their effort to unlearn racism at work to the home. Home and work are not only experienced as different worlds; White women reinforce the difference through a symbolic boundary, an imaginary line that signifies they make sense of these two domains of daily life in different and contrasting ways, between home and work. To manage the differences between the two spaces, they represent the home as having a different set of rules than the workplace; it should be free of effort and the challenge to adapt to multicultural South Africa. The women say they do not want to talk about work at home, and vice versa; worries about work are not allowed to spill over into the home, and co-workers must remain in the dark about life at home. Some women depict themselves as machines that have learned to turn themselves on and off, a metaphor that not only reflects a desire to contain the emotional stress at work but also the strategy of ignoring—even resisting—scrutiny into the racial origins of their emotional stress.

The women compartmentalize their lives. Outside of work, beyond the physical borders of the workplace, in the city and at home, racism rules their perceptions of Black people. Rosita De Klerk enjoys good relations with her Black co-workers. Like other women, she describes how she has adjusted over the years and really gotten to know them; she now likes to call her co-workers "family." But when she describes unfamiliar Black people, she says:

When you are outside, you do not work together with them, you do not know them. You still feel that outside they are barbaric. If you read the newspapers, if you listen to the news, then you feel as if you can still hate them, even though you are not allowed to do so. You feel you want to protest against them. They will not care if they smash you in your car. They will not care if they steal your purse from under your arm. They will not care to steal from you. For me it feels like that is in their nature. It is part of their humanity. But like I said, it is totally different to work together with them, as it is to be together with them outside.[42]

De Klerk draws a strong distinction between the Black co-workers she is now familiar with and the Black Africans outside of work. They are, to her, still threatening, as she links them to crime and hate. She suggests that Black people have different beliefs and cultural values; their supposed violent tendencies are even rooted in their biology.

The pronounced gender dimension of this separation of spheres is revealed in Sarie de Wet's comments, which make clear that her husband does not allow racial tolerance at home: "My husband also does not believe in this. I differ a lot from him, but I also believe that in every culture, the housewife stands together with her husband."[43] At work, she adheres to the new nonracial norms, but at home her husband is in charge. The husbands sometimes demand that people of color stay out of the house, which explains the women's narrative tension in creating an artificial boundary between home and work.

The Moral Order of Golden Sun

The gated community of Golden Sun in Pretoria, with its six thousand residents, is a small city in itself. The residents describe the community as pleasant to live in and very beautiful. Moreover, they depict Golden Sun not only as a place free of fear but in moral terms: they take pride in their estate because they see it as an "ideal" community, a place where "everybody knows everybody" and "nobody locks the door," where "kids can play in the streets." In Golden Sun, the residents say, "people still have respect for each other" and "care about each other"; it's a place of "dignity" and "respect." They say that neighbors "show up in the middle of the night" if your child is sick and that people "greet each other"; as one woman said, "You can borrow some sugar or walk over and drink a glass of wine." In other words, "It's an ideal place to live."

However, strict regulations are needed to maintain the aesthetic beauty, community order, and control over the private spaces of the estate—regulations that are laid down and enforced by the aesthetic committee.[44] The committee's work consists in the maintenance of the green areas and parks of Golden Sun in order to assure its aesthetic appearance. Ingrid Le Roux, the *omgewing* trustee (environment trustee) of the Home Owners Association, heads the committee. When I talked with her, she told me that the aesthetic appearance of the community symbolizes the care people take in their surroundings:

> You see, in an estate it is very much about whether we care. We care about Golden Sun right up to the gates. We don't worry too much about what is going on outside. But we've fixed our own roads, all those years, even though this isn't our job. Because in the rules it says that every owner has to look after the roads. And this is where I say we have the psychological network in place to keep the roads clean, because it is for the whole of Golden Sun. People are part of their environment. To make sure the environment looks—how should I call it—friendly, we do all these physical things to the houses, streets, and the surroundings, because there is a psychological surrounding too, namely, the feeling you get when you come inside. The people inside Golden Sun create the social surrounding themselves in which they interact. And from the beginning they have made an effort to say that people are important. . . . This makes Golden Sun a very nice estate for everybody.[45]

For Le Roux, estate living is about "whether you care." It is important to her that residents care about Golden Sun "right up to the gates." Concern for one's surroundings and the community is turned inward; as she acknowledges, residents don't worry very much about "what is going on outside." In this way, she links aesthetics with community order and security. She is a firm believer in the idea that physical surroundings influence behavior; for her, the aesthetic appearance is almost a stand-in for community harmony. Moreover, the estate rules mean that people control each other, to the point that, she says, the rules encourage people to take action if they become "annoyed" with their neighbor. In the end, in her view, it is all about caring about Golden Sun. For its upper-class residents, the estate represents a renewed sense of moral order—a spotless, beautiful estate, ordered by uniform, aesthetic standards, symbolizing stability and decency.

Whiteness and Memory

At Golden Sun, the romantic and nostalgic language the White residents use to describe the community draws directly on their memories of apartheid and eerily resembles the anti-urban discourses so prevalent at that time. They celebrate the rural idyll, focus on the quality of life, and refer to the past positively. They say that the community has a "countryside feel," that it feels as if you live "outside of the city." It has a "very nice and warm" atmosphere and is "a little like paradise." The estate is depicted as a *klein boeregemeenskap*, or "small farmers' village," where everyone lives together and "in harmony." The aesthetic look of Golden Sun makes the historical parallels possible. Implausibly, they imagine their community to embody both the apartheid past and the future of South Africa.

Surprisingly, the White residents forgo a neoliberal discourse of ownership and lifestyle, thus revealing how White South Africans' experience of home is bound up with Whiteness and the apartheid history. They don't see or experience the gated community as a neoliberal lifestyle choice or a private corporation, which in fact Golden Sun is. The aesthetic look and logic of the private community render their experience of home and community continuous between apartheid and post-apartheid.

To compare the romantic image of the community to the world outside the estate would involve negative depictions such as "chaotic," "dangerous," and "wild." Indeed, much of the positive social, aesthetic, and moral community discourse can be read as a mirror image of the negative views many White residents have of post-apartheid South Africa: its community versus anomie, beauty versus ugliness, order versus chaos, and safety versus danger. Le Roux, the environmental trustee, continues:

If I come in at the gate, I open my window because it feels good. I can drive with my windows open because the Golden Sun environment feels safer for me than outside the gate. When I come in, the people of Golden Sun will open the gate, and you don't have to lock your car anymore. But if you drive out of the gate, you lock your car and you close all your windows. Like it is a war outside, that is how you drive out. But inside you feel safe.[46]

As Le Roux makes evident, the world beyond the estate is seen as a "war zone" in comparison with the "people environment" inside the estate. The contrast between the worlds outside and inside is also marked by the difference between cleanliness and dirt. Outside the estate, residents experience the city as "dirty," "uncared for," and "chaotic"; inside, things are perceived as "beautiful," "well taken care of," and "clean." This is attributed to the fact that Golden Sun has rules—and rules that are actually enforced.

While the romantic and rural identity of the Golden Sun community is perceived in contrast to the purported negativity of the outside world, it is related positively to the White residents' youth during apartheid. Many of them feel that it's much like the old, small Afrikaans communities where they grew up, where you could simply walk over to a neighbor's house. They say they want to "give their children the same experience" as they had. Although this is often said in direct reference to the feeling of safety they experience inside the gate, it also alludes to the White privileges they had during the apartheid past, establishing a continuity with that past rather than the rupture experienced in other areas of life. Indeed, one man did say in so many words that the community of Golden Sun is like "the old Afrikaner culture." Such talk of "a small farmers' village" conveys a distinct air of cultural nostalgia for the apartheid days, rooted in nostalgic Whiteness.

The romantic nostalgia the estate evokes among the White residents of Golden Sun relates to how they remember apartheid. There is a wide gap between the residents' perceptions of apartheid as a crime against humanity and their personal memories of family life in those days. They readily admit that apartheid was a "wrong system," that it was "not right." They recall how police enforced the evening curfew and regularly used violence against Black "offenders," including their own maids. Many acknowledge the inequality of race relations then and recount situations where they experienced the racial divide: different rules for Black servants in the house and the consequences of violations of those rules. Antjie Kruger shared the following:

> I was a young child. So, what was very funny for me was that this went totally against your being human, that people were treated totally different. I grew up in a house where my dad said, "Everybody is the same." And then you arrive at a garage and then there are restrooms just for Black people, and there are restrooms just for Whites. Or you arrive at a restaurant and you are not at all allowed to eat together . . . , to eat with a Black person at the same table in the restaurant. This was very wrong to me. What was bad is that the church supported this and in sermons (apartheid) was legitimized.[47]

In recalling the inconsistencies between her father's words and the reality of South Africa during apartheid, the apartheid past for White residents like Kruger is unacceptable, and they admit apartheid was wrong. However, their representations of family life during apartheid often stand in stark contrast to a system they depict as wrong. What they recall of apartheid is the agreeable situation in their parents' home: the old *plaas*, or farm, is idealized for its harmonious racial relations and the general benevolence of their parents toward Black people. Whether their families were conservative, liberal, or somewhere in between, White residents argue that their parents were *ordentlik*, or decent people, and not racists; that they treated their Black servants "well" and "with respect"; and that they often "bent over backwards" to assist them:

> We were very liberal. So, my father worked together with Blacks and they came over to our house to relax and drink coffee out of the same cup, which was strange at the time. Most Blacks had their own cup. I grew up learning to respect them and that they were part of our life. My father was in the National Party a little and at school I represented the Democratic Party. So no . . . we did not. . . . We

treated the house servant with respect and she was not a rag to mop the floor. We have never been anti-Black but I have to say, I don't like those who murder and that kind of thing.[48]

Smith stresses that her parents were liberals, yet at the same time her father was an active member of the National Party. The inclusion of the phrase "a little" downplays her father's political activities and his complicity in the system; the past is acknowledged in the same breath as it is excused. Thus the private, personal memory of home is placed outside the public history of apartheid.

Black Residents

The Whiteness of these discourses became apparent as I spoke to the Black residents of Golden Sun. In contrast to the White residents, Black residents straightforwardly use the neoliberal language of privatization, lifestyle, and ownership to describe their feelings of community and to explain why they appreciate living in Golden Sun. They do not make positive references to apartheid's past; their evaluation of the quality of life in the estate is related to their feelings of ownership within the community. This becomes evident in the testimony of Gigi Nkruma, a Black resident. Like the White residents, she feels at home in the Golden Sun estate and appreciates the "community feeling," but she voiced her vision of the community in a distinctly different language from that of the White residents:

> I like the lifestyle. I would not want to live anywhere else. I feel comfortable. I am happy around the area. And I feel like a part owner of it. When I am sitting at the club and looking at the view, I love it. Feels to me like I am part of everything. . . . I, for instance, feel that the club is for the people who live in the club. That is the kind of feeling I have. When I am driving inside I feel pride . . . like I am now at home. . . . I think it is because I love the place. Here you feel like you own part of the golf course. You can go there anytime.[49]

Nkruma speaks of "lifestyle" and "ownership" in relation to the community. Note how for her the idea of "owning the place" contributes to her feeling of pride and being at home and comfortable; she appreciates the community feel of the estate and its aesthetics. But she does not re-fer back to an idealized past, which for her is nonexistent. Instead, she frames her feelings about home and belonging in the neoliberal language that connects her to the private community that is Golden Sun.

Unsurprisingly, Black South Africans who live in Golden Sun do not share in the nostalgic White narratives about the apartheid past, nor do they seem especially eager to romanticize the dream of a new multicultural South Africa. Instead, they employ the neoliberal language of belonging as ownership and freedom as lifestyle to express their satisfaction with living in the community. They feel they belong in the estate—they legitimize their feelings of belonging—because they own a piece of property that they have worked hard for to be able to buy. Furthermore, they feel at home because they enjoy the lifestyle of the community; for the first time in South Africa's history, they have the freedom to pursue their dreams in this capitalistic and consumerist way. Yet they overlook the potential negative consequences of this lifestyle: the racial inequality produced by the politics of aesthetics and privatization that underlies the community remains invisible to Black as well as to White residents, though for very different reasons.

It is revealing how Whites view and discuss their fellow upper-class residents who are Black. Some of the wealthiest residents of Golden Sun are Black executives, and their houses have a prominent place in the es-tate. White residents are highly aware of this and often bring these resi-dents up in conversation. From American research, we know that the economic fragility of the Black middle class and the racism they have to confront makes them more concerned with status than the White middle class because Whites tend to stigmatize Black people as poor and unde-serving.[50] But Whites also mask their own privilege, status, and entitle-ment by overemphasizing Black upper-class residents' alleged concerns with status. Karin Jacobus, for instance, says that she "has no problems with Black people living in Golden Sun" and speaks positively of Black people who live inside the estate. She says that the Black South Africans in the estate have "a certain standard" and in general are perceived as "very nice." Some White residents call them "cultivated" or "educated." To Jacobus, it is encouraging to see how far some Black people have come and how much money they are able to earn:

They are, I think, the richest in the estate. I think these are people who have the most status. For me, it is like the Whites have gone through this whole development cycle. First, they wanted to be rich, they wanted to earn a lot and prove they have money, and now the circle is half completed. Now, it is just, "I want to live and live nicely." But I think Blacks are still under pressure to first say, "You know I want money." I just want to point out they don't feel they have the choice to say, "I want to stay here because it is nice." It is still about status.[51]

Jacobus says that it is natural for Whites to "live nicely" in Golden Sun, that it's convenient and enjoyable. For Black people, however, Jacobus and other Whites portray it as a status investment. For Whites, of course, living in Golden Sun is a status investment too, but White residents like Jacobus are able to mask their privilege. They sing the praises of the estate's appearance and connect it to fuzzy memories of apartheid, while at the same time claiming they are so "developed" that status is supposedly no longer a concern for them. The White residents seem oblivious to how aestheticization as a management technique of the estate naturalizes their White privilege. Furthermore, the White residents' romantic and anti-urbanism discourses—the discourses of Whiteness—obscure the logic of privatization underlying the community, so visible in the narratives of the Black residents.

Neoliberal Logics and Racialization

Despite the centrality of aesthetic discourse to how White residents talk about the estate, another defining feature of living in an estate like Golden Sun is its being a private community. Golden Sun is "governed" by the Home Owners Association (HOA), a Section 21 company that functions as an intermediary between the neighborhood and the municipality. This legal firm provides great authority to an elected but small governing body.[52] The HOA runs its operation as a neoliberal private enterprise, binding concerns about security and aesthetics together while in turn making these concerns inseparable from privatization.

The discourse of privatization has far-reaching consequences for how "problems" in the estate are perceived. For example, within this discourse, community management depicts racial incidents as "a PR problem." Residents claim that "they run their own government." According to one woman, "We bought a piece of exclusivity and security, and now we run and govern it." The most important consequence of the logic of privatization, as well as the difference between a gated community and a non-gated suburb, is that a house in an estate is bought as a "package deal": by buying into an estate, homeowners do not just obtain a "different way of living" but underwrite the privatization logic, in which privatization, security concerns, and aesthetic appearance become inseparably linked.

Specifically, privatization provides residents a neoliberal language of legitimacy, while it assures that their preferences are prioritized over other people's rights. The aesthetic appearance of the community arouses sincere feelings of comfort and relaxation in residents, but it also hides how the implementation of strict security impacts workers, visitors, and the outside community, imposing restrictions on their lives. The estate can only do this because it is run as a private entity. Whereas aesthetics visually and emotionally conceal the negative effects on outsiders, privatization discourses assure that security and aesthetic concerns overrule outsiders' concerns about public space and citizenship rights.

The difficulty of satisfying the desire to keep outsiders outside the gates is made evident by how security is organized and operates within the estate, and how the process is racialized. Crime and fear of crime is an important reason why the White residents live in Golden Sun. Many of them moved to the estate for security reasons. Many also experienced incidents firsthand or had family or friends who were victims of a burglary or assault; one interviewee was carjacked. The stories of crime and assaults are numerous and disturbing.

Life inside the gates is considerably safer than that outside, but fear of crime does not disappear inside the gates. It continues to shape the residents' everyday conversations, racial attitudes, and views of post-apartheid society. Indeed, although some aesthetic discourses obscure how deeply the security apparatus permeates the collective social life and can mute residents' concerns about order and chaos outside the estate, fear of crime remains a concern for people even after they move into the estate. The desire for security is self-perpetuating: improvements in security measures tend to increase rather than decrease the fear of crime, as such systems remind residents of their fears in the first place. This logic calls for ever stricter and tighter controls, which tends to trump other concerns.

Security concerns immediately surface when residents talk about the workers who are employed on the estate. Talk about (Black) construction workers, gardeners, housemaids, and the many other servants is always accompanied by concerns about crime and security. I asked Hannelie Toonder about the working conditions of the gardeners, and she immediately started talking about her safety concerns:

> There is a good security system and I am really quick to call security. So, any person has to keep their eyes open but the security screening is really good so I am really not scared. Of course, there will be times that you see a taxi driving and then I call security and then they immediately react. Security is always a point of concern. I think if a person does not call them, they don't know what bothers us. So, you have to call for even small things, because small things can become big things.[53]

Toonder's first concern when she talks about the workers in the estate is safety—her own. For her, security takes precedence over everything else. She worries that if you are not constantly vigilant, security will weaken. Living in the estate in fact increases concerns for security: the possibility of workers being unreliable or unsavory poses a constant threat to the residents' care- and crime-free world.

For the estate to operate as a privileged fantasy world, White residents have to rely on Black workers, which is a constant source of tension for them, since the fear of crime is always present. This of course could be seen as racist, so the residents feel a need to prove they are not:

> If I drive into the gate, this is a feeling of upliftment. You come in; it is like you are at the front door of your house. It is the same feeling. It is not that you feel bad on the other side of the door. But I have to say, yes, I love South Africa. I am friends with every newspaperman from whom I buy the paper. What I want to say is, I know there are people who don't even open their window to talk to someone, but I do. I talk to

them, and for me this is a feeling of . . . this is a thing I have to do. They say a person has six senses in South Africa—you have one more. A person develops a feeling of what is safe and what is unsafe. In Golden Sun, my bag can lie anywhere. This does not matter. But you don't do this in South Africa. You don't do that. You don't carry around this big jewelry when you walk in the middle of town. This is just how it is.[54]

Golden Sun obviously makes Matthews feel good; as she puts it, it has become synonymous with home. But she emphasizes that this doesn't mean that she doesn't feel good outside of the estate or that she would be too fearful of crime to have interracial interactions. She emphasizes that she talks to Black workers, as if to show that she is not afraid of them because of crime; indeed, she works hard to disentangle the fear of crime from race. But as her lament about South Africa makes clear, such posturing seems to lessen the anxiety routinely experienced outside the gate only slightly if at all. If the promise of good race relations in post-apartheid South Africa has narrowed to being friendly to a Black servant, little progress has been made.

Security is achieved at a high price when it comes to the mostly Black workers who support the luxurious, secure, and ordered existence of Golden Sun residents. Although in principle everyone is subjected to security checks, nonresidents and especially workers and employees are screened through a more extensive procedure, including an identity documentation check. There are also separate rules for employees living in the estate. Gardeners, domestic workers, and people working at the golf club must wear a uniform while walking in the estate and a photo identification badge on their suit. The security regime has become stricter over time. When the houses of the different phases were being constructed, construction workers still enjoyed a rest on the golf course; since then, workers are no longer allowed to leave the building site.

Most domestic workers experience living in Golden Sun as extremely restricted. Since 2008, the estate has arranged special transport for domestics so that they no longer walk around the estate. They are also discouraged from living together with their families or even inviting them for visits. And they are not allowed to provide access to the estate by themselves; if they wish to receive visitors, they must make an appointment—their employers have to grant access to their visitors. As one domestic said:

> In the community of Golden Sun, everything is strict. It is not easy like the townships, which is your place. No one is going to control you there. But in Golden Sun, they can say to you, "You mustn't do this, you mustn't do that. You mustn't drive the golf cart if you don't have a license." That is what I don't like. You can't bring a lot of people to come to visit you without contacting other people. You are allowed no more than three or four visitors at a time. You can't come here and ask, "Can I go to . . . ?" They say no. Only one or two is okay. Or you have to come with a car.[55]

In Golden Sun, residents completely control the work and social life of their domestics. These workers regularly have to travel more than four hours back and forth to their family homes in the townships and thus end up spending most of their weekdays in social isolation in the estate.

The HOA routinely legitimizes and justifies the regulation of social life in and outside the estate on the basis of concerns about security and the prevention of crime. The chairman of the HOA argues that Golden Sun respects the rights of people "like any other company." Screening measures for "undesirables" are legitimized on the grounds of being "all for the greater good" and making the community a "safer place for everybody." "Everybody," however, refers only to the inhabitants and owners of homes in the estate. Within Golden Sun, all movements by people apart from the residents are seen as possible risks to security:

> You must understand: the more people walking around, the higher the risk profile becomes . . . and that is an ongoing challenge because it is a big estate. We try, where possible, to reduce the number of people walking around, because it becomes a risk issue. Especially like domestics, friends of domestics, et cetera. We just put procedures in place now that they cannot walk on the estate. They've got to be fetched by the homeowner and taken back by the homeowner, because they don't live on the estate. Once they are inside the gate

they can be anywhere. At the end of the day we are not prepared to compromise security for something that might be a relatively small item, which it is when you look at it in absolute isolation.[56]

In the eyes of the general manager, all activities of nonresidents are viewed in terms of "risk profiles" and "security concerns." In this view, people who walk around become a "risk issue." According to this logic, all social relationships are viewed through the lens of risk and security, and the possible repercussions for nonresidents are either downplayed or denied.

In the narratives of White South Africans in post-apartheid South Africa, institutional racism and individual racial ideologies are no longer as tightly connected as they once were. Neoliberal policies such as securitization and privatization have changed the relationship between race and space. Aestheticization and the importance in neoliberal urbanism of consumers' tastes, motivations, and what appeals to them have made the politics of aesthetics central to Whites' racial narratives. Class is essential to the politics of aesthetics, but Whiteness is equally central to people's spatial imagination, collective memory of place, and cultural narratives about the urban landscape.

After apartheid, lower-middle-class White South Africans could no longer rely on the state and its resources to translate their racial anxieties into spatial policies; they had to confront their anxieties on their own. Crime is a problem in the neighborhoods of the women I interviewed, but fear of crime does not completely explain their broader views about urban disorder, race and class threats, and loss of political control. They experience chaos as encroaching upon them. They feel threatened by their proximity to Black poverty, and they sense a loss of control over the city. Their narratives echo apartheid discourses about "Black peril," but it is newly anchored in the democratic transition of 1994. The end of official racial desegregation is, for the White lower middle class, the only plausible explanation for the visible and invisible deterioration of the city. They are unable to access alternative explanations such as a lack of government funding for public space, perhaps because these are downplayed by the popular White identity politics of the Solidarity Movement, which also legitimizes the women's White grievances. While White women in particular have been able to unlearn racism at work, their views of the city remain racialized and often flat-out racist.

In contrast, the members of the White upper class who live in gated communities have unlearned the overt racism of apartheid days. The women I interviewed vocally support multicultural South Africa and even portray their community as exemplary of the country's moral and multiracial future. They imagine, albeit implausibly, that their gated communities embody both the apartheid past and the multicultural future of South Africa: their feelings of safety and intimacy are rooted in their youth during apartheid, while the estate's beautiful appearance encourages them to believe that the dream of a multicultural South Africa is possible.

Yet these White mythical dreams of a racially integrated South Africa are at variance with how these communities impose and justify racial inequality. White residents accept people of color inside the estate, it seems to me, because they are not forced to develop personal ties with them. In their narratives, the few residents of color are viewed in a tokenistic way, as evidence of the diversity and moral high ground of the community. Aestheticization disguises, to residents and outsiders alike, how strict regulations govern the sight and proximity of racial others—the undeserving—as an inconvenience and risk. Those rights can be taken away without repercussions, reinscribing racial inequality and exclusion into the South African landscape. Whiteness rooted in racialized aesthetic discourses has replaced overt racism and coded racist ideologies. White residents practice a White identity politics that normalizes Whiteness as part of a multiracial South Africa, without giving up the old and new privileges attached to it.

Thus far, this book has explored the lives and views of White South African adults at work and at home. But what about the new generation of White South Africans? Are they unlearning racism, or do they hold on to Whiteness? How should we understand the role of schools and socialization in the process of unlearning racism? And do we see class differences among the youth similar to those we have identified among adults? These questions are the subject of the next chapter.

Unlearning Racism at School

The Story of Sandra and Alex

"I am glad that I have opportunities," Sandra says, "because I know I will do something with mine." Sandra is a bright, young, sixteen-year-old, White Afrikaans-speaking girl in the honors class of the eleventh grade at an elite White Afrikaans high school, Hoërskool De la Rey. The school is located just outside the city center of Cape Town in an affluent White neighborhood. It is still predominantly White and Afrikaans-speaking, although it has a small minority of Coloured students. Here, students are trained to achieve top grades and move on to elite universities.

Sandra appreciates her school and Cape Town. She feels that the school community is "unique" and "diverse," and she loves the "cosmopolitan" character of the city:

> I would say the majority of South Africa is still bitter about apartheid, even though we want to deny it. But it is no longer here at school. People don't base their prejudice or judgment on your skin color or nationality. It is the personality that counts. Here we are all basically the same.[1]

Sandra professes a belief in multicultural South Africa and argues that her generation has overcome racism. She does not identify as a White Afrikaner or with Afrikaner nationalism; instead, she posits that people are equal. Sandra's identity narrative of change is typical for her peer culture, the culture created by the circle of girls she is part of at this upper-income school. As members of the Born Free generation,[2] they seem to exemplify a young, White South African generation who are changing their racial outlook.

Perhaps surprisingly, this transformation is happening independent of the school. The school itself has changed little since apartheid, when it was White only; it breathes tradition. It is a three-centuries-old Dutch colonial-style building, and the marks of the apartheid history are everywhere. The corridors are decorated with a century's worth of pictures of the previous sports teams. Foremost are the boys' rugby teams, standing tall in their uniforms, along with the girls' netball teams and the swimming teams—all of them White. It still practices strict discipline and a traditional leadership style. There is a collection of portraits depicting all the principals of the school, reaching back for more than a century; all of them are White, male, and stern-looking. Twenty years after the end of apartheid, Hoërskool De la Rey still has a White, male principal with executive powers.

Sandra's description of the school and her identity, however, displays some fault lines. When she talks about being White in the new South Africa, she tells a different story, which has to do with her being upper class and a woman. Sandra is self-conscious about the color of her skin, especially when there are "Black" people around. The "Black" people she refers to are the Coloured workers at her school who do the gardening and maintenance or work as security guards and parking assistants in the neighborhood. Race relations at De la Rey are extremely unequal, and students have to make sense of them. Racial inequality is manifested by who is able to attend school but also by who services and works on its extensive grounds.

Apart from class, gender is important in how students experience race. Sandra has little contact with the workers, but she often feels she's being stared at, that the men watch her. This feeling—of being watched or scrutinized—is common among the privileged White girls at De la Rey. It gives rise to a particular understanding of racial inequality:

> I know they think (of me) as this little rich girl that has an education and a future. They know . . . that many [of them] are not going to have an effect on the world like I will do. They will have an effect on me, but not on the world, even when it is a negative effect. . . . They just sit there and resent, because that is all they do.[3]

Despite her belief in multiculturalism, Sandra is highly aware of the race of the people around her and expects that they be similarly focused on hers. She assumes her Whiteness is a symbol to Coloured workers of the unequal opportunities awarded to different races. Race, class, and gender intersect here. She feels the male gaze specifically as an upper-class White female, so this gaze is classed and racialized. In her mind, the gaze of Coloured workers exposes her White privilege, and she reacts by defending herself. The scrutiny she feels from the Coloured workers does not lead her to question her White privilege; instead, she mixes race and class prejudices to justify her domination and position of power.

Sandra's identification with a diversity narrative has not ended her racism. In her monologue, Sandra implies that only White people like her—privileged and educated—are able to change the world. Coloured people are not just powerless in her eyes but also idle. The only thing they do, she argues, is resent White people's privileges. Of course, Sandra does not really know if the Coloured workers resent her; she merely projects all those thoughts and feelings onto racial others.

On the other side of the city, Alex lives in a lower-income area at the outskirts of Cape Town, where he attends Hoërskool Malan. Institutions like Malan changed rapidly after apartheid; the location of the school and its affordability contributed to rapid desegregation. However, since Alex began attending Malan, the school has resegregated—White flight has meant a rapid decline in White students. Many Whites perceive the school as unsafe, even though it is located in a "good" area of Cape Town and only borders on neighborhoods where crime is high.

Hoërskool Malan is a place where White privilege has a different meaning for young Whites of the Born Free generation. Like Sandra, Alex is in the eleventh grade and sixteen years old. He is one of the few White boys left at school. Many current students note that their older sisters or brothers went to the same school but that their siblings had a different experience. When asked about the changes in the school, Alex expounds on what has been lost since his sister went to Malan:

> My sister used to be in this school. It was a very good school. It used to have athletics. It used to have netball. Netball was the best team. We had the best rugby team in the Western Cape. We played each school. It is not good anymore. It was a good school seven years ago. It had a lot of discipline. It was very different.[4]

For lower-middle-class White youth like Alex, White privilege has become relative. Malan has lost a lot of amenities because of the changing student population. It now receives less financial support from the state and has a less well-to-do student population. Lower-middle-class White youth are forced to adjust to integrated schools and White flight.

Among the small White minority that remains at Malan, the responses of the boys and the girls differ because of their starkly different peer cultures. Race and gender both play a role in their reactions. The White girls at Malan adopt and embrace integration at school; they fit their experience into a broader narrative about the diverse new South Africa. In contrast to the girls, Alex and his friends do not identify with South Africa's new multiculturalism. Racial boundaries have hardened among the White boys at Malan. Alex is drawn to the apartheid past, with its stories of Afrikaner military power. The boys carry the label "Boer" with pride. Alex says that he "likes" his culture (his culture being White and Afrikaans) and where he comes from (both literally and figuratively). He enjoys Afrikaans music and hangs out with Afrikaans people. "I am White Afrikaans," Alex says. "There is not much I can do about it." He can't claim the White privileges of the past, but he can claim its solid sense of White Afrikaner identity.

Despite Alex's strong identification with Afrikanerdom, he is introspective about his racial prejudices. A few weeks before my interview with him, a Black person mugged him near the school, and he struggles to make sense of the experience: Why would a Black guy attack him for his bike? "I don't know why they do the wrong things," Alex says. "But I am not a racist. I don't go around calling people racial names." "Sometimes," he confesses, "when I see a Black guy on a bike, I feel like a racist, and that I am a 'true Boer.'" A true Boer, to him, is a White Afrikaner of the apartheid past. "But I wouldn't show when I'm feeling something racist happening. I keep it for myself."[5] Alex doesn't want to be thought of as a racist.

Alex's parents belong to the lower middle class, and he lives in the borderlands of White Cape Town. It is one of the few racially mixed areas in the city, where the wealthy, White southern neighborhoods border the Coloured neighborhoods of the Cape flats. Alex had many Coloured and

Black friends when he was younger. He used to be part of a mixed-race group of BMX riders and still jokes and has fun with his Coloured classmates. Alex understands how apartheid caused poverty and inequality.

> Sometimes, yeah, when I see how people struggle and what their lives are like, like shacks and stuff, squatter camps and stuff. How did it originate? Where did it come from? Mostly from apartheid. Those people could not get jobs and their children couldn't have their education and now they're sitting there with children without food, shelter, or anything and then they must suffer the consequences.[6]

Unlike Sandra, Alex sees and understands the roots of poverty and the ongoing consequences of apartheid for the Coloured population.

Sandra's and Alex's stories impel us to think about the challenges that young, White South Africans face in confronting the history of White supremacy and racism. The differences in their narratives prevent us from drawing any simple conclusions about generational change. Their accounts reveal how unlearning racism involves more than raising awareness about racial inequality and White privilege. Both Sandra and Alex are decidedly aware of their own White skins—this is something they share. What distinguishes these two individuals, however, is how their self-described identities relate—or do not relate—to their racial outlook: Sandra sees herself as a cosmopolitan urbanite, while Alex identifies as an Afrikaner nationalist.

Racism and Socialization

American race scholars, who study education and the socialization of youth, have long been concerned with the reproduction of racism. Racial disparities in the American educational system continued to be high at the start of the twenty-first century. After the civil rights movement, scholars were especially puzzled by the question of how racial inequality was maintained, even after *Brown v Board of Education* officially ended racial segregation in public schools in 1954. Racism, they hypothesized, had not disappeared but undergone significant transformation, and they asked how racism was reproduced through the school system.

American educationalists have been particularly inspired by the work of Eduardo Bonilla-Silva, who not only continued to foreground the systemic nature of racial oppression but also pointed to the pernicious influence of the ideology of color blindness.[7] White teachers and parents, these scholars have shown, avoid race in their talk in order to mask a reality of racialized practices.[8] School management chooses to speak as though race does not matter, and when they do address race, White people in positions of power use oppressive stereotypes to characterize other races. Racism is thus reproduced through a color-blind ideology among staff, teachers, and parents, who do not take historical and contemporary socioeconomic inequalities into account. The strength of studies on color-blind racism is that they apply an ideological lens to the study of racism and look for cohesion in the varied stories that White people tell themselves about the way race works in the world.

A second group of sociologists of education have been inspired by Whiteness studies.[9] They ask what it means to be young and White at the beginning of the twenty-first century. These studies show that in schools, merely interacting with students of different races is not enough to counter the forces of racism in White students.[10] They also find large differences in identities between White youth in majority-White and minority-White schools. If being White means different things in different schools, this challenges the assumption of a uniform color-blind ideology impacting White high school students. The strength of Whiteness studies is that it centers on people's own role—their agency—and ability to change.

In South Africa, sociologist Melissa Steyn has been particularly influential in her focus on White identity change.[11] Educationalists following in her footsteps have emphasized the analysis of the learning and unlearning of racism and highlighted the possibility of social change rather than social reproduction among White adolescents.[12]

Sandra's and Alex's stories provide a starting point for examining the socialization of racism—how children learn racism and also how they *un*learn it.[13] Their accounts call into question both theoretical approaches. The problem is that Sandra's and Alex's narratives show that White identity change is not indicative of young White South Africans unlearning racism. The Whiteness studies approach in South Africa has been undercut by its singular focus on racial identity over racial ideology and its failure to conceptualize the politics of White identity. Conversely, color-blind racism cannot explain how Sandra and Alex approach the topic of race. White youth do not avoid talking about race or argue that race does not matter; Sandra and Alex are, albeit in different ways, highly aware of their own Whiteness. Studies on color-blind racism also overemphasize the role of school management, teachers, and parents, vis-à-vis the agency of White youth.[14] It is a mistake to see White youth as passively reproducing what is received from teachers or parents.[15]

The narratives of Sandra and Alex thus present us with a puzzle. Outwardly, Sandra's White identity has shifted, while Alex embraces a pre-1994 Afrikaner identity. Sandra professes a belief in multicultural South Africa, but upon further discussion she legitimizes her privileged position and justifies White dominance. By contrast, Alex confronts his loss of White privilege and checks his racial bias. Sandra's identification with diversity does not lead her to question her privilege; Alex's identification with Afrikaner nationalism does not prevent him from problematizing his racism. Sandra's and Alex's stories show us that the relationship between White identity change and unlearning racism is at best a tenuous one. If White identity change means unlearning racism, we would expect Sandra to be the antiracist and Alex to be the racist. Yet their stories do not bear out this theoretical premise.

Looking at the stories of Sandra and Alex through the eyes of White identity politics solves this puzzle, because it demonstrates how Whiteness is relevant to White youth far beyond their identity narratives. Moreover, it explains something that color-blind racism cannot: how the importance of race does not have to be denied for racialized practices and a racialized view of the world to be justified. As demonstrated in the previous chapters, White identity politics has succeeded color blindness as the new racism in South Africa. Its politics is marked by the strategic politicization of White identity and the adoption of the language of marginalized communities. White youth use White identity politics to endorse multiculturalism and a limited form of antiracism, while simultaneously positioning White South Africans as the new victims in South Africa. Sandra and Alex practice White identity politics in different ways, because of their different class and gender and how this makes Whiteness emotionally resonate; but ultimately they endorse the same politics.

Sandra and Alex write their own racial narratives with their peers. While they do so against the backdrop of their schools and broader society, they nevertheless do so independently. I propose the analytical concept of *peer culture* to better understand the process of unlearning racism for youth at schools, defining it as a set of activities, values, and concerns that youth produce and share with peers. The concept is a productive alternative to identity because it is not static but process oriented, capturing both the social (peer) and meaning-making (culture) aspects of the unlearning process.[16] White youth in South Africa socialize primarily with one another; they construct their own norms and valued identities within the peer group through talk and cultural production. Youth playfully transform and actively resist existing cultural categories through peer talk and resistance to adult culture.[17] They make meanings that evolve over time through interactional and performative cultural processes with each other.

My cultural approach to analyzing race in schools and the focus on peer culture allow for the incorporation of cultural processes happening beyond school grounds.[18] However, I am not just interested in the question "What does it mean to be White, young, and South African?" but also in "How does it feel to be White, young, and South African?" Students do not only interpret what Whiteness means; they also live and experience it. As discussed in Chapter 5, Whiteness is about cultural knowledge and knowledge in the body; socialization is inscribed in the body. Scholars have demonstrated how privilege and disadvantage are embodied.[19] The contingent relationship between meanings and feelings among White youth can only be explored if we analyze how class positions are intimately linked with race and gender through embodiment.

White youth make sense of race against the institutional backdrop of a South African educational system in transition. Since 1994, racial desegregation has dramatically transformed the South African educational landscape, reshaping many public high schools, but it has done so unevenly. By law, all schools in South Africa are desegregated; in reality, this process is taking place primarily in formerly White schools where high educational standards attracted new Black and Coloured students.

School-governing bodies, dominated by White parents, were able to make desegregation and racial integration a class issue through imposing high school fees. Nevertheless, even in elite White schools in Cape Town, student bodies are now at least a quarter to a fifth nonwhite students. Still, most desegregated South African schools do not explicitly address race and difference in their policies or curricula.[20]

My analysis focuses on two groups of White youth who attend two formerly White-only schools.[21] The first school, De la Rey, is a predominantly White, Afrikaans, upper-middle-class school. The school has remained predominantly White, although like most formerly White schools, it has accepted a small percentage of students of color, who are all upwardly mobile or have received sports scholarships. The second school, Malan, is a lower-middle-class school where teaching occurs both in Afrikaans and English. Until recently, the school offered a similar level of education as De la Rey. In the last few years, this school has not only desegregated but also seen its White Afrikaans-speaking students disappear, so it is resegregating.[22]

The De la Rey School: Continuity and Change

For all its traditions, De la Rey has had to change, and that change has been incremental and controlled. While the school has remained an elite, single-medium Afrikaans school, which means that Afrikaans is the only language of instruction, the school officially desegregated in 1992. Nonwhite staff are employed, and nonwhite students are now admitted to the school. Indeed, some changes have been more far-reaching, as reflected in the new Coloured female vice-principal, hired in 2006, and the Coloured *hoofseun* elected in 2007 (a star of the rugby team).[23] To the outside world, De la Rey has definitely altered, but the question is not whether De la Rey has desegregated, but why this change has been as limited and uneven as it has been. The admission of Coloured students has been highly selective and tightly regulated. The school admits most Coloured students based on sports criteria; only a few are accepted on the basis of other criteria such as academic merit or musical talent. Almost twenty years after desegregation, this result is almost unique for a school in the inner city of Cape Town: most former Afrikaans schools in the city that desegregated in the early 1990s have not been able to slow-walk integration and have experienced White flight. They no longer have any White students.

However, De la Rey has not experienced White flight from the school, and it has not become resegregated as an all-Black or Coloured school. There are three reasons for this. First, the school has expanded its catchment area and extended the operation of their boys' and girls' hostels, which now house students from all over the Western Cape. Second, the school ensures that it attracts only a limited number of specially selected Afrikaans-speaking Coloured students. Most of them obtain a sports bursary and boost the sports reputation of the school, which is still an important way to remain competitive in the educational market.[24] Third, and most important, the school started to operate an affordable and elaborate bus system that transports students to the school from White neighborhoods and areas as far away as Langebaan on the West Coast (nearly an hour's drive outside of Cape Town). The bus system has offered students who normally would have been too far from the school a chance to go to De la Rey. The bus system negatively affects other schools by facilitating White flight in these locales. The student body of De la Rey, therefore, consists of many whites who have avoided neighborhood schools that have a "bad reputation" (another term often used for schools with a large influx of nonwhite students), together with gifted Coloureds.

The Fragile Balance of Whiteness

In the unequal and competitive educational landscape of post-apartheid South Africa, reputation management is essential for schools, and reputation is strongly based on the racial composition of the school. De la Rey remained a traditional, mostly White, and single-medium Afrikaans school after apartheid, and has even attained maximum occupancy. Nevertheless, the school's management is constantly aware of the fragility of its position and the need to keep up its (racial) reputation in competition with other schools. The school manages its (racial) reputation largely through two types of policies: first, it has installed a mix of policies that help to limit the possible influx of Coloured students, often expressed in economic language about supply and demand and justified by the need to keep up "standards"; second, to handle diversity, it strongly regulates racial life inside the school by stratifying school classes, which produces a racial hierarchy that isolates most White students from Coloured students.

By means of the first set of policies, the school simultaneously controls the admissions process and tries to obscure the ethnic composition of its student body. Because admission to the school cannot be based on racial or ethnic criteria anymore, a new language has been devised to legitimize the selection of students that prioritizes the preferred White Afrikaans students. At De la Rey, as well as many other former Afrikaans schools, the criteria for admission are now wrapped in the economic language of "benchmarks," "supply and demand," and the need to uphold "standards." For instance, the school principal explains that prospective students should all have to meet the "same standards." The language of standards has the ring of neutrality and works effectively; but in application the racial logic of this language becomes evident. Take the principal's example of music education, used to explain his educational philosophy. De la Rey is well known for its department of drama and music, but it only teaches classical music.

> You achieve the best education if people who have the same standards surround you. For me it would be impossible to put people who . . . experience hip-hop in the same class as those who study classical music, like Bach and Beethoven. . . . Those are two different influences. It is a question of supply and demand: What does the cultural (ethos) of De la Rey offer? This will determine who is interested in De la Rey. This is a natural process. Other people, who have an interest in hip-hop or rock, if I may use that example . . . If De la Rey has a focus on classical music, then we will attract the candidates who have an interest in that, a love for and socialization in this. But the school that is in Harlem or New York, like the school from the movie "Fame," they will attract the rock 'n' roll and hip-hop youth.[25]

By drawing a contrast between Cape Town and Harlem and between classical music and hip-hop, the racial logic of the school principal is evident. Students who "experience hip-hop," he argues, do not belong together with students who "study classical music." The principal deemphasizes his own role in the selection process, instead, presenting the process as an economic one—a process in which the school offers a certain product and where rules of supply and demand simply play out. In other words, the school operates in the educational "market" and has its "natural" customers.

Second, the educational philosophy that prescribes that students with the same "standards" learn together has resulted in internal segregation, with a hierarchy of classes in De la Rey that has strong racial repercussions. Once admitted to the school, the students follow different academic tracks. For instance, in eleventh grade, the school divides the students into four classes, named after the first letters of the name of the school: H(oerskool) D(e) L(a) R(ey). The H-class is the honors class, for students whose first language is both Afrikaans and English and take mathematics at the highest academic level. Students of color, many of whom are selected for their athletic talents and recipients of a bursary, often perform poorly academically. They are selected to go into the lowest class, the R class, with the poorest-performing students. In 2007, the R class had thirty students, of which only seven were white; the other three classes together had only three students of color. In this way, De la Rey creates segregation within a desegregated school; it produces a racialized hierarchy in the school that is never openly addressed but rather hidden or denied. Thus the management can proudly present the school as traditional Afrikaans and Christian.

Diversity Talk

Students at De la Rey are very positive about the school and celebrate its pleasant atmosphere. Girls and boys both paint a picture of the school as a progressive and open place. They call it "unique," "liberal," and "special." They think it has a lot of "respect for culture" and that "everybody" can come to the school. Students can be "who they are" and "everybody is accepted" and "treated the same." Everybody "talks to each other" and is "flexible" and "an individual"—nobody "judges you."

> I wouldn't say we experience differences naturally. . . . We don't see any differences, I mean, apart from the color of our skin, nothing else is really different. They play the same sports as us, they do the same things. . . . We tend to learn from each other. We listen to the

same things. They have the same things, they wear the same clothes, so there's nothing really different. . . . We're together a lot. We work in the same groups, we work with the Coloureds; they work with us. We don't discriminate against anyone. So I think because we're so open to other cultures, we tend to be very . . . free.[26]

Most students share Annelie's views. They say they are part of a unique and diverse student body. While there may be an element of flattering self-presentation here, such discourse is nevertheless remarkably distinct from the focus of the management on tradition, on being Afrikaans and Christian. Students present an image of the school that is all their own. They claim that it embodies the values with which they want to identify. Many feel the school to be a community that is strongly unified, with few subgroups that really matter: the school has few cliques and no one gets bullied. It is a "close knit" school where "everybody is friends" and "everybody stands together."

They link the image they have of the school and themselves to the broader geographical area where they live: Cape Town. Students connect a positive, liberal view of the school with idealistic images of Cape Town. They see it as a progressive city. Most of all, they feel the city is different from other parts of South Africa, like the former South African capital Pretoria or the *platteland*, the countryside:

Because it is also in Cape Town, the school allows much more flex-ibility for your own personality and your own identity. I mean, our motto is "Wees jouself," yeah . . . be yourself. And people do live up to that in this school. You are not an outcast because you do not dress the same. And because you do not talk the same or think the same. . . . When you come here, you can't really be like all your friends, because all your friends are different. So, I was forced to cre-ate my own identity, to form it. And in that way I cannot thank the school enough.[27]

Students like Ineke say that Cape Town is "cosmopolitan" and has no "racist stuff." They think the city allows you to develop your identity without "any culture forced upon you."

The active embrace of multiculturalism and diversity marks the White identity politics of the students at De la Rey. They do not deny differences exist but actively celebrate them and try to fit the White Afrikaans minority into this picture as "just another group." Patsy says: "It is not the Black people (who are different), it is us. We are different."[28] They playfully transform the traditional way the school promotes pride in being and speaking Afrikaans, as most believe Afrikaans is "fading" and "dying out." They do want to be proud of who they are, but they are aware of the fine line between "I am a proud Afrikaner" and "I am White and I am proud." Petronella says: "We are the rainbow nation, very diverse. We all feel proud of who we are."[29] Ultimately, most students argue that they cannot help being White and Afrikaans. Jeanne says: "I am White Afrikaans, I mean, I cannot change that. I was raised Afrikaans so it's part of me."[30] The students' White identity politics does not deny the reality of race, as would be the case in color-blind racism, but gives it new meaning.

Policing Racial Prejudice

The school desegregated after 1994, but the number of Coloured and Black students is still below 20 percent. Nevertheless, as in most of the public sphere in South Africa, antiracism has become the social norm at Hoërskool De la Rey. Many students, particularly the girls, say they actively police the new norm, both at home and at school. Some argue explicitly that Coloured students are the same as Afrikaans-speaking White persons. But most girls go even one step further: they adamantly and strongly condemn racism—that is, racism as they define it: open, derogatory remarks about people of color. Ronel talks about what happens if one of the boys says something inappropriate:

> One of the boys would say like "Ja, I don't want that piece here." Or whatever, just something inappropriate, and then all the girls would just be like "What are you talking about?" And the guys would just keep quiet. Ja, that is usually what would happen. . . . He would refer to a worker, which is very racist and I don't approve. . . . But I think that if we all help the guys that are racist . . . if we talked to them, and show them, they might change their minds.[31]

Ronel attributes racist remarks to boys but notes that the girls, particularly in a group, actively and successfully police them. She says that the boys actually do listen and hopes that in the end such policing will change their minds and help them improve.

White identity politics distinguishes itself from color-blind racism by not denying racial difference but actively presenting itself as antiracist. The White girls of De la Rey present themselves as a generation that is "friends" with Coloureds. They do not say that they do not see color but stress that they welcome Coloureds at school. The students see themselves not as racist but as antiracist. Their self-identification, however, is based on a very narrow understanding of racism as racial prejudice.

Talking about race does not come easily to White Afrikaans students, in part precisely because of the changed social norms and the new self-representation of being a generation that has moved beyond race. Answers to questions on race are qualified by sentences such as "I do not want to be rude" or "I don't want to look arrogant." Students are visibly uncomfortable talking about race and often exhibit a sense of uncertainty about their thoughts as they verbalize their thinking. There is an astute awareness that talking about race and difference may cause them to be perceived as offensive and racist. Many qualify any remark they make about race and offer assurances that they are "not a racist." The problem has become how to explain difference without making distinctions.

What the norm of antiracism has provided is the necessary impulse for the students to rethink old prejudices. Students have found creative ways in which to restate the old prejudices about Coloureds. One way is to deny them—to simply stress that there are no differences. For instance, some students say that Whites and Coloureds perform the same academically, even though that hardly seems true at De la Rey. Sometimes prejudices are not denied but simply questioned while being stated. Maretha, for example, says that she wrestles with stereotypes: "Some people say White people plan better for the future. . . . I do not know what to think of it. White people are maybe more sophisticated."[32] Another way is to say that there are differences but that they don't matter. For example, some students note that Coloured students listen to different music, and while this distinction is not entirely innocent, it need not be prejudiced.

But these are merely the most obvious ways to deal with prejudice and difference—to deny them, question them, or say they do not matter.

Some students believe they can restyle prejudices by inverting them or revaluing them, apparently unaware that thereby they are reproducing another set of old stereotypes of Black people as "always happy" or only defined by their physical traits. Students stress that they see the "loud character" of Coloureds as a good thing, not a bad thing; they say they love that Coloureds are "outgoing," "start the party," and "do crazy stuff." Such distinctions draw a fine line, as the students steer their comments between admiration and amusement, mixing appreciation for difference with prejudice. In other words, do they laugh *with* them, or *at* them? It is sometimes hard to tell; what seem to be admiring comments about Coloured students can also be read as code for their not being viewed as very smart, serious, or hardworking.

Feeling Whiteness

The condemnation of open racism almost obscures the fact that race is present not only in students' talk but also in their being, seeing, and feeling. Whiteness is about performance at De la Rey. This became evident to me when White students would comment on the behavior of Coloured students. Where racism in talk seems easy to police, it is more difficult for the students to escape a White worldview that "colors" their judgment of the world. Whiteness is thus embodied, but this embodiment is not only about performing appropriately: it is, specifically for female students, also fundamentally about being and feeling seen.

Racial difference at De la Rey is experienced in terms of performance, both inside and outside the school. This is evident in how judgments of Coloureds are mostly based on behavior that deviates from the White norm. Students describe Coloureds as "eccentric" and "exciting," ambivalent characterizations that reveal the fine line between fascination and deprecation. Others are less ambiguous, referring to Coloureds as acting "crazy" or "mental" and "willing to do anything." Girls also feel intimidated by Coloured boys: Zola, for instance, sometimes finds it hard simply to pass a group of Coloured boys, as they will "squeeze you and everything."[33] This form of sexual harassment is rightfully condemned, but the way these complaints are racialized speaks also to a more problematic White norm of what is appropriate and correct behavior in the school. White students judge racial differences on the basis of performance and how a person is supposed to act. They see Coloureds as displaying different behavior—mostly deviant behavior; acting like a White person is the norm.

Dawid is the only boy who says he regularly hangs out with Coloured boys. Actually, he is part of the only racially mixed group of male friends at school. He says that he switches his language when he speaks just among whites or in a mixed-race group:

> You have to speak different because when you are with your White friends and you say: "Ja, die Coloured ou het dit vir my so gesê . . ." [Yes, that Coloured guy just told me . . .]—if there is a Coloured around, it sounds to me offensive to say "Ja, that Coloured ou did that . . ." I would say "ou" when he was with me. . . . You get used to it, when they are there and when they aren't. You look for them, basically, in a way. You think before you speak. It comes naturally. . . . If they were to hear it, they would smack you! . . . It is like a bond that you have that you can sense. You can sense it. . . . You can feel when they are watching.[34]

Dawid watches what he says around Coloured people. But he has developed a strategy by which he automatically changes his way of talking from "White talk" to what he deems as more appropriate race talk. Interestingly, he says that knowing this—when to switch and what to change—creates a bond among his White friends. A "sixth sense" that tells them when "they" watch him and how to speak in those moments, how to sound acceptable for Coloureds and when to let go among your White friends. You have race talk but you also have White talk. Dawid is exceptional in articulating the existence of White talk, but note how he depicts his switching back and forth as the racially sensible thing to do; he does not seem aware that he could stop his White talk altogether.

Like Dawid, many White students mention the experience of feeling observed and watched because of being White. Being White is not only a way of acting or talking but also a way of feeling. Partly because of fears of crime, students rarely venture into areas where the majority is not White or where they would have to navigate a multicultural society on more equal footing. While living in "cosmopolitan" Cape Town, White students live predominantly in a White world. When they do recount experiences beyond their White world, their White feelings quickly show.

Students' feelings of being watched are evoked by the racialized landscape of their daily lives and the inequality embedded in their racial relationships. For White students, school and daily life involve many unequal interactions with Coloureds in service jobs, such as security guards, parking attendants, and traffic controllers. Most interactions with people of color, in fact, are highly unequal; students rarely meet people of color with a similar lifestyle or education. Students often say "Black" workers make them feel uneasy, and most of these workers are men; feeling White is therefore also heavily gendered and sexualized. White girls will say they feel sexually intimidated or scared, based on the looks they receive but also from being whistled at and shouted at on school grounds.

The students' belief in diversity sits uneasily with their segregated lifestyle both in and outside school. When it comes to race, the girls implicitly use themselves—their privileged Whiteness—as the norm. But their belief in diversity is not supported by intimate interracial experiences in daily life; instead, it depends on a set of positive self-images and racial fantasies that can only exist in their White world—a world in which the girls' White identities and racial views are not often challenged.

When White female students recall feeling their Whiteness, it turns out to have been an unpleasant experience. But it is also through such experiences that many girls feel guilt for being privileged and White in post-apartheid South Africa. They acknowledge that this affects their interactions with Black or Coloured South Africans, that they are being labeled as wealthy, sexually desirable, and privileged. It is striking how in their narratives they mix their own feelings with readings of the feelings of the racial other:

> With the builders here at school, they do not have proper education. I feel they resent me, because I have enough money for school; that I can go to school. They think I am better than them. When I sit with

my backpack, reading before I go to music class. . . . You think they look down on you. When they look at you . . . you know . . . just . . . when they stop and stare. They do that because in that moment they know they have some little effect on you.[35]

For Sandra, privilege comes with a burden. She thinks that the Black people in her surroundings think negatively of her, that they resent her for her good education and her possibilities. She thinks that by staring at her they are trying to get back at her. She feels guilt and tries to diminish this feeling by negotiating her privileged position:

It is not racist. It has nothing to do with me or with them. I only play some part in it. If I am clever or if I deserve it, I can't claim it, it is not my doing. Some people in my class throw away their potential; they can do so much.[36]

Sandra argues that her chances in life have nothing to do with racism; she cannot be held responsible for her privileged position. All she can do is to either make use of her potential or fail to do so, like some other students. She argues that for her not to make use of her potential would be a waste, and that for Blacks to enjoy such a thing would be wrong. But if she does make use of her potential, she feels that Blacks will be resentful of her. As a consequence, interactions with the racial other are tense and anxious:

You are afraid to offend them. You don't know what to say. By saying something plain like what I want to do, they might be resentful about that, so you are careful about what you say. I'd rather not say anything than lie, if it makes them feel bad. . . . I feel bad, and guilty, for everything. I do. Sometimes I am angry for what I feel, because I feel guilty. I played no part in my opportunities.[37]

Sandra constantly feels emotionally strained. She argues that it is always better to make use of her opportunities than to fail, yet she still feels guilty about her privileges and wants to get rid of the feeling. She feels damned if she does and damned if she doesn't make use of her chances.

Sandra's thoughts and feelings reveal how Afrikaner nationalist ideas about middle-class femininity and White embodiment continue to resonate in the present. During Afrikaner nationalism, White women determined the purity of the White race; specifically, they had to dress, present, and organize their bodies as *ordentlik*, an Afrikaans word meaning "decency" that helped organize women bodies in accordance with nationalist respectability politics.[38] The bodies of White women were seen as the carriers of White supremacist ideology. At De la Rey, the school management still imposes discipline on how White youth present themselves. The school polices the clothing, movement, and appearance of all its students. The vice-principal checks the length of everyone's hair weekly; students are not allowed to walk too slowly inside the school; and any kind of sexually loaded exchanges, such as kissing, are forbidden. This helps to explain Sandra's emphasis in her narrative on her White embodiment—her feelings about being seen—and how her sexuality, being a White woman, and being privileged are interwoven both in her thinking and in her projections onto the racial other. She might consider herself a modern and freethinking White girl who is no longer beholden to White supremacist thinking, but her thoughts betray a constant self-surveillance of her White body as being that of a respectable White girl.

What has changed after apartheid is Sandra's emphasis on the upper-middle-class value of self-actualization, through which she justifies her privileged position. Ultimately, Sandra's logic rests on a lack of recognition of the historical advantages that benefited the White group to which she belongs. Feeling uneasy about her privilege but failing to see the historical roots of it, she has to manage the troubled feelings that come with unequal race relations. She is exceptional in articulating these feelings, but her sentiment is hardly rare. Indeed, Sandra's preoccupations are characteristic of her peer group of female students at De la Rey, a group whose narrative about identity and race is marked by a tension between their belief in diversity and their Whiteness that legitimizes the racial inequality they observe in their surroundings. What results is a nagging feeling of anxiety about their privileged position, an emotion sustained by the discrepancy between the reality in which they live and their ambition to be the first White generation that is beyond racism. As much as these girls say they want to achieve this goal, their experience and feelings are distinctly White. To be young, White, and privileged in post-apartheid South Africa is a constant source of ambivalence and unease.

The White boys of De la Rey do not experience White embodiment in the same way as the girls. This does not mean that they never feel White; when they venture beyond the immediate setting of the school and their White neighborhoods, they are shocked to learn that they are part of a small White minority in South Africa, even in Cape Town. Many recounted the experience of having to visit the Department of Home Affairs for the first time to obtain documentation such as a driving license or a passport. Students must collect these documents in person, meaning that they join a long queue with their fellow, nonwhite South Africans. The students have experienced this as very unpleasant. "Where has everybody gone?" Hendrik Louw, a male student, recalls thinking.[39] Students felt fearful, embarrassed, and irritated. Carel Naude, another male student, says: "There were ten Black people and only two White people. We were the only White people for a hundred kilometers. It got creepy for a while."[40] They felt they were treated "unfairly" and "dismissed" by Black people working at the department; they felt "out of place" and that they "did not belong." But according to many of these White male students, these experiences are rare, which reinforces the impression that these students exist in a White world.

More so than the girls, the boys reference the history of Afrikaner nationalism. White identity politics, as we have seen in the previous chapters, retells this history in a way such that White Afrikaans-speaking South Africans are presented as similar to Black South Africans:

> Afrikaners had a really tough history, with the South African war. We share some of the history with Black South Africans. Afrikaners have suffered also financially. It is kind of funny, when you think of it how we are the same.[41]

Theron uses the supposedly historical parallel between White Afrikaans-speaking South Africans and Black South Africans to deny the history of White supremacy and to position White Afrikaners as victims.

The majority of White students at De la Rey are well-to-do by South African standards and could be considered the winners of the post-apartheid democratic transition. Attending the upper-middle-class school provides them with excellent chances of attending one of South Africa's top universities. Nevertheless, students are fearful of the future and present themselves as victims of affirmative action. They do not deny the wrongs of apartheid; Carel Naude, for example, says he often feels "angry towards the White man" and that apartheid was "forty-five years of all wrong." He thinks his parents' generation was "flippin' stupid," and he feels "sorry for the Coloureds and how they were handled and how unfair apartheid was."[42]

Nevertheless, students at De la Rey present themselves as the new victims when it comes to sports, education, and the economy. White identity politics, the students show, is just as much driven by White South Africans who fear losing their privileges as by those who have already lost them. Students claim that in South Africa "Black women are at the top" and that White youth are "right at the bottom of the food chain." Jurie van Wyk, a male White student, says: "It will not matter if I get 90 percent at school, I still will not get into university,"[43] despite the fact that elite universities such as the University of Cape Town and Stellenbosch University still had a majority of White students at the time of the interviews. Students argue that "apartheid should not affect the youth of today" and that they were "very young" when it ended. The current affluence and happiness the students experience seem to hardly mitigate their fears of the future. Jurie says, "I am happy here. I love it. I have good friends. I feel safe. When I am older I will emigrate, because there are no opportunities in South Africa to survive as a White male."[44] Jurie's use of the word "survival" when he speaks about "opportunities" echoes Afrikaner nationalists' concerns about the survival of the Volk. Given the class position of these students, their fear of what might happen to them is remarkable. Here is Jaco Niekerk, a male White student:

I guess we don't know enough about the future to say something definitely about what is going to happen, but it is scary. I mean: a White chick or White guy living in a Black populated country. It will be scary if it was like apartheid again or if they wanted to have us all killed. I don't know. They would not, but I'm just saying. It could be scary.[45]

The Malan School: United by Loss

The small group of White students attending the Malan school are acutely aware of the changes happening at their school. In their stories, they mention many activities and practices that have disappeared or lost their essential meaning at their school. Few talk about their lifestyle or their sport activities as the basis of their identity; instead, the students are united by feelings of loss. What is striking is how girls and boys respond differently to loss: while the girls are able to name their feelings and to admit how the loss has affected them, the boys pretend not to care. Nevertheless, in the boys' discourse about change, there is plenty of evidence that they care more than others around them.

Students feel that the changes have come quickly. Like Alex, many remember their sisters or brothers going to the same school yet having a very different experience. The students feel that they have lost a wide variety of activities and amenities previously provided by the school. Many activities, including sports, have had to stop owing to lack of participation or money; several courses have been terminated. But more important, traditions, practices, and rituals that many White students used to take pride in have now withered away or lost their meaning, including the school's once high academic standards.

Traditionally, academic achievement was given value through specific symbols—symbols that in the past meant something to students but have now lost their value. Marie Mostert says that the insignia she wears used to signify that you were one of the top ten students in the school, but that now it means nothing to her:

> Previously, the highest academic-achievement award went to someone who got 90 percent. Now the standard had dropped and all you need is a 70 or a 60 percent average and you will make it into the top ten. It has become easier . . . I don't know why, maybe the work has just become easier or maybe I just work harder. I think the academic standards have lowered but I don't know why. I think the kids are just not motivated anymore. It could be also that the curriculum has changed and it has become easier for us to get higher marks like 70

percent or so. My mum is very disappointed with the drop in standards. She wants the school to go back to the way it was when it was fun and we used to have activities after school and stuff like that. Sometimes I think the quality of education has lowered. It's not like it used to be.[46]

Marie's sadness about all the changes and the loss that has resulted is evident. But behind these particulars, something else has been lost as well for the students. This comes to the forefront when they talk in more abstract terms about what is lost. They will say that the school "is not what is used to be" or that "sports are dying out" and "there is no more sports in the school." Some rhetorically ask: "What is a school without sports?" They say similar things about culture. They say that it is good "to have culture" in a school but that their school "does not have culture anymore." Factually, such statements are clearly not entirely true, as the school still has a rugby team and of course has "a culture." But they hint at something else: that sports activities do not have the same cultural meaning anymore. They have lost their relevance and their value.

Gendered Response

Although the students do not know why the school has changed, they do know that the changes took place at the same time as the new students of color entered the school. This is evident in their discourse of loss. Students attribute the cause to an unspecified "they": "it is loud" becomes "they are loud"; "there is no respect" becomes "they are rude"; and "there is no safety" becomes "as long as they don't do anything to me."

This attribution is mostly implicit owing to the social norm of antiracism. Explicitly attributing the changes and losses at the school to the Coloured students would be considered racist. And if the White Afrikaans-speaking students want to avoid one label more than any other, it is that of racist. They already feel stigmatized because of the apartheid past. Students therefore tread carefully when they try to explain what happened to their school.

In any case, the response to change and loss is decidedly different for boys and girls. All the White students notice that the school has changed, but for boys like Alex, the Malan school represents what they feel has been lost: morality, discipline, and ethnic pride. The boys vehemently denounce what has happened to the school much more than the girls; their identity is what is most under stress. They not only deplore the situation, they morally condemn it and rebel against it:

> The White kids, I don't know, but suddenly they disappeared from the school. You only see White people in grades 11 and 12. Most of the guys, the proper guys, the proper people, go to De la Rey, because that is the more popular school, the more expensive school also. There won't be any trashy kids there, kids with trashy background coming there destroying your life. . . . You have a lot of them here. There was a guy that stabbed me with a pen. His father died a few years ago, and his mother died when he was in grade 8 as well. So that is classified as trashy. But my mother also died a few years ago and I am not a rebel. I don't do stuff like that. Stab people, and things like that.[47]

In line with the antiracist norm, Alex does not speak of "Black" or "Coloured" kids (the two new groups present at school) but makes a distinction between "proper kids" and "trashy kids," which double as racial categories for White and nonwhite youth. He stresses that what he perceives as bad behavior is not necessarily caused by race but from the circumstances the Coloureds live in. He does not want to be seen as a racist, but he clearly connects the changes in the school with the new student population of "trashy kids" and the violent experiences he has had with them. The connections and oppositions Alex makes are noteworthy: proper people versus trashy kids; popular versus violent; rich versus poor. He connects class and social issues, along with social mobility, which he doesn't have. In Alex's perception, the school has two types of students: the "proper" (White) youth, who do their work and have discipline, and those he categorizes as the "rude and trashy" youth, who have no discipline, are bad-mannered, and "destroy" his life. He justifies this moralistic framework by directly challenging, with anecdotal evidence of his own struggles during his upbringing, the idea that someone's background and hardships should be taken into account when judging their immoral behavior. In other words, he creates a moral boundary between the two positions: whether you are "proper" or "trashy" depends on your moral choices.

Alex and his friends clearly condemn the Coloured and Black students for "destroying 'their' school," but they claim to be indifferent to the changing racial composition of the school. Le Roux, one of Alex's friends, has a different history with nonwhite youth from that of the children who grew up in the city. Until the age of ten, Le Roux Pienaar lived on a farm in the Eastern Cape with his grandfather and grandmother. Like his friends, he says he does not care about the racial change at the school:

> Well, it doesn't bother me. I don't care. . . . I don't care about how many White or Coloured or Black people are in the school. As long as I have my friends I'm happy. . . . I don't see why I have to care about it . . . because I'm not like a racist or anything. . . . Actually when I was like six or seven till about the age of ten, I lived in the Eastern Cape and then . . . I went to like a Black school and then I learned to speak Xhosa and stuff like that. My best friends were Africans and I really miss them, because I don't know where they are.[48]

Le Roux says that he does not care about the changes in the school; his reason seems to be that he feels comfortable with the influx of students of a different race. If he were to care about these changes, he seems to think, he would be seen as a racist, so he preempts such accusations by using his personal history as proof that he is not a racist.

In regard to the girls at Malan, a very different picture emerges. They do not blame the new students for the changes they have experienced. In general, the girls are more eloquent in explaining how the school has changed and how sad that makes them. Of course, just like the boys, they wrestle with what the changes mean and how to deal with them, but they find different interpretations of the changes and different solutions for the problems they confront. Most remarkably, the girls never say they do not care; loss is named instead of denied. Their responses to the changes are twofold. On the one hand, the girls often admit that the changes have made them sad, thereby dealing with the emotional consequences of loss upfront. They will say openly that the changes are "actually sad" and that you "have to get used to it." On the other hand, they interpret the changes more positively, legitimizing and neutralizing them. For instance, they will stress the necessity of the changes in the school, or at least some of them. They say, "You just cannot have a White Afrikaans school anymore." They say change isn't that bad because "it is still a very good school" and "every school has its problems and ups and downs." Both strategies make them less judgmental in their causal attribution.

Unlearning racism is about emotions but also about the management of emotions. Desegregation and racial integration demand that the White working-class youth at the Malan school adjust, culturally and emotionally, but girls and boys manage their emotions very differently. Girls do so by confronting their loss. White working-class boys do something different. They do not deny the racial reality of the school—which would be color-blind racism—even though they sometimes avoid racial categories. They practice White identity politics to give new meaning to what it means to be a young White man, a process fuelled by their angry emotional response to their loss and precarious Whiteness.

Alex and Friends

Although Alex and his friends now hang out with only White friends, they did not grow up doing so. They were not born in one of Cape Town's relatively safe, all-White neighborhoods, and while growing up, many had some tough experiences with crime. Nor was their primary school all White; they were often part of mixed-race groups: for instance, Alex with his BMX bike riders. Moreover, much more than the girls at school, the boys hang out in the racially mixed neighborhoods surrounding the school. Every now and then they go to bars, including what they call "Coloured" bars. They drive themselves to their after-school jobs, where they work with Coloured clients, and spend time just exploring the streets. Alex and Le Roux, for example, work in a store that rents out suits and dresses to a largely Coloured clientele. They assist customers with finding the right suit or dress and in making personal adjustments. In other words, they have always hung out with Coloureds and continue to work with Coloured people, and until recently they were not known at school for racism or explicitly identifying as White.

The White identity politics of Alex and his friends represents a change for them too. Whiteness has only recently become a central concern in their peer group. Young people become aware of racial differences at a very early age, but during their teenage years their racial identity takes on a new meaning. In the Malan school, White boys see their fragile White privilege eroding and their working-class masculinity being challenged. They embrace a White, masculine, Afrikaner identity not because the school or their parents told them to do so—or socialized them into it—but because White identity politics allows them to reimagine themselves as the new victims at school.

If Alex and his friends are to be believed, the problem with racial relationships at school is not so much that they do not like the new Coloured boys in the school but rather the opposite: that the Coloureds do not like Alex and his friends. They say the prevailing social norm of antiracism gives the Coloured boys a new edge: they are able to discriminate against White boys, while White boys cannot discriminate against them. The White boys present themselves as a vulnerable White minority who are in need of and entitled to protection, that with the new composition of the school they are regularly challenged and even harassed:

> They [the Coloured students] don't want to hang with you. You are seen as a whitey. They blame us for apartheid. Now they don't want to be friends with us. . . . I know that. And you can't call them on their racial names, like the k-word, because then you are a racist. You keep your mouth shut and stay out of their way. Not that you are scared of them. It is a daily experience, but I'm used to it now. I've been here for four years now.[49]

The power has shifted, and Alex clearly voices his discontent with how the changing social norms in the school work to his disadvantage, both verbally and physically. He faces intimidation by Coloured boys and feels he has to keep a low profile. Recently, Alex and his friends had to move from their favorite place in the courtyard because a group of Coloured boys wanted their place. It is evident that he feels he is now in the disadvantaged position and that the Coloured boys, who often come from the rougher neighborhoods in Cape Town, have the upper hand. One way in which Alex and his friends try to continue to exercise their power is through controlling the dating behavior of the White girls in the school. The White girls hang out with Coloured students and attend their parties, but when one of the White girls kissed a Coloured boy, Alex and his friends could not stop pestering her about it, calling her a "Coloured" and telling her she mustn't kiss Coloured guys.

Racial integration at the Malan school challenges the White boys' budding masculinity. White working-class masculinity has always been performed through physical horseplay, and it is here that the White boys are losing to the Coloured boys. But masculinity is also judged through the lens of authenticity. In their race talk, Alex and his friends like to challenge the new hierarchy by subverting it, making accusations that Coloureds are "posers" and "not for real":

> There's a lot more people who think they can rule the school, students who think, yeah, they're the boss and nobody should mess with them and stuff and try and show that they're the man . . . and in the old day, like when in grade 8 everyone was getting along fine and everything, and now it's like . . . it's not like gangsterism and stuff. It's people that try to be gangsters . . . they try and act and be something that they're not. And maybe that's the problem with this school. It's people who try to be something that they're not and then it causes trouble in the school and stuff.[50]

Chris argues that the new boys only try to act like gangsters, thereby suggesting that they are poseurs and have not actually obtained power and the upper hand in school. They only like "to play" the boss, Alex and his friends say, imagining themselves to still be at the top of the racial and gender hierarchy despite many signs of distress.

Alex and his friends practice White identity politics to reposition themselves as a threatened White minority. Their interpretation of what is happening at their school dovetails with their assessment of what is happening in the rest of South Africa. In an assignment for his English class on the question whether he is happy with democracy, Alex wrote: "We all know that the majority of our country is the African [Black] people. . . . Democracy brought about many changes but very little improvement. The worst is still to come for my fellow White people and me."

Bridging the Racial Divide

The story most of the girls at Malan tell about race is remarkably different. In fact, it is not so much a story but a set of bridging arguments in their race talk to establish that they think everyone at school is the same. What ties their stories together is neither moral condemnation of the newcomers nor complaints about loss of power and racial inauthenticity; Instead, they argue for equality between students and for the value of sameness. They say that "you are who you are" and that whether or not they like you does not depend on what language you speak. They say that everyone has the same problems and talks about similar things, because on the inside "everybody is the same." They are aware of the prejudices—and they counter them. They say that "you shouldn't judge a book by its cover" and that they don't judge anyone by the color of their skin. Instead, they are positive about the value of diversity; they say they like to learn about other cultures. In regard to friendships, they express pragmatism:

> You can be White, Black, or Coloured. It really doesn't matter to me. It's about how you feel about the person. If we get along, if we click, then I'm going to be friends with you.[51]

Girls see their fellow Coloured students in a very different light than the boys. There is no hint of the jockeying for power and no sense of the loss of status or position; again and again, they stress sameness and equality. Some of the girls still express prejudice, but most of them say that they often feel uncomfortable with other people's prejudices. They sometimes feel that they have to police other people:

> I felt ashamed a number of times, by the way other people act or the way they talk about Blacks or Coloureds or Muslims or whichever different religions. Then I feel ashamed of them, because they don't want to try to get to know these people. . . . They're judging them before they get to know them. . . . It's like judging a book by its cover. I mean some of the plainest books can be the most interesting . . . and that sort of happens regularly, no matter what color your skin.[52]

White working-class girls celebrate diversity, despite having seen their White privileges eroded at the Malan school. They do so not from the safe position of being a powerful White majority, like the upper-class students at De la Rey, but by confronting their loss and forging durable interracial friendships. They accept integration, embrace multiculturalism, and bridge the racial divide. The boys' nostalgia for Afrikaner nationalism does not appeal to them because this history symbolizes the old patriarchy. They are not interested in the heroic Afrikaner past but praise how democracy has enshrined women's rights into law. As Fanie wrote in her essay on democracy: "Women are treated more as equals today than they were in the apartheid past."

The end of Afrikaner nationalism exposed its foundations not just in White supremacy but also in "male supremacy." As we have seen in previous chapters, young White working-class women have thus made the most progress in unlearning racism. Their struggle to unlearn racism is complemented by their gains through the rollback of patriarchal ideology. Post-apartheid South Africa provides them with a freedom and equality of opportunity that the White patriarchy never did. Young White women of all classes share a positive outlook toward the future. What is different, however, is that young White working-class women actually share their school with others and think of themselves as part of a multicultural South Africa without White or class privileges or claims to victimhood.

Sandra's and Alex's stories (as well as many others) push us to think about the challenges that young White South Africans continue to face in confronting the history of White supremacy and unlearning racism. The differences in their narratives reflect the differences in their schools. These findings prevent us from drawing any quick conclusions about hope in the new generation; their accounts reveal how unlearning racism involves much more than raising awareness about racial inequality and White privilege. Both Sandra and Alex are decidedly aware of their own White skins—this is something they share. What distinguishes them is how their self-described identities relate—or decidedly do not relate—to their racist ideologies. Sandra casts herself as a cosmopolitan urbanite, while Alex identifies as an Afrikaner nationalist.

Both Sandra and Alex, however, practice White identity politics. Unlearning racism at school is not a happy case of generational change: racism can be unlearned but can also be relearned. It is a mistake to see White youth as passively reproducing what is received from teachers or parents, but we must not assume that they automatically change for the better. White identity change turns out to be an unreliable indicator of unlearning racism. The focus of this book on peer culture to understand how race, class, and gender intersect at schools has revealed the importance of emotions and emotion management to unlearning and relearning racism. White identity politics, which accepts multiculturalism but positions White youth as the new victims, is driven by the way Sandra and Alex, respectively, poorly manage their feelings of White guilt and their White resentment.

Unlearning racism must take place not only in the head but also in the heart. Perhaps we do not want to center White feelings in our fight against racism, but if these feelings are ignored, we cannot address how racism reinvents itself successfully. Young White South Africans need to confront their negative feelings to truly unlearn racism. The young White working-class women at the Malan school offer some hope again, also in this regard. Unlike their peers, they have come to terms with what it feels like to lose some White privilege, to accept this loss and embrace multicultural South Africa with their heads and hearts.

Learning from South Africa

WHAT DOES A WHITE MINORITY at the tip of Africa have to teach us about racism and Whiteness? If one is interested in the American and European experience of racism, then South Africa does not demographically offer a mirror, but perhaps it does offer a lens, telling us something about the character of American racism. Racism is a global phenomenon, and mining the similarities and differences between specific places may provide great insight. I will leave the reader with some lessons that I have drawn from my time spent in South Africa. I will resist the urge to suggest any institutional changes for policy makers to follow. But I will draw some conclusions that are as concise as they are challenging. I will think beyond South Africa so as to make sense of what White identity politics might mean for unlearning racism in other countries.

The Meaning of Racism after the Death of White Nationalism

One of the ironic consequences of the end of apartheid was the uncertainty it bore with it about the meaning and usefulness of the concept of racism. Few thought that racism had disappeared, but many believed that systemic racial discrimination had ended. Scholars were dissatisfied with the politicization of racism by the government and found little analytical use for the term. Whiteness offered an alternative way of understanding racism and unlearning racism: to analyze whites as a racial group and study how their identity changed. Whiteness was a new word for a simple idea: that racism is not only about how whites think about others but also about how they think about themselves. Out of the study of Whiteness came the idea of White privilege. Despite critical debates about Whiteness, scholars united around the idea of White privilege, arguing that racism was not about prejudice but about unearned advantages. To

South Africans, Whiteness promised a new way of thinking about un-learning racism, and this was framed as a collective challenge. Scholars found Whiteness more useful than racism in understanding unlearning racism and showing White South Africans how to accept responsibility, integrate, and change their identities.

South Africa's White minority largely adopted this stance of change and took up the challenge to unlearn racism. They have gone from seeing themselves as a nationalist collective and an ethnic group that supports White supremacy to seeing themselves as a group that accepts a multi-cultural, integrated, and diverse South Africa. In the counterpublic, the White Afrikaans-speaking community has tried to come to terms with its past. The White business elite admitted guilt to the TRC, and their organization AHI looks more diverse, that is, it now includes members that they formerly excluded. The White working-class union rejected the idea of a color bar and White rights, instead making their political claims through the multicultural language of civil and minority rights; it accepted South Africa's liberal democracy and its constitutional frame-work. White South Africans living in gated communities and White youth at elite schools celebrate South Africa's cultural diversity and argue that their social environments embody the ideals of a new South Africa. Some would argue that these changes are mostly rhetorical, but they are sub-stantial nonetheless.

White South Africans appear to have unlearned racism, but to a large extent they have not. Coming to terms with the past and self-reflections on ancestral wrongs are not the same as unlearning racism: they are only a necessary first step of a longer process. The White business elite's cooperation with the process of transitional justice did constitute an ac-knowledgment of responsibility for apartheid, but it was also a costless admission that helped them reclaim legitimacy. Moreover, racial integra-tion at the elite business level served to tell a story about the past that whitewashed Afrikaner nationalists' history of White supremacy. As I found, racial integration could be accepted at work while being rejected at home. Indeed, racial prejudice can be unlearned while feelings of su-periority remain unshaken. Speaking the language of minority rights can mask a politics that preserves White privilege and power. Furthermore, the celebration of diversity and multiculturalism by White youth can coexist with White privilege and new forms of segregation. As much as this study has documented the changes that have taken place, it has also outlined the limits of White South Africans thinking about unlearning racism and their practice of it. And it has exposed something else: Whiteness can no longer hide behind nationalism.

White nationalism is dead. In South Africa, White people's dreams of a White nation are over. During apartheid, South African politics had been a rivalry between Afrikaner nationalism and African nationalism, and one could not understand South Africa except in terms of nationalism. After apartheid, scholars argued that trying to understand the country through the lens of White nationalism no longer made sense; in the new multiracial democracy, the White minority is just one of many. Whiteness became marked and showed its naked face; the Whiteness of Afrikaner nationalism became visible together with its class and gender faultlines. None was more noticeable than Afrikaner men who decry their visibility by presenting themselves as the new victims in post-apartheid South Africa. The death of White nationalism has not meant the death of White privilege—it has instead made it patently discernible.

As Whiteness was exposed, South Africans concluded that racism would become less important after apartheid. Despite continued racial inequality, Marxist scholars argued that racial apartheid had changed to class apartheid. Notwithstanding the continuing omnipresence of racial identities, liberals promoted unlearning race over unlearning racism, while scholars abandoned the analysis of racism altogether. Although some unlearning of racism has taken place, and Whiteness is more visible, the conclusion that racism is no longer relevant seems premature at best.

Racism continues to be at the heart of post-apartheid public debate, and racial inequality remains very high. Despite twenty-five years of democracy, South Africa remains the most economically unequal country in the world along racial fault lines.[1] One in three Black South Africans was unemployed in 2017, while among White South Africans the rate was one in ten. On average, Black South Africans make five times less than White South Africans. Racial inequality also means less access to essential public services, like electricity and water.[2] More than half of South

Africa's population lives in poverty, while only a few thousand White households do so.[3] Some say that apartheid has essentially persisted in economic form, but what they mean is that racial inequality remains an undeniable fact of South African life.

This is not where South Africans thought they would be after ending apartheid. The end of racism should not go hand in hand with the continuation of racial inequality. Multiracial democracy seemed a far more desirable politics than white nationalism—so how did South Africans get to this place?

They got here because White South Africans have adapted their political strategy to multiracialism and the politics of identity. The end of White supremacy and White nationalism forced White South Africans to rethink racism. It made the White minority—acutely aware of the pressure to unlearn racism—change their politics so they could newly defend their interests. The irony of South Africa's idea of unlearning racism is that the White minority has unlearned the old racism but at the same time learned a new racism: a politics based on a visible Whiteness that has co-opted minority rights and applied them to the new circumstances of a multicultural South African polity where racial identities are the key to political power. This has made racism not necessarily worse but more confounding and more difficult to address.

South Africa is also here because of one of the key features of South African exceptionalism: nonracialism. This ideology has remained popular among South Africans as a way to celebrate the multicultural and diverse character of their society. Nevertheless, both the ANC and the opposition have struggled to fulfill the promise of nonracialism, albeit for different reasons. On the one hand, the government's program of racial redress cannot easily be connected with nonracialism. On the other hand, the opposition, specifically the DA, has co-opted it to mean color blindness. South African academics rushed to unlearn race before they had unlearned racism. Nonracialism may be cherished as having been a brilliant antiracist strategy for confronting the apartheid years, but its legacy should be celebrated through innovation. Considering the struggle to define racism, the unfinished business of unlearning racism, and the continuation of racial inequality, we are left to wonder about South Africa's racial progress.

The Trick of Racism: The Global Rise of White Identity Politics

Racism reinvents itself by co-opting and misappropriating antiracist strategies. In South Africa in the 1950s, Afrikaner nationalists used Franz Boas's theory of cultural relativism to justify apartheid based on cultural differences. In the United States in the 1970s, conservative Republicans co-opted Martin Luther King Jr.'s arguments against judgments based on skin color to profess color blindness and object to race-based remedies for historical injustice and affirmative action. In France in the 1980s, the National Front seized immigrant groups' demands for the recognition of cultural differences to argue that European culture was also "different" and therefore incompatible with immigrant cultures. In the United Kingdom in the 1990s, British nationalists relabeled White British people as indigenous to claim special rights for the majority. No matter the context, racism takes new forms; the trick is that those forms always resemble antiracism.

The new racism in South Africa co-opts minority rights and reimagines identity politics for the benefit of White people. I call this White identity politics. After 2000, White South Africa embraced the visibility of Whiteness to claim special rights for their group. They no longer denied the relevance of race or coded their race talk, nor did they object to identity politics. Instead, they embraced identity politics to claim "racial interests" that are framed as different from racism. The White elite and populists both promote multiculturalism and minority rights; racial inequality remains hidden. Meanwhile, assimilation is turned on its head: it is now the White group who demand protection. The political goal of practitioners of White identity politics is to make White identity legitimate again, at a time when Whiteness has become synonymous with racism. By replacing White nationalism with White identity politics, a move to achieve the normalization of Whiteness, Whiteness seems reasonable again and not a racist ideology defending power and privilege as critical Whiteness scholars originally intended. South Africa has long been a bellwether for race relationships in the world, and it still is today.

Few foresaw the rise of White identity politics, particularly in the United States. At the beginning of the twentieth century, the United States saw the expansion of the White racial category to include Irish, Jewish, and Italian immigrants; many predicted demographic trends would lead to another expansion of the White racial category at the beginning of the twenty-first century. The current White majority is set to become a demographic minority by 2042. Many thought that the Republican Party, given its majority White base, would be forced to expand the category of Whiteness and embrace Asians and Latinos as "honorary whites" to maintain its political viability.[4] But my analysis suggests that White identity politics offers them an alternative political strategy to hold on to power.

In retrospect, White identity politics has long been in the making, masking itself by its opposition to identity politics. The silent majority, which President Richard Nixon spoke about in 1969, was said to be a "White backlash" against the African American and women's liberation movements. However, identity politics was always about the meaning of Whiteness and masculinity, as well as Blackness and femininity. In the 1970s, John Updike wrote that "being a White man is no picnic either" to highlight how White masculinity had become marked after the sixties.[5] The character Archie Bunker from the TV sitcom *All in the Family* turned the angry White male into a cultural icon. During the 1980s, President Ronald Reagan cultivated the concept of "reverse discrimination," which depicted affirmative action as anti-White racism and White men as victims. Reagan successfully tied the White working class to the Republic Party.[6] In the 1990s, White identity politics openly surfaced in the conservative campaign against affirmative action at the University of California: from the explicit use in the media of "angry White men" to the institutionalization of White men as victims and the misappropriation of civil rights language.[7] The modern conservative movement is often depicted as a White backlash against the civil rights movement, but White backlash is too simple a term for the new racist politics.

White identity politics is the successor of color-blind racism. The new visibility of Whiteness enables a symbolic re-empowerment of White people. Whereas color-blind racism was a rearticulation of liberalism and individual rights, White identity politics is a rearticulation of identity politics and group rights. White identity politics does not rest on abstract liberalism, as color-blind racism does. According to Bonilla-Silva, abstract liberalism means that White people support ideas such as "equal oppor-tunity" but oppose "concrete" proposals to reduce inequality.[8] White identity politics promotes an abstract expression of identity politics along with a perversion of multiculturalism. It is abstract because its politics is not rooted in the oppression of White identity: the language of abstract identity politics—"whites also have interests"; "White people are just an-other group"—allows White people to sound reasonable and just while masking how they continue to accrue power, wealth, and privilege in the United States through systems that exploit and unfairly disadvantage oth-ers. White identity politics does not rely on cultural racism, as color-blind racism did. It is not constructed around essentialist cultural differences but around White favoritism. Advantages that White people provide to other White people are the primary mechanism by which racial inequal-ity is reproduced. White identity politics presents itself in the language of love rather than hate; its proponents rhetorically ask: "What is wrong with liking your own group and why can't I stand up for my own kind?"

White identity politics in the United States has not completely over-taken color-blind racism, but it has gained prominence as America tran-sitions away from White nationalism.

The practitioners of color-blind racism and White identity politics both deny that discrimination remains a central factor affecting minorities. But White identity politics makes racism harmless by defining it in extremely narrow terms, as the "supreme" evil. It strategically acknowledges that racism exists and affirms that it is wrong, but at the same time it raises the bar extremely high for who can be called a racist, supposedly because it is so evil. As a consequence, no White person is a racist. Practitioners of White identity politics assert that racial equality has been achieved be-cause only this assertion allows them to claim a White identity without being regarded as racist. They claim that being White merely represents their identity through language and action, something other racially de-fined groups have always done. In order for White identity politics to work, Whiteness needs to be normalized—an illusion that being White is no different than belonging to any other racial group in the United States.

In Europe, White identity politics has emerged as an explicit and maybe even more successful political strategy than in the United States. In the United Kingdom, the media and academia present "White self-interests" and "White grievances" as legitimate political claims not rooted in racism. In contrast to the United States, Whiteness in Europe is no longer euphemistically framed in political terms as the "silent majority," "Middle America," or "left behinds." Instead, White identity politics tries to sell us openly "racial self-interest" without racism. In *White Shift*, Canadian sociologist Eric Kaufmann uses new demographic data to make an old racist argument: that White people will no longer be the majority in their historic "homelands" such as the United Kingdom.[9] The problem with this argument is that it relies on a static and therefore racist idea of who is White. Kaufmann's thesis on White demographic decline assumes that we know who is White or must remain White. He normalizes people's attachment to White identity instead of acknowledging how White identity historically has been the means through which racism was promoted. Nonetheless, Kaufman sets up his argument for White identity politics as explicitly antiracist. He argues that because some people are irredeemably racist, we need to stop them from violence by mainstreaming his brand of "mildly" racist politics that does not challenge White grievances but rather wants to validate them. In fact, Kaufman calls for more tolerance for those who want to express pride in their Whiteness.

In the Netherlands, practitioners of White identity politics also use demographic anxieties. In *Minderheid in Eigen Land* (Minority in your own country), politician Martin Bosma presents a right-wing revisionist history of South Africa, in which he focuses solely on the ANC's use of violence and Dutch left-wing support of the anti-apartheid struggle, without exploring White supremacy and White nationalism. Bosma, the former right-hand man of Freedom Party leader Geert Wilders, used South Africa as a warning for White Dutch people that they will become a minority in their own country. Dutch sociologist Ruud Koopmans went so far as to propose "majority rights" to practice his version of White identity politics.[10] Warnings about a new White minority in the Netherlands are hard to take seriously in a country where almost 90 percent of the population considers themselves to be White. Koopmans therefore applies the logic of identity politics in another way: by adopting minorities' call for group rights for an unspecified "majority," a term that all too easily reads as a White majority.[11]

While the global triumph of identity politics made Whiteness visible in liberal democracies, it has also made White identity politics possible. Liberal democracy was a key condition for the emergence of identity politics. The Black feminists of the Combahee River Collective in 1982 coined the term "identity politics"—"the most profound and potentially most radical politics come directly out of our own identity"—and this politics has allowed all kinds of previously marginalized groups to mobilize against the White polity.[12] The Black freedom struggle, second-wave feminism, and LGBTQ liberation in the United States have illuminated our understanding of how liberal democracy is historically rooted in White supremacy. Groups who practice identity politics have argued that the neutral citizen of liberal democracy has a default identity that is implicitly and explicitly coded as being White, male, middle-class, and heterosexual. Whiteness scholars have built on identity politics to expose the invisibility, normativity, and universality of Whiteness in Western societies. Despite the broad scope of political movements under the umbrella of identity politics, few predicted the emergence of White identity politics. Once these groups had made Whiteness visible, it could no longer hide within White nationalism. White identity politics succeeded White nationalism precisely because marginalized groups were so successful in marking Whiteness and making it noticeable. This is the warning of South Africa.

The Identity Politics Conundrum: The Prospect of Unlearning Racism

The rise of White identity politics presents us with a challenge when it comes to unlearning racism. The choice to confront Whiteness has long been framed as somewhere between the abolishing of Whiteness and reforming White identity.[13] One problem with the first solution is that Whiteness as an ideology is always about more than privilege and socioeconomic status. As shown in this book, it involves history, skin color, culture, ethnicity, language, and place. White people might not have a discrete, "positive" content for their racial identities, but Whiteness certainly has meaning.[14] The call to abolish Whiteness also misconstrues the problem, because what is needed is not direct abolishment but a process that disentangles the many historical threads between Whiteness and culture, ethnicity, and language through critique and introspection. This is a process South Africans have embarked on but have yet to complete. The risk involved in this process is clear: one result of disentangling Whiteness from nationalism is the birth of White identity politics. It is often out of the battle against the old racism that a new racism emerges.

The more attractive option seems to be to create a positive, proud, and attractive antiracist White identity and reimagine Whiteness in a nonracist way, to substitute a "good" antiracist Whiteness for the old "bad" racist version. However, this solution implies that racism only stems primarily from misunderstanding and ignorance, yet unlearning racism is also about confronting interests and not just changing minds. Because people have a possessive investment in Whiteness (it pays for people to stay White because Whiteness means privilege), reforming Whiteness cannot be the solution. Encouraging a reimagined sense of Whiteness is unlikely to promote a more equitable or harmonious social order.

White identity politics allows White people to continue their possessive investment in Whiteness because it normalizes White advocacy groups and erases historical oppression, injustice, and inequality. Paradoxically, it presents White people as without Whiteness, a powerful ideology and privileged identity. It undermines the ideal of "White without Whiteness" by claiming to already embody it. Those who employ White identity politics represent themselves as Whites without Whiteness, a people without history, because they claim to be just like other groups. Practitioners of White identity politics have found a way to claim that Whiteness has changed without changing it. It is the politics used to defend White interests that has changed. White people are using White identity politics and the new visibility of Whiteness to empower themselves.

What must we do if neither the abolishment of Whiteness nor its reform is appealing? This is the conundrum of unlearning racism. It seems we are back to square one, where unlearning racism may be impossible without unlearning race. However, this book demonstrates that the opposite is also true: we cannot unlearn race without unlearning racism.

Utopian visions about unlearning race too often overlook the reality of racism and its dynamic of continuously reinventing itself. Fantasies about unlearning race are harmful if we do not first address unlearning racism, because we are left without the tools to address and remedy racial inequality.

Raising the question whether we can unlearn racism has exposed why it is so difficult in the first place: racism continually takes different forms. Despite this, I believe that my detailed description of White identity politics in South Africa provides new tools with which we can continue the fight against racism. Exposing the rise of White identity politics can help us to challenge claims about White people having become "just like any other group." Arguments that we are "Whites without Whiteness" must be treated with suspicion and are often simply false. Portrayals of White people as the new victims must be thoroughly deconstructed and empirically appraised. White identity politics is impossible without the assertion of victimhood. If Whites cannot claim they are oppressed or treated unjustly, it is impossible to make political claims. The co-opting of identity politics by White people presents a new challenge and gives us a reason to rethink identity politics from the perspective of its success.

We must remember that antiracism is an attitude rather than an identity. To the question "Can we unlearn racism?" my answer will always be yes. The lesson of this book, however, is that the real work begins after the "yes." To unlearn racism on an individual level requires a degree of faith in the feasibility of that outcome, but beyond that, what is needed is a commitment to the collective process—a commitment of time and energy; a commitment to steady, methodical progress; and the simultaneous commitment of those around you. Success is by no means assured and undoubtedly difficult.

But who said hope is supposed to be easy?

Methodological and Theoretical Considerations

I CAN'T REMEMBER THE EXACT MOMENT it dawned on me that writing about Whiteness in South Africa, this ideology of racial superiority and privilege, mostly on the part of those who call themselves White, poses a fundamental problem for the ethnographer. The art of ethnography rests on the assumption that people's understanding of themselves in their own terms must be foregrounded in the analysis of their lives. Ethnographers habitually align themselves, methodologically if not always ideologically, with the common sense of the common people. What if, however, at the heart of this "common sense" are the many distortions, lies, and false assumptions about race that three centuries of White supremacy have left behind? White supremacy and racism have profoundly shaped South Africa's past. This problem goes beyond just the opportunities and pitfalls of ethnography. What I needed to address—before anything else—was how to overcome the tension between the analysis of Whiteness through the study of White South Africans in their own words and the need to deconstruct the myths at the heart of Whiteness. Or to state the problem in another way: how to be a good ethnographer and a good race scholar at the same time.

In this study, I started with understanding how White South Africans themselves see the world and to document their own accounts of life after apartheid. I employ the ethnographic method that is committed to deep immersion in the everyday life practices of other people as a means of learning, knowing, and accurately representing them and their view of the world. Such an approach highlights the agency of people—their independent actions and free choices. However, ethnographers of Whiteness must critically engage with people's understanding of the world. They must compare and contrast people's views with data obtained through other methods, such as historical records and documents. Only then can they critically examine whether and how White people's changing stories in the aftermath of apartheid—about themselves, their history, and their place in the world—still remain rooted in an ideology of Whiteness, a set of ideas and ideals that help to elide, distort, and deny the power and privilege of White people and South Africa's racial reality and racist history. In order to understand how Whiteness as an ideology is transforming in South Africa, a critical ethnographic approach is necessary.

When I arrived in South Africa in 2007, I wanted to chart White South Africa's racial odyssey after apartheid. Because my aim was to understand how the crisis of Whiteness impinged on people's intimate lives, I relied on intensive personal interviews. At the heart of this book is a body of interviews I conducted with over 160 White South Africans, the majority of which were in Afrikaans and on average lasted one-and-a-half hours. All of the interviews were held between January 2007 and February 2010. I spent six months, from January to June 2007, doing ethnographic fieldwork in two schools in Cape Town and another six months, from January to July 2008, living in a gated community and interning with the Solidarity Movement. All but a few of the quotations in this book are from interviews with White South Africans, recorded on tape or, if preferred, in writing at the time. With the help of others, I have translated the interviews into English. In the first part of the book, Chapters 1–4, all of the interview quotations use the actual names of the interviewees, as these chapters concern public debates and representatives of organizations functioning in the public sphere. In Chapters 5–7, I use pseudonyms for the interviewees in order to abide by the ethical imperatives of confidentiality and to respect the privacy that White South Africans relinquished on a personal basis when they took me into their world.

During my initial fieldwork among White South Africans, I spent much of my analysis parsing the differences and conflicts between White Afrikaans-speaking and White English-speaking South Africans, as this was what White South Africans themselves emphasized. As American race scholar Tiffany Willoughby-Herard argues, however, the analysis of White supremacy and Whiteness in South Africa has for too long been hampered by focusing on the intrawhite rivalry between Afrikaners and

English South Africans rather than excavating the White supremacist assumptions that unite both White groups.[1] South African sociologist Zina Magubane similarly warns against adopting the analytical categories and concepts that rule South Africa's public discourse if we want to critically engage with the issues of White power and privilege.[2] This study moves beyond the ethnic lens to focus squarely on Whiteness. Deeply inspired by Melissa Steyn's *Whiteness Just Isn't What It Used to Be*, I present a number of new analytical concepts, such as White identity politics, to upend the terms prevalent in South Africa's public discourse and introduce a new critical vocabulary.[3]

My study principally concerns the country of South Africa, but this country also provides a good starting point for critically engaging with the methodological assumptions prevalent in the growing field of sociology that studies right-wing political parties, conservative movements, populism, and nationalism in the West. This book poses a challenge to those who hold that we need to understand the Trump supporter and Brexit voter, despite their racism, on their own terms. American sociologist Arlie Hochschild speaks of the need as researchers to climb the "empathy wall" to truly understand people who have feelings and beliefs that differ from our own.[4] Supporters of racist ideologies must indeed not be denied agency and the capacity to act and think on their own. As early as 1971, American psychiatrist Robert Coles observed that all people, even racists, "deserve to be described with a vocabulary that does not dismiss them all as brainwashed dupes, but takes into consideration their ability to look into their minds analytically and examine their own society critically."[5] It is one thing to stop depicting White people as unthinking mouthpieces of a racist ideology. It is quite another thing, however, to sacrifice our abilities as sociologists to critically analyze Whiteness and racism as ideologies and overlook the centrality of race to ideologies of populism and nationalism.

Understanding White people on their own terms is not unimportant, but the demand for empathy too often decenters Whiteness and leaves White subjects' power and privilege unexamined. American sociologists Tufuku Zuberi and Eduardo Bonilla-Silva warn against methodological approaches to the study of racism that confirm White racial "common sense."[6] Specifically, they critique survey researchers who analyze racial phenomena as individual attitudes instead of racial ideologies. Ethnographers of Whiteness face methodological challenges that are both similar and different. First, White racial common sense tends to decenter Whiteness; yet in order to understand the problem of unlearning racism, Whiteness must be analytically centered. Second, sociologists must not limit themselves to the (historical) study of Whiteness and racism as social constructions but acknowledge how Whiteness and racism as ideologies actively construct—that they are productive in the present.[7] In the past, sociologists and historians demonstrated how White supremacy and Afrikaner nationalism in South Africa produced powerful historical myths and imagined its national space as a "White country." There is no reason to assume Whiteness has lost all of its power to produce new histories and imagined spaces in the present. My ethnography specifically explores and deconstructs contemporary Whiteness.

The ethnographic method is a powerful tool for making visible how South Africa's racist past lives on in the present. Its focus on the act of interpretation opens up people's cultural and racial views to critical scrutiny.[8] Ethnographers have long studied how people's meaning-making and cultural practices are geographically and historically specific. They highlight the act of interpretation—what people see and do not see, which explanations they use and do not use, what matters to them or does not matter—to understand how people give meaning to their world. Ethnography emphasizes social interactions, the importance of time and place, and material support for maintaining identities and ideologies. It also examines how people give racial meaning to the world around them in talk and actions. It can make the implicit racial aspects of White people's talk and actions explicit, enabling us to trace the seemingly nonracial back to racist ideological constructs. My analyses of people's acts of interpretation—as well as my specific focus on Whiteness—may surprise and even dismay some White South Africans, but the words themselves are quoted extensively and verbatim in this ethnography.

Through my critical attention to the interpretive work of my ethnographic subjects, I make people's ideological work legible and tangible. Ethnography must not naïvely rely on people's opinions about their world but carefully analyze their acts of interpretation to trace how their meaning-making practices are connected to existing power structures, status struggles, and material conditions,[9] thus exposing how people's Whiteness is maintained discursively and materially. Precisely because I understand Whiteness to be rooted in time and place—Whiteness is not situated somewhere metaphysical—the ethnographic approach exposes variations. My methodology provides a nuanced understanding of the ideology of Whiteness, which is coherent but not applied by everyone everywhere in the same way.

Ethnographers have been reluctant to address Whiteness and racism as ideologies.[10] Some social scientists, like Canadian sociologist Michèle Lamont, prefer to steer away from an ideological approach because in their view the study of race alone is not sufficient to explain how and why race matters.[11] Thinking in terms of race, sociologists like Lamont stress, must not obscure how race intersects with nation, ethnicity, class, and gender. They argue that an ideological approach flattens our understanding of how race works in reality.[12] These sociologists emphasize the complexity and contradictory workings of culture and warn against the risks of overdetermination if we understand race as an ideological discourse. But perhaps the larger problem in sociology has been that sociological thinking in terms of nationalism, ethnicity, class, and culture has discounted the importance of race and racism. This is what race scholars have long argued.[13] My approach also suggests that we do not have to decenter race to analyze it in conjunction with other social forces. Ethnographers of Whiteness have mainly focused on people's different racial sensibilities and the various meanings of Whiteness to various people. My approach also appreciates the diffuse range of signifying practices and the subtle interplay between meaning-making practices and societal structures. I demonstrate the breadth, depth, and variety in the ways in which Whiteness pervades society's structures and people's consciousness—even their bodies. This does not mean, however, that we have to give up on studying Whiteness as an ideology.

My systematic analysis of differently situated groups of White South Africans allows for conflicting interpretations and a range of positions within the White community, but it also works toward understanding

Whiteness as a single ideological construct. Through my selection of six case studies, I validate the variety of people's racial explanations for how the world works and their different levels of awareness. The workings of Whiteness are varied but also patterned and regularly shaped by class, gender, and generation. The incorporation of a variety of different social contexts enables me to identify both site-specific phenomena and racial processes that transcend a single locale. My ethnographic sensitivity to the heterogeneity of Whiteness does not preclude a careful analysis of how different groups of White South Africans apply similar strategies, albeit in different ways, to promote Whiteness as an ideology. Indeed, I highlight how Whiteness works similarly among groups in different contexts. Whiteness, I conclude, is a dynamic but shared ideology among White South Africans.

In this ethnography, I also carefully explore White emotions. Some social scientists have replaced the focus on racial ideology with an approach that centers on the politics of emotions.[14] Race scholars have long emphasized the centrality of emotions to the study of race, but scholars such as American historian Carol Anderson and Whiteness scholar Robin DiAngelo have also warned against racism shaping our interpretations of emotions in politics.[15] A legitimate focus on emotions must not replace the focus on Whiteness as an ideology. It is here where my approach again diverges from Hochschild's, whose otherwise laudable methodological emphasis on emotions decenters, if not completely replaces, the analysis of Whiteness and racism. By contrast, my ethnographic approach uses the lens of Whiteness to analyze how intimately ideological, identity, and emotional concerns are connected, and how Whiteness as a felt ideology is rooted in history and place. In fact, we cannot analyze what I call White embodiment—the relationship between Whiteness and feelings—outside of the historical and spatial context. I explore people's emotions in part to show how Whiteness as an ideology is embodied but also rooted in time and place.

As an ethnographer of Whiteness, I want to make the reader feel the politics of Whiteness while providing a critical historical and geographical perspective, to show how White South Africans live after apartheid and how Whiteness continues to be anchored in history and rooted in place.

One inspiration for this perspective was the American race scholars and historians who documented how after the civil rights movement White Americans shifted from a White supremacist to a color-blind reading of America's racist history.[16] Color-blind racism became the racial ideology through which the history of Whiteness in America was remade,[17] allowing White Americans to deny that White privilege played a central role in the fortunes of White Americans. Informed by this perspective, I focus on how White South Africans use historical knowledge in their stories. My analysis suggests that they have moved beyond color blindness. They practice White identity politics—a politics that does not deny South Africa's racist past but ideologically repurposes it to normalize Whiteness. Another inspiration for me was American ethnographers of White communities in the United States. Race scholars have long emphasized the connection between racism and place: racial hierarchies mean spatial hierarchies.[18] Ethnographers have also long been concerned with people's racialized understanding of place but have been reluctant to connect it to racism.[19] Their reluctance, I show in this book, isn't warranted. Ethnographers of Whiteness are well placed to provide a nuanced and situational account of racism and Whiteness as ideologies. Racism is always shaped by people's social and physical location in space. Ethnographers correctly emphasize the need to take White people's location vis-à-vis the racial other into account, both socially and physically, but must also analyze how Whiteness and racism as ideologies always actively construct places and spaces. During apartheid, South Africa's White supremacist regime created homelands, townships, and many other segregated spaces. And Whiteness after apartheid continues to construct places and spaces.

As an outsider to South Africa, I was wary of the lure of becoming a heroic researcher who travels to the "heart of Whiteness" to come back to tell the tale,[20] a trope that builds on the false idea that racism is always located elsewhere. My methodological choice of a multi-sited ethnography among different groups of White Afrikaans-speaking South Africans was also intended to avoid the appearance of a journey to the heart of Whiteness.[21] Whiteness in South Africa was never confined to a specific place. But after apartheid it seemed especially important to analyze how Whiteness intersected with class, gender, and generations in different institutional spaces and to situate my research subjects' stories in the broader institutional context of racial inequality. A multi-sited ethnography approach helped me to map the varieties of Whiteness despite the ethnographic advantages of analyzing Whiteness in a specific location, as well as to avoid giving the impression of Whiteness as being a single blanket hanging over the White community in South Africa. This also means that my approach relies more on ethnographic interviews than on observations, focusing less on discrepancies between attitudes and behavior and more on the similarities and differences in ideology. Ultimately, my ethnographic journey to White South Africa taught me as much about Whiteness in South Africa as it did about the future of Whiteness in the United States.

Whiteness matters in South Africa because how White South Africans understand themselves—their history and position in contemporary society—is closely connected to how they see others and how they exercise power over others. To analyze unlearning racism as a social process is not about measuring whether people are more or less racist but rather analyzing how Whiteness as an ideology after apartheid continues to operate. I wanted to know whether and how Whiteness is transformed, whether and how White power and privilege continued to be defended, and what it meant to lose Whiteness. In the end, my methodological approach focuses on how the cultural process of giving racial meanings is ideologically translated to the defense of White privilege and the exercise of power. This approach uses Whiteness as a conceptual lens to theorize racism and unlearning racism. Whiteness theory emerged out of the study of racism and the dissatisfaction with both individual and institutional approaches to the analysis of racism. It offers a new and promising way to understand unlearning racism.

Notes

Preface

1. Crapanzano 1985.
2. Crapanzano 1985, xiii.
3. Essed 1991.
4. Fredrickson 2002, 152.
5. Fields and Fields 2012.

Chapter 1: White without Whiteness

1. Barack Obama, Twitter, August 12, 2017, 8:06 p.m., //twitter.com/ BarackObama/status/896523232098078720.
2. It attracted more than 3.3 million likes and 1.3 million retweets.
3. It wasn't the first time that Obama had turned to South Africa as an alternate model of race relations. At Mandela's memorial in 2013, Obama drew a parallel between the United States and Mandela's country and argued, "South Africa shows us we can change." Five years later, at a lecture that marked Mandela's one hundredth birthday, Obama said that the movement he had led had come to signify something beyond South Africa: "the possibility of a moral transformation in the conduct of human affairs." See Barack Obama, "Speech at Nelson Mandela's memorial" (speech, Johannesburg [SA], December 10, 2013), CNN, https://www.cnn.com/2013/12/10/politics/mandela-obama-remarks/ index.html; and also Barack Obama, "The Nelson Mandela Annual Lecture" (speech, Johannesburg [SA], July 17, 2018), National Public Radio, https://www. npr.org/2018/07/17/629862434/transcript-obamas-speech-at-the-2018-nelson-mandela-annual-lecture.
4. Mandela 1995, 512.
5. Derrida 1985.
6. Van den Berghe 1967, 18.
7. Wolpe 1972, 451; Adam 1971, 79.
8. Seekings and Nattrass 2008, 254.
9. Christopher 2001.
10. Turok 1994.
11. Bill Keller, "Mandela Shares Nobel Accolade with De Klerk," *New York Times*, October 16, 1993.

12. TRC 1997.

13. Adorno 1959; 2010.

14. South African educationalist Jonathan Jansen is probably the most influential public intellectual working in this tradition. In *Knowledge in the Blood: Confronting Race and the Apartheid Past*, he provocatively draws on German research on second-generation Holocaust survivors to analyze how racial knowledge in South African is passed on between different generations of White South Africans, who are often seen as perpetrators (Jansen 2009).

15. Hacker 1993.

16. In 2000, he held the first Steve Biko Memorial Lecture: "'Iph' Indlela? Finding Our Way into the Future." *Iph'indlehla* is a phrase in the South African language Xhosa that means, "Where is the way?"

17. Krog 1999.

18. In an interview, Krog credits Ndebele's Steve Biko lecture, which "helped a lot of us to see that there is a difference between being white and Whiteness. The latter word refers to a construct, a thing that you make." Krog qtd. in Sean OToole, "Burden of Whiteness," Mail & Guardian, April 5, 2004.

19. Krog 2003,128–29.

20. Krog 2009, 93.

21. It is unlikely that Morrison would agree with Krog. She writes: "It is no accident and no mistake that immigrant populations (and much immigrant literature) understood their Americanness as an opposition to the resident Black population. Race in fact now functions as a metaphor so necessary to the construction of Americanness that it rivals the old pseudo-scientific and class-informed racisms whose dynamics we are more used to deciphering. . . . Deep within the word 'American' is its association with race. To identify someone as South African is to say very little; we need the adjective 'White' or 'black' or 'colored' to make our meaning clear. In this country, it is quite the reverse. American means white" (Morrison 1992, 46–47).

22. By the time the ANC adopted "nonracialism" in the mid-1950s, various alliances between Black and White anti-apartheid activists outside of the ANC had been using the term to argue that race should not be a basis for governing. The ANC adopted nonracialism as a strategic response to Afrikaner nationalist descriptions of apartheid as being "racialist" instead of explicitly racist (Rassool 2019, 370).

23. MacDonald 2013.

24. Dubow 1992.

25. Everatt 2009.

26. Bass et al. 2012.

27. In 1993 its GINI index was 59.3; in 2014 it had grown to 63.

28. R300,000 for Whites versus R70,000 for Africans (UNU-WIDER 2019).

29. Fanon 1967.

30. Harris 1993.

31. Melissa Steyn, for example, in her brilliant study of Whiteness after apartheid hardly mentions the word "racism"; the word doesn't even have an entry in her book's subject index (Steyn 2001).

32. Crenshaw and Race 1988.

33. Jung 2000; Minow 1998; Wilson 2001.

34. The definition is in the Black Economic Empowerment Act of 2003, which states that "Black people" is a generic term meaning Black Africans, Coloureds, and Indians and includes provisions to ensure that they must have been South African citizens prior to 1994.

35. Telles 2004.

36. DeGloma 2014.

37. hooks 1984.

38. In South Africa, Steven Otter's *Khayelitsha: Umlungu in a Township* is an example of this genre. Otter writes about moving to Cape Town's township Khayelitsha and how he as a White man—*umlungu* in Zulu—comes to newly understand his Whiteness and the meaning of community (Otter 2012).

39. Warren 2010.

40. White nationalism is often defined narrowly as a type of nationalism that explicitly espouses the belief that White people are a superior race. However, I understand it more broadly as the historical intertwinement of nationalism, Whiteness, and racism dominant in the United States and Europe.

41. Marx 1997.

42. Ashforth 1990.

43. For a study on divorce and marriage dissolution (Cronjé 1933).

44. In books such as *'N Tuiste vir die nageslag* (A home for the future generation; 1945) and *Regverdige rasse-apartheid* (Just racial segregation; 1947), Cronjé provided the crude but vibrant theoretical justification for apartheid (Cronjé 1945; 1947; Cronjé and Venter 1958). The South African politician and Afrikaner Nationalist, D. F. Malan, who also received his PhD in the Netherlands, drew heavily on Cronjé's thinking in the election speeches that made him the first apartheid president in 1948.

45. Verwoerd got his PhD at Stellenbosch University in 1923 for his dissertation "The Blunting of Emotions." He became a professor of sociology in 1932.

46. In the late 1920s, Verwoerd traveled through the United States for a study tour. At a time when American sociologists proclaimed the innate intellectual differences between the White and Black races, based on "scientific" IQ scores, Verwoerd explicitly rejected these ideas (R. Miller 1993).

47. Bottomley 2017.

48. Bell 2000; Magubane 2008.

49. Willoughby-Herard 2015.

50. Tayler 1992.

51. Dubow 2001.

52. Posel 1991.

53. Cronjé and Venter 1958; see also Van der Westhuizen 2017.

54. Roos 2015.

55. But see DiAngelo 2018; Kendi 2019.

56. Horowitz 1992; Sparks 1996; Gevisser 1996; Ramphele 2008.

57. The prominent South African sociologist Neville Alexander argues in *An Ordinary Country: Issues in the Transition from Apartheid to Democracy* that South Africa remains a deeply divided society but that class now determines the divisions. Among South African scholars who were part of the anti-apartheid struggle, such as Alexander, Marxism has long been popular. They tend to emphasize the importance of class struggle over race in explaining apartheid and White supremacy in South Africa. After apartheid, many tend to emphasize how the country's inequality is growing along class lines (Alexander 2003, 16).

58. Also notable are book titles that express a defensive posture when it comes to the importance of race matters, such as a volume edited by Xolela Mangcu, *The Colour of Our Future: Does Race Still Matter in Post-apartheid South Africa?* (2015), and American political scientist Michael MacDonald's *Why Race Matters in South Africa* (2006).

59. Jung 2000; Wasserman and Jacobs 2003; Distiller and Steyn 2004.

60. Durrheim, Mtose, and Brown 2011.

61. Mangcu 2012.

62. In *Realizing the Dream: Unlearning the Logic of Race in the South African School*, educationalist Crain Soudien critiques how race is used to reiterate the naturalness of the category and how unlearning this logic is "central to our becoming fully human" (Soudien 2012, 7). It is important to note that Soudien never denies the significance of race. In *Declassified: Moving beyond the Dead End of Race in South Africa* (2014), sociologist Gerhard Maré provides a historical overview of the conflicting uses of nonracialism to argue against the ANC government's persistent use of apartheid racial categories for affirmative action, because it would reinforce "the racialization of society." Finally, in *Race Otherwise: Forging a New Humanism for South Africa*, sociologist Zimitri Erasmus asks how we can recognize the pervasiveness of race thinking without submitting to its power. In trying to "think and write towards the future," she wants South Africa to no longer be trapped in the racial categorization of apartheid (Erasmus 2017, 47). She also quotes British race scholar Paul Gilroy approvingly: "Coming to know *otherwise* posits where race lives, politics ends" (145).

63. Coetzee 1988; Dolby 2001a; Steyn 2001; Nuttall 2001; Verwey and Quayle 2012; Nyamnjoh 2012; Posel 1999; Ndebele 2000.

64. Biko 1978, 65.

65. McGee 2017; Fredrickson 1997; Cone and Hordern 1971. In the 1980s, James Cone's Black Liberation Theology became also influential in South Africa, for instance in the work of Barney Pityana and Allan Boesak.

66. Coetzee also writes: "I have two concerns in this book: with certain ideas, the great intellectual schémas, through which South Africa has been thought

by Europe; and the land itself, South Africa as landscape and landed property" (Coetzee 1988, 11).

67. Du Bois 1935; Baldwin 1964; Wellman 1977; Frankenberg 1991; Morrison 1992.

68. Jardina 2019.

69. American sociologist Joe Feagin has long argued for systemic racism being foundational to White supremacist societies such as the United States. He defines the White racial frame as "an overarching White worldview" that includes "a broad and persisting set of racial stereotypes, prejudices, images, interpretations and narratives, emotions, and reactions to language accents, as well as racialized inclinations to discriminate" (Feagin 2013, 3).

70. Omi and Winant 1994, 55.

71. Omi and Winant did not theorize how racism itself as a concept, and not just race, is politically contested. They concluded that the meaning of racism had become unclear after the civil rights movement and that it had become unstable and constantly challenged—but they never explored why. They did not recognize how this confusion about racism is not a natural phenomenon but actively produced by political struggle. I am thereby inspired by the critique of American sociologist Joe Feagin, who brought the unsatisfactory place of racism in Omi and Winant's theory to my attention (although my critique of racial formation theory is very different from Feagin's) (Feagin and Elias 2013).

72. Kendi 2019.

73. Durrheim, Mtose, and Brown 2011; Mangcu 2015.

74. Lewis 2004; Hughey 2012.

75. Ahmed 2004; 2007.

76. Bonilla-Silva 2006.

77. Ansell 2006; Milazzo 2015; Mangcu 2017.

78. Lake and Reynolds 2008.

79. Pearson 1894.

80. Dyer 1992.

81. Bonnett 2004.

82. This section benefited greatly from the work of historians in and outside of South Africa who are revising the history of Whiteness in that country.

83. These included the South African Republics (the SAR and the Orange Free State [OFS]), founded in 1852 and 1875, as the most important ones. However, the discovery of gold and diamonds stimulated British interest in the Boer republics, and two wars followed: the First Boer War (1880–81) and the Second Boer War (1899–1902). The British Army was particular brutal during these wars and in its concentration camps. In the end, an estimated 27,000 Boers died.

84. Willoughby-Herard 2015.

85. Hyslop 1999.

86. Seekings 2007.

87. Bell 2000; Magubane 2008; Willoughby-Herard 2015.

88. Dubow 1989; Seekings 2008.

89. Giliomee 2003b.

90. Retief 2013.

91. Tayler 1992.

92. Dubow 2001.

93. Furlong 1991.

94. Posel 1991.

95. Dubow 1992.

96. Adhikari 2005; Viljoen 2001.

97. Rassool 2004, 320–24.

98. Soske 2015.

99. Everatt 2009.

100. Dubow 2014.

101. Giliomee 2003a.

102. Lodge 2011.

103. MacDonald 2013.

104. J. Miller 2016, 16.

105. During apartheid, as South African historian Danelle van Zyl-Hermann argues, the lessening of race-based job reservation—the setting aside by law of certain (skilled) grades of employment for white South Africans—in the 1970s and 1980s had given legitimacy to the White elite and to Black labor but not to the White working class, those who held the majority of supervisory and skilled jobs (van Zyl-Hermann 2020).

106. Compared to 41 percent in 1946 and 29 percent in 1991 (Sadie 2002, 54).

107. Van Zyl-Hermann 2020; 2021.

108. Biko 1972; Arnold 1978; Lodge 1983.

109. Hirschmann 1990.

110. Fredrickson 1997.

111. Frederikse 1990.

112. Lodge and Nasson 1991; Seekings 2000; Van Kessel 2000.

113. Love 1985; Thörn 2006.

114. Giliomee 2003a.

115. Lodge 2007.

116. Carlin 2008.

117. Boraine and Plummer 2000; Tutu 2009.

118. Johnstone 2001; Theissen 1996; Giliomee 2003a; Krog 1999.

119. Theissen and Hamber 1998.

120. Asmal, Hadland, and Levy 2011.

Chapter 2: Coming to Terms with Whiteness

1. Asmal, Hadland, and Levy 2011, 154.

2. Asmal, Hadland, and Levy 2011.

3. Jelin 2003.

4. Tutu 2009, 254.

5. Asmal, Asmal, and Roberts 1997.

6. Tent 1982; Olick 2005; Pollock and Adorno 2011.

7. This term, originating with American sociologist and race scholar Chrystal Fleming, highlights how the problem of race always has a temporal dimension that takes on different configurations (Fleming 2017).

8. Scott 2004.

9. Adorno 2010.

10. Fraser 1990.

11. Boraine and Levy 1995.

12. TRC 1997.

13. Minow 2015, 1621.

14. Boraine and Levy 1995.

15. Asmal, Asmal, and Roberts 1997.

16. Van Vugt and Cloete 2000, 196.

17. TRC 1997.

18. Hayner 2000; Krog 1999; Gibson 2006.

19. Minow 1998.

20. Krog 1999.

21. Mamdani 1998, 3.

22. Giliomee 2003a, 651.

23. Johnstone 2001; Theissen 1996; Giliomee 2003a; Krog 1999.

24. Half of the English-speaking South Africans approved the activities of the TRC, but only a third of the Afrikaners did (Giliomee 2003a, 652).

25. Boraine and Plummer 2000; Meiring 2014.

26. Du Preez 2004.

27. Wilson 2001.

28. Fraser 1990.

29. Habermas 1991.

30. Fraser 1990, 67.

31. Van der Westhuizen 2007, 285.

32. Botma 2008.

33. Dawson 1994.

34. Statement of Deputy President Thabo Mbeki at the opening of the debate in the National Assembly on "Reconciliation and Nation Building," National Assembly Cape Town, May 29, 1998.

35. See www.anc.org.za/ancdocs/history/mandela/mandela/1994/sp940427.html.

36. S. Daley, "With Rare Bitterness, Mandela Attacks White Elite," *New York Times*, December 17, 1997. See also *Business Day*, December 17, 1997.

37. Blaser 2004.

38. *National Conference on Racism Final Report*, March 2001.

39. C. Niehaus, "White Racists Raise Your Hands," *City Press*, October 2, 2002.

40. White South Africans used the word *kaffir* in a denigrating way to describe Black South Africans during apartheid. One could see it as the equivalent of the American "n-word."

41. Thabo Mbeki "State of the Nation," address to parliament, February 9, 2001, www.sahistory.org.za/archive/2001-president-mbeki-state-nation-address-9-february-2001.

42. "The Politician Who Sells Absolution," *The Guardian*, May 20, 1999.

43. Ndahinda 2011.

44. Van Zyl Slabbert 1999; Du Preez 2004.

45. Krog 1999, 442.

46. "Malema Elected as New ANCYL Leader," *Mail & Guardian*, April 7, 2008.

47. Jenni O'Grady, Natasha Marrian "Zuma: 'It's Only the Afrikaners Who Are Truly South African,'" *Mail & Guardian*, April 3, 2009.

48. See www.praag.co.uk, April 22, 2009.

49. Hunter 2011.

50. Gunner 2008.

51. G. Hart 2014.

52. Wasserman and de Beer 2009.

53. "Malema: Without Land, Voting Means Nothing," *Mail & Guardian*, April 18, 2010.

54. Joel Stein, "Least Influential People of 2010: MORONS," *Time*, April 29, 2010.

55. Posel 2013.

56. "Malema: Helen Zille a 'Racist Little Girl,'" *Mail & Guardian*, May 1, 2009.

57. "De Klerk Not a Hero," *News21*, January 11, 2010.

58. David Smith, "ANC's Julius Malema Lashes Out at 'Misbehaving' BBC Journalist," *The Guardian*, April 8, 2010.

59. Jonny Steinberg "Malema's Theory of White Power Caches Resounds," *Sunday Times*, September 11, 2011.

60. Anciano 2016.

61. "A New Vision for the Democratic Alliance," speech of DA leader Tony Leon at the DA federal congress, Durban, November 20, 2004.

62. Anciano 2016, 204.

63. "AfriForum Demands Apology from Malema," *Mail & Guardian*, March 25, 2010

64. See the ruling of Lamont J. in *AfriForum v Malema* 2011 (6) SA 240 (EqC), specifically para. 35.

65. De Klerk 2000.

66. De Klerk 2000, 9.

67. De Klerk 2000, 13.

68. C. Louw, "Boetman is die bliksem in," *Beeld*, December 20, 2000.

69. The title refers to an early encounter between then-powerful De Klerk and young journalist Louw. De Klerk, the newspaper's editor, greeted him in the hallway with "Goodbye, Boetman," which means "young chap." Boetman felt it was condescending and insulted his masculinity (he was married then and already had two children).

70. W. de Klerk, "De Klerk reaksie," *Beeld*, May 18, 2000.

71. Louw 2001.

72. Klopper 2011a.

73. A. Blyburg, "Fokofpolisiekar Revolution," June 6, 2004.

74. A. Bezuidenhout, "From Voëlvry to De la Rey—Popular Music, Afrikaner Nationalism and Lost Irony," *Beeld*, May 5, 2005.

75. Klopper 2011b, 187.

76. A. Blyburg, "Fokofpolisiekar Revolution," June 6, 2004.

77. B. van Blerk, "De la Rey" (Pretoria: Mozi Records, 2006).

78. N. Nell, "Popular Bok Drives 'Em Wild," *Beeld*, February 5, 2007; P. McDowall, "Afrikaners Go 'Bok.'" *The Times*, January 29, 2007; Y. Groenewald, "The De la Rey Uprising," *Mail & Guardian*, February 16, 2007.

79. Kombuis, an alias for André le Roux du Toit. Koos A. Kombuis, "Bok van Blerk en die bagasie van veertig jaar," www.litnet.co.za, November 28, 2006.

80. A. Krog, "De la Rey: Afrikaner Absolution," *Mail & Guardian*, April 1, 2007.

81. N. Nell, "Popular Bok Drives 'Em Wild," *Beeld*, February 5, 2007.

Chapter 3: Elites and White Identity Politics

1. Thabo Mbeki, "Speech at the Afrikaanse Handelsinstituut Awards Gala Dinner," Johannesburg, August 1, 2003), https://www.polity.org.za/article/mbeki-afrikaanse-handelsinstituut-awards-gala-dinner-01082003-2003-08-01.

2. "Mbeki's History Lesson," *Mail and Guardian*, August 2, 2003.

3. Thabo Mbeki, "Statement at the Opening of the Debate in the National Assembly on 'Reconciliation and Nation Building,'" Cape Town, May 29, 1998, http://www.mbeki.org/2016/06/08/statement-at-the-opening-of-the-debate-in-the-national-assembly-on-reconciliation-and-nation-building-cape-town-19980529/.

4. Bond 2006.

5. Godsell 1991.

6. Mamdani 2015.

7. Bond 2000; Habib and Padayachee 2000.

8. Wasserman and de Beer 2009.

9. Thabo Mbeki, "Speech at the Annual National Conference of the Black Management Forum," Kempton Park, November 20, 1999, http://www.mbeki.org/2016/06/09/speech-at-the-annual-national-conference-of-the-black-management-forum-kempton-park-19991120/.

10. Lorde 2007.

11. Scholars mostly focus on the early 1990s to show that the ANC initially

promoted racial reconciliation and was fixated on establishing the "correct" macroeconomic fundamentals to gain international legitimacy (Bond 2000; 2003a; Marais 1999; 2011; Gumede 2007; MacDonald 2006). They are less clear about how President Mbeki's shift to a more explicit racial politics in the late 1990s fits their story.

12. Such an analysis uses a mainly Marxist vocabulary and terminology and emphasizes the influence of "global pressures" on South Africa and the changing "state-capital relations." South African political economist Hein Marais traces the growing distance between state and capital during the 1980s to explain the transition to democracy. He affirms that business elites remain central in South Africa's trajectory after apartheid. However, he mainly points to the influence of the elite on structural changes, not cultural narratives such as capital flight and divestment, the globalization of corporations, or corporate restructuring (Alexander 2003; Marais 2011).

13. Omi and Winant 1994.

14. Veblen 1899; Mills 1956; Bourdieu 1984.

15. Lamont 1992; Lareau 2003; Khan 2012a, 2012c.

16. Beckert 2003; Kendall 2008; Khan 2012b; Salverda and Abbink 2013; Sherman 2019.

17. Shamus Khan's excellent *Privilege: The Making of an Adolescent Elite* (2011) devotes considerable attention to race and Black elite students but has surprisingly little to say about Whiteness for an ethnographic study of a dominantly White school.

18. Feagin 2003; 2017.

19. Davies 2012, 392.

20. Van der Westhuizen 2007.

21. These so-called Transformation Bills included the Preferential Procurement Policy Framework Act of 2000, which targeted Black economic inequalities and underdevelopment, and the Promotion of Equality and Prevention of Unfair Discrimination Act of 2001, which targeted businesses in real estate, insurance, pensions, banking, and transport for monitoring in terms of their transformation and deracialization.

22. *Executive Summary Report of the BEEC 2001* (2001), http://www.bmfonline.co.za/bee_rep.htm.

23. Southall 2008.

24. Tangri and Southall 2008.

25. Ponte, Roberts, and Van Sittert 2007.

26. Iheduru 2004; 2008.

27. Mbeki qtd. in Iheduru 2004, 4.

28. MacDonald 2006.

29. Everatt 2009.

30. S'Thembiso Msomi, "Black Empowerment's Lone Heretic," *Sunday Times*, April 6, 2003.

31. Alexander 2003, 49.
32. Southall 2004.
33. Giliomee 2003a.
34. Brits 2008.
35. Verhoef 2016.
36. MacDonald 2006.
37. Du Toit, Kruger, and Ponte 2008.
38. O'Meara 1983.
39. The future CEO of Anglo American Corporation, Bobby Godsell, one of South Africa's largest mining companies, worked with American sociologist Peter Berger on the book *Africa beyond Apartheid*, which was published in 1988; it featured a wide range of essays on the future of South Africa and was a bestseller in South Africa.
40. Interview with Johan Naudé de Villiers, May 2008.
41. Interview with Theo van Wyk, June 2000.
42. Interview with Johan Naudé de Villiers.
43. Interview with Theo van Wyk.
44. Afrikaanse Handelsinstituut, "Submission to the Truth and Reconciliation Commission," October 9, 1997.
45. Interview with Theo van Wyk.
46. Interview with André Lamprecht, June 2008.
47. Sonn 1993, 2.
48. Sonn 1993, 7.
49. Du Toit 1935, 31.
50. Sonn 1993, 8.
51. Sonn 1993, 8.
52. Franklin Sonn, "How Can International Business Contribute to Trade and Industry in the Republic of South Africa?" Presidential address given at the annual congress of the Afrikaanse Handelsinstituut in Bellville, South Africa, October 24, 2001.
53. Sonn, "How Can International Business Contribute?"
54. Interview with André Lamprecht.
55. Anton Botha, "Presidential Address Given at the Annual Congress of the Afrikaanse Handelsinstituut," Vanderbijlpark, South Africa, October 21, 2004.
56. Interview with Japie Steenkamp, May 2008.
57. Interview with Japie Steenkamp.
58. Nakedi Mathews Phosa, "Presidential Address Given at the Annual Congress of the Afrikaanse Handelsinstituut, Johannesburg, South Africa, October 19, 2006.
59. Interview with Eltie Links, June 2008.
60. Interview with Eltie Links.
61. Interview with Venete Klein, May 2008.

Chapter 4: Populism and White Minoritization

1. Flip Buys, "The Future of Multiculturalism in South Africa: An Afrikaner Perspective," speech given in Cape Town, South Africa, February 2, 2016, F. W. de Klerk Foundation, http://www.fwdeklerk.org/index.php/en/document-library/speeches?start=25.

2. By racial tokenism I mean recruiting a small number of businessmen and women of color in order to give the appearance of racial integration.

3. I want to thank Danelle van Zyl-Hermann for her idea of thinking of the Solidarity Movement as a populist movement (see also van Zyl-Hermann, 2018b).

4. Flip Buys, "The Future of Multiculturalism in South Africa: An Afrikaner Perspective," speech given in Cape Town, South Africa, February 2, 2016, F. W. de Klerk Foundation, http://www.fwdeklerk.org/index.php/en/document-library/speeches?start=25.

5. Gest 2016; Frey 2018.

6. Bosma 2015.

7. A typical, if unusually direct, headline on the opinion pages of the *New York Times* in December reads "Does Racism Explain Donald Trump's Victory?," https://www.nytimes.com/2016/12/28/opinion/does-racism-explain-donald-trumps-victory.html.

8. Lamont, Park, and Ayala-Hurtado 2017.

9. Rydgren 2007; Mudde 2016.

10. Notably, *The Oxford Handbook of Populism* (Kaltwasser et al. 2017) has no chapter on racism.

11. Brubaker 2017.

12. Scholars point to the nonracist left-wing populism of the People's Party in nineteenth-century America, the emergence of ethnopopulism in Latin America in the early 2000s, and the left-wing populist parties in southern Europe in the 2010s in order to suggest that racism is not essential to populism. European scholars are reluctant to explicitly use the term "racism" and to draw on race theory (Mudde 2007; Goodwin and Evans 2012; Makovicky 2013; Norris and Inglehart 2019).

13. The reluctance to center racism in populism stands in marked contrast to the substantial literature on the relationship between nationalism and racism (Fredrickson 1997).

14. Bonikowski 2017.

15. Rosa and Bonilla 2017.

16. Taguieff 2001. In his work on France, Pierre-André Taguieff particularly focuses on the extreme right's appropriation of left-wing concepts for exclusionary purposes, such as *droit à la différence*, the right to difference. The French sociologist actually introduced the term "national populism" to describe the new racism of the far-right National Front in France. However, this seems to confuse matters. I use the analytical terms "populism" and "racism" separately and analyze how one impacts the other. Moreover, Taguieff's understanding of racism is too specific to the French case and generally problematic when it comes to his critique and

lack of understanding of the antiracism activism of people of color.

17. Kazin 1998; Himmelstein 1992; Brinkley 1994.

18. Lo 1982.

19. Formisano 2004.

20. Sugrue 1995.

21. "Beweging stel Helpmekaarplan van R3, 5 miljard bekend," *Solidariteit/ Solidarity* 6 (2015): 16–17.

22. M. Du Preez, "AfriForum 'Hijacking the Afrikaner Mainstream,'" *News24*, July 26, 2016, http://www.news24.com/Columnists/MaxduPreez/ afriforum-hijacking-theafrikaner-mainstream-20160726.

23. Visser 2008.

24. Interview with Dirk Hermann, May 2008.

25. For example, Brubaker has suggested that the idea of threat was specific, maybe even unique, to populist politics (Kaltwasser et al. 2017).

26. Stultz 1974.

27. Lubbe 1997.

28. Brown 1987; Cornwell 1996.

29. "Dr. T Roep Werkers Op," *Die Mynwerker*, January 1990, 1. It is important to note that the MWU not only protested against increased access for Blacks to jobs but also against mixed facilities and new programs for educating Black employees for employment in the mines.

30. *MWU-NUUS* (newsletter of the MWU), "Manifes van die blanke werker," October 1991, p. 11.

31. Hermann 2007, 14.

32. Hermann 2013.

33. The court indicated that Solidarity should have disputed the affirmative action plan and not the individual case. Subsequently, Solidarity approached the Labour Court in an attempt to compel the SAPS to consult the union on its new affirmative action plan.

34. https://www.politicsweb.co.za/party/solidarity-goes-to-court-to-compel- saps-to-consult.

35. Solidariteits Akademia, "Solidariteitskunde," 3.

36. Interview with Dirk Hermann.

37. Blade Nzimande, the general secretary of the SACP, is well known in South Africa for his racial critique of (White) politicians and (White) businessmen. For example, in 2012, he called the Democratic Alliance (DA) "a party of white madams and baases (white bosses)," a reference to then party leader Helen Zille, https://www.news24.com/SouthAfrica/Politics/DA-a-party-of-white-madams- Nzimande-20121124?cpid=5. See also https://forumnuus.co.za/afrikaners-moet- n-visie-anderkant-die-woestyn/.

38. Albertazzi and McDonnell 2007, 3.

39. Interview with Dirk Hermann.

40. F. Buys, "Wie en wat is 'n Afrikaner?," Maroela Media, June 3, 2013,

https://maroelamedia.co.za/debat/meningsvormers/wie-en-wat-is-n-afrikaner/.

41. "Krisisberaad besin oor groeiende krisis in land," Maroela Media, May 4, 2015, http:// maroelamedia.co.za/nuus/sa-nuus/krisisberaad-besin-oor-die-groeiende-krisis-inland/.

42. "Solidariteit hou krisisberaad," Maroela Media, April 27, 2015, http:// maroelamedia.co. za/nuus/sa-nuus/solidariteit-hou-krisisberaad/.

43. *South Africa Police Service (SAPS) Annual Crime Report 2016/17.*

44. However, the idea that White poverty is an unrecognized problem in South Africa is false. According to Statistics South Africa (SSA), there were 47,494 White people living below the poverty line in 2015. This represented 1 percent of the White population of South Africa. SSA also estimates that in 2015, a little less than 50 percent of Black South Africans lived below the poverty line.

45. However, in the balance between minority protection and accommodation of population diversity, on the one hand, with unity and nation-building, on the other, emphasis in the South African constitution is often on the latter rather than the former (Henrard 2002).

46. Kallie Kriel, "AfriForum Now 210 000 Members Strong," *AfriForum* (blog), July 25, 2018, https://www.afriforum.co.za/afriforum-now-210-000-members-strong/.

47. M. Trapido, "Afrikaner Aspirations: An Hour with AfriForum's Kallie Kriel, *Mail & Guardian*, April 16, 2008, https://thoughtleader.co.za/traps/2008/04/16/afrikaner-aspirations-%E2%80%93-an-hour-with-afriforums-kallie-kriel/.

48. Kallie Kriel, "Racism: Definition, Causes & Manifestations." Short introductory remarks by the CEO of AfriForum.

49. AfriForum's Kallie Kriel had long focused on the song's use. In my interview in 2008, he told me that the ANC parliamentarian Patrick Choke had rallied a crowd against whites by singing the same song. However, Julius Malema had also made it a habit to sing the song during political gatherings.

50. Eugène Terre'Blanche had led this extreme right-wing organization in the late 1980s and early 1990s. At his farm in Ventersdorp, he was found clubbed and hacked to death. The police arrested two farm workers at the scene, who apparently had a wage dispute with Terre'Blanche. The AWB accused Malema of having "blood on his hands" for singing the song.

51. In South Africa, hate speech is excluded from the protection of free speech in the constitution by the Promotion of Equality and Prevention of Unfair Discrimination Act. AfriForum's application was based on Section 10 of the Equality Act (see also Section 16 of the Constitution of the Republic of South Africa), which provides that "no person may publish, propagate, advocate or communicate words based on one or more of the prohibited grounds, against any person, that could reasonably be construed to demonstrate a clear intention to (a) be hurtful; (b) be harmful or to incite harm; (c) promote or propagate hatred."

52. In the lawsuit, AfriForum claimed that the lyrics of the song "Ayesaba Amagwala" (The cowards are scared) were a form of hate speech that targeted

White people. In particular, AfriForum focused on the "objectionable utterances" contained in the song, such as the call to "Dubula ibhunu" (Shoot the Boer) and "Dubula amabhunu baya raypha Dubula" (Shoot the Boers, they rape).

53. See the ruling of Lamont J. in *AfriForum v Malema* 2011 (6) SA 240 (EqC), specifically para. 35.

54. https://nolstuijt.wordpress.com/tag/human-rights/.

55. Interview with Flip Buys, May 2008.

56. Kretzer and Kaschula 2021.

57. Interview with Flip Buys.

58. A government land audit released in 2017 showed that farms and agricultural holdings comprised 97 percent of the 121.9 million hectares of the nation's area, and that whites owned 72 percent of the 37 million hectares held by individuals.

59. "Farm-Attacks National Crisis," *News24*, November 27, 2012, https://www.news24.com/SouthAfrica/News/Farm-attacks-national-crisis-Solidarity-20121127; https://www.afriforum.co.za/afriforum-says-facts-show-disregard-property-rights-farm-murders-serious-threat-south-africa/.

60. https://www.killtheboerbook.com/about-the-book/.

61. Data released by the South African government in 2018 showed that the number of farm attacks had increased between 2012 and 2018, but that the number of murders on farms had decreased year by year during the same period. Farming organization AgriSA also reported that the murder rate on farms had declined to its lowest level in twenty years, from a little over a one thousand at its peak in 2001 to twenty in 2017, https://www.news24.com/SouthAfrica/News/farm-murder-rate-lowest-in-20-years-remoteness-the-reason-for-brutality-20180531.

62. "Beweging stel Helpmekaarplan van R3, 5 miljard bekend," *Solidariteit/Solidarity* 6 (2015): 16–17.

Chapter 5: White Embodiment and the Working Class

1. Interview with Eric Sommers, May 2008. All names in this chapter are pseudonyms.

2. Interview with Eric Sommers.

3. Steensland 2014.

4. Rothmann et al. 1932.

5. Interview with Eric Sommers.

6. Interview with Eric Sommers.

7. Interview with Eric Sommers.

8. Cramer 2016; Gest 2016; Salmela and von Scheve 2017; Norris and Inglehart 2019.

9. A. Hochschild 2016.

10. Arlie Hochschild mentions the word "racism" just once in her book on the Tea Party and Trump voters in Louisiana, in a passage on White Americans talking about "reverse racism," a term invented in the 1970s by conservative

opposition to color-conscious policies aimed at addressing racial inequality, such as affirmative action.

11. McDonnell, Bail, and Tavory 2017.

12. Hall et al. 1978, 394.

13. Fanon 1952.

14. Hook 2005; 2006, 212.

15. Ahmed 2007.

16. Morrell 1998.

17. Giliomee 2003a.

18. Posel 1999.

19. Du Bois 1935. American sociologist W. E. B. Du Bois argued that Whiteness allowed the "White worker" to move through the world with ease and feelings of access, belonging, and agency. Whiteness to Du Bois was about having a job but also about newspapers writing favorably about you and your group.

20. Du Pisani 2001.

21. At the turn of the twentieth century, stories by the journalist Gustav Peller portrayed the Boer as the quintessential pioneer, or *Voortrekker*, who left the Cape Colony in the late nineteenth century in an ox wagon to become a frontiersman. After the South African War, the Boer was portrayed as a heroic leader and stubborn fighter. Nationalists sought to depict Afrikaners as an ethnic group with rural origins. The image of the Boer embodied the illusion of continuity in history and the unchanging Afrikaner identity. In the 1920s, the *plaasroman*, or farm novel, depicted the Boer as the benevolent patriarch of the family farm, who valued hard work and family life, and passed his legacy on to his sons.

22. In reality, the Boer society as mythologized in Afrikaner nationalism never existed: not in the Cape, the Karoo, or the Transvaal area of South Africa. During the late 1800s and early 1900s, South Africa's agricultural society radically changed through the combined forces of commercialization, capitalization, and urbanization, processes that forced many small White farmers and sharecroppers into poverty and off the land to move to the city. Agriculture came to be concentrated in the hands of fewer, wealthier White landowners, who increasingly relied on mechanization and Black labor.

23. Australian sociologist R. W. Connell introduced the concept of hegemonic masculinity to define the culturally idealized form of masculine character, which is always constructed in relation to various subordinate masculinities and to women (Connell and Messerschmidt 2005).

24. As South African historian Sandra Swart explains, there was originally no shame in being a *bywoner*. Landowners welcomed them for their help. She argues that during most of the eighteenth century, Boer society was characterized by a rhetoric of equality and a form of republican *gelykheid*, or equality between White men. Only toward the end of the nineteenth century did this started to change (Swart 1998). See also Keegan 1986.

25. South African sociologist Ann Steensland demonstrates that social scientists in the 1930s pathologized the *bywoner* and his White habitat (Steensland 2014).

26. The 1932 *Carnegie Report* spoke about the "poor White disease," which was induced by the "unhealthy" ecological and socioeconomic environment in which poor whites lived.

27. Willoughby-Herard 2015.

28. Cronjé 1945, 58.

29. Van Zyl-Hermann 2018a; 2021.

30. Fredrickson 1982; Chanock 2001.

31. Kinder and Sears 1981; Sears and Henry 2003.

32. Sears, Sidanius, and Bobo 2000; Lamont 2000; Kefalas 2003.

33. Willoughby-Herard 2007.

34. Interview with Henk Sadie, June 2008.

35. Interview with Flip Meyer, February 2010.

36. Interview with Jady Schalkwyk, June 2008.

37. Interview with Chris Rensburg, May 2008.

38. Interview with Andre Durandt, April 2008.

39. Interview with Roche Gerlach, April 2008.

40. Interview with Johan Faurie, May 2008.

41. Interview with Johan Naude, June 2008.

42. Interview with Jady Schalkwyk.

43. Interview with Johan Faurie.

44. Lamont 2000.

45. Interview with Johan Faurie.

46. Interview with Henk Niekerk, June 2008.

47. Interview with Andre Durandt.

48. Interview with Chris Rensburg.

49. Interview with Johan Naude.

50. Interview with Johan Faurie.

51. Interview with Andre Durandt.

52. Interview with Andre Durandt.

53. McDowell 2011; Weis 2004.

54. In her work Lamont shows how the American White working class demands dignity in different ways than the French White working class, but she never questions why dignity is required in the first place (Lamont 2000).

55. Vandello, Bosson, and Cohen 2008.

56. Interview with Marie Nell, June 2008.

57. Interview with Rita Schoeman, June 2008.

58. Interview with Sonja Hattingh, May 2008.

59. Interview with Lana Gouws, May 2008.

60. Interview with Rania Scholtz, May 2008.

Chapter 6: Whiteness at Home

1. Interview with Sonja Hattingh. All names in this chapter are pseudonyms.

2. Christopher 2001.

3. Interview with Sonja Hattingh, May 2008.

4. Interview with Karin Jacobus, May 2008.

5. McClintock 1991; Westhuizen 2017.

6. These communities emerged in the late 1980s in the United States but since then have become a dominant urban form in countries as diverse as Brazil, Turkey, and China (Atkinson and Blandy 2013).

7. Kempa and Shearing 2000.

8. As Edward Blakely and Mary Gail Snyder's pioneering study of the emergence of gated communities in the United States shows, these residential environments are the latest innovation in the suburbanization movement, resulting in even more privatized, secured, aesthetically appealing, and exclusive communities (Blakely and Snyder 1997). Their work has been invaluable in shedding light on the process of privatization and the emergent "fortress mentality" that responds to fear of crime and loss of privilege. Their study suggests that gated communities create a strong barrier against interaction among people of different cultures and classes. One problem with their assessment, however, is that Blakely and Snyder did not address race or racism, either directly or indirectly. In contrast to their work, contemporary research in Brazil has addressed gating and the new politics of race and place. In her work on São Paulo in Brazil, Brazilian sociologist Teresa Caldeira links the development of gating to economic inequality, the transition from dictatorship to democracy, and the fear of crime (Caldeira 2000). According to Caldeira, the continuing unequal distribution of wealth, in combination with a failing criminal justice system, leads to an increase in violent crime, and thus those who can afford it have opted for gated communities.

9. Bond 2003b.

10. Lipsitz 2007.

11. White residents of gated communities, Low claims, reject pluralism and pursue homogeneity through coded race talk to protect their community and lifestyle (Low 2004). See also Simon 2007.

12. Lemanski 2004, 101. However, Lemanski provides very little data for these assertions, only a few anecdotes.

13. Harrison, Todes, and Watson 2007.

14. Duyvendak 2011.

15. Duncan and Duncan 2004; 2006; Harvey 1985.

16. Ioanide 2015.

17. Lo 1995; Avila 2004.

18. Lipsitz 2011.

19. To understand how race operates in different institutional spheres, Telles makes a helpful distinction between two kinds of social relationships: vertical relationships that are defined by hierarchy and inequality and are dominant in

the spheres of work, education, and politics; and horizontal relationships that are defined by equality and conviviality that are dominant in the spheres of family, friendship, and neighborhood community (Telles 2004).

20. Mabin and Smit 1997.
21. Maylam 1990.
22. Maylam 1995.
23. Dubow and Beinart 1995.
24. Dooling 2018.
25. Bickford-Smith 1995.
26. Dubow and Beinart 1995.
27. Bickford-Smith 1995.
28. Parnell 1988a.
29. Parnell 1988b.
30. Nauright 1998.
31. D. Hart 1988.
32. Mabin 1992.
33. Interview with Bernadet Blignaut, June 2008.
34. Interview with Rosita de Klerk, June 2008.
35. Interview with Marie Nell.
36. Interview with Antjie du Plessis, May 2008.
37. Interview with Marie Nell.
38. Interview with Bernadet Blignaut.
39. Interview with Sarie de Wet, May 2008.
40. Interview with Lana Giliomee, May 2008.
41. Interview with Marie Nell.
42. Interview with Rosida de Kerlk, June 2008.
43. Interview with Sarie de Wet.
44. There are rules and restrictions for the type of materials, the height of walls, the plot size, and the wall surrounding the golf course. Apart from rules pertaining to the architecture of buildings, there are various other regulations, dealing with such diverse issues as building and house maintenance, house-selling practices, and garden and road maintenance, as well as pet animal rules. Residents can complain to the committee about violations of the rules or other disputes with their neighbors, and the committee deals with these matters. Things are further complicated because of the golf course and a game park on the estate; the golf course is particularly a source of community friction, as only 40 percent of the residents use the golf course for golfing, while other residents enjoy it as a recreational area. The environment committee regulates aesthetic concerns at the estate.
45. Interview with Ingrid Le Roux, May 2008.
46. Interview with Ingrid Le Roux.
47. Interview with Antjie Kruger, May 2008.
48. Interview with Hannie Smith, June 2008.

49. Interview with Gigi Nkruma, May 2008.

50. Landry and Marsh 2011.

51. Interview with Karin Jacobus.

52. The HOA is a Section 22 Nonprofit Company, which, simply put, means that all levies and fees need to be reinvested in the estate. On the board there is a chairman, vice-chairman, security trustee, financial trustee, and environmental trustee. Being a trustee on the board used to be a voluntary job, but since early 2000, trustees are paid a monthly fee. The trustee supervises different committees, such as the security committee, levy-determining committee, aesthetics committee, environmental committee, social responsibility committee, and estate agents committee. See also Kaltwasser et al. 2017.

53. Interview with Hannelie Toonder, June 2008.

54. Interview with Cornelia Matthews, June 2008.

55. Interview with Thandie Kumalo, June 2008.

56. Interview with the general manager of Golden Sun, Adam Cobbledick, May 2008.

Chapter 7: Unlearning Racism at School

1. Interview with Sandra Witbooi, April 2007. All names in this chapter are pseudonyms. I use first names in this chapter to emphasize that my interviewees are adolescents between the age of 15 and 17 years old.

2. "Born Frees" are the generation born in the 1980s or thereafter, who became politically active after 1996 (Mattes 2012).

3. Interview with Sandra Witbooi.

4. Interview with Alex Strydom, April 2007.

5. Interview with Alex Strydom.

6. Interview with Alex Strydom.

7. Bonilla-Silva 2006.

8. Lewis 2003; Pollock 2009.

9. Roediger 1999; Frankenberg 1991.

10. Perry 2002; Morris 2006.

11. Steyn 2001.

12. Sociologists of education such as Nadine Dolby and Crain Soudien have used the Whiteness perspective to explore the opportunities for identity change after apartheid (Dolby 2002; Soudien 2007; 2012).

13. The interviews for this study were gathered over a six-month period between January and June 2007 at two high schools in the greater Cape Town metropolitan area. I conducted semi-structured interviews with a total of thirty-two people in both schools, including students, teachers, and staff. At Malan, I interviewed six White boys and five White girls, and at De la Rey, nine White boys and eight White girls. All interviews were conducted in English. In my analysis, I focus on small peer groups that attended the same class in the eleventh grade. At De la Rey, the group of girls I interviewed were those with the highest grades; I refer

also to the boys but argue that the gender differences at the school were small. At Malan, I focus on a small group of boys that are in the same class. Because I found the gender differences at Malan significant, I specifically contrast the talk of the boys with that of the girls in the same class.

14. See, for example, the work of South African sociologist Chana Teeger, who presents a convincing case that a specific South African color-blind ideology is influential among teachers at elite schools. She shows how in history classes, young South Africans are taught to ignore the contemporary effects of apartheid. She demonstrates how teachers actively limit students' ability to make connections between past and present. She speaks of the "both sides of the story" narrative, which emphasizes that not all whites were perpetrators and that not all Blacks were victims during apartheid. The TRC itself, she argues, represented an earlier institutionalized version of this narrative, as it constructed a story of moral equivalence by requiring members of resistance movements to apply for amnesty in the same way as members of the apartheid regime (Teeger 2015).

15. The youth exercise more autonomy vis-à-vis socialization agents than the literature on the socialization and reproduction of racism suggest. Scholars overemphasize the role of adults in the socialization process and overlook the agency of youth. In that sense, my approach is markedly different from that of South African educationalist Jonathan Jansen, who in *Knowledge in the Blood* makes the case that it is White parents who transmit knowledge indirectly to youth about their privileged place in society (Jansen 2009). My approach is based on the work of American sociologist Joe R. Feagin, who in *The First R*, in 2001, together with American sociologist Debra Van Ausdale, argued that we could not assume that what adults teach is what children learn about race (Feagin and Van Ausdale 2001). South African educationalist Crain Soudien also writes: "[Youth] are in much more active dialogue with the conditions of their socialization than one might assume" (Soudien 2007, 100). See also the study of American sociologist Margaret Hagerman (Hagerman 2018).

16. Following American sociologist Peggy Giordano, I stress the independence of young people's cultural interpretations and the importance of peer groups for the process of socialization (Giordano 2003).

17. Kyratzis 2004.

18. South African educationalist Crain Soudien argues that scholars are often out of touch with the cultural resources that are available to youth (Soudien 2007). In her study of a South African school, American sociologist Nadine Dolby demonstrates how cultural forces outside the school, such as popular culture and the media, shape the process of racial socialization (Dolby 2001b). For the cultural approach to studying race in schools, see Carter 2012; Warikoo 2011.

19. Paulle 2013; Khan 2011.

20. Soudien 2007.

21. The ANC government struggled to address segregation and integration because it had limited control over educational institutions (Moodley and Adam

2000; Motala and Singh 2002; Christie 2006). Nevertheless, continuing efforts to achieve control, for instance over language policies to increase access, have resulted in significant but uneven desegregation at formerly White schools. The large majority of formerly Afrikaans schools have changed to double-medium or single-medium English, partly through pressure from the Department of Basic Education. The number of schools that remain single-medium Afrikaans dropped from 1,800 in 1994 to 1,279 in 2018, or 5 percent of the total number of schools. The challenge remains for the government to push beyond desegregation and devise strategies for integration at schools.

22. Evidence, both anecdotal and academic, suggests that White flight from desegregated schools in South Africa after apartheid was an issue in cities such as Cape Town, Durban, and Pretoria. In separate case studies, both Chisholm and Dolby show how schools near Durban, which they researched and qualified as desegregating and integrating in the mid-1990s, have subsequently resegregated and had been abandoned by the White lower-middle class by the mid-2000s (Chisholm 2004; Dolby 2001b). Resegregation of schools through White flight is a general problem and in Cape Town, where various formerly White lower-middle-class schools have resegregated.

23. Traditionally, the head boy has been an honorable function for the most successful male student, chosen by the students. Organizationally, the school has its own tradition in student representation. The school has a student cabinet, which consists of twelve members. They are the prefects of their class. Every prefect chairs a committee that focuses on a particular topical issue—like culture, drama, hockey, or dancing—and is assisted by two other students. Prefects are voted in every year, with a system of weighted votes. The votes of the students in grade 11 count the most, while the votes from teachers and from students in grades 12 and 8 count the least. Each year, the school chooses a *hoofseun* and a *hoofmeissie* of grade 12, *matriek*.

24. Central to the school's image to the outside world is the performance of sports. The school is in competition with other (elite) schools in the Western Cape that are often much larger—up to two thousand pupils—and often equally or better endowed. Rugby is the most important sport, at least for boys, while netball is for girls. Athletics also stands in high regard, with the school investing a considerable amount of time and money to recruit the best coaches, often the same who are responsible for training at the provincial level. It is in sports where the changes after 1994 are most visible. The competitive nature of school sports and the prestige invested in it by schools have—after desegregation—opened up a market where students are lured to schools based on their athletic abilities, where they receive a scholarship and housing in the school's hostel. At De la Rey, scholarships are mostly awarded to top-performing Coloured athletes, who are being drafted from all over the Western and Northern Cape. That such students perform poorly academically seems of less concern.

25. Interview with school principal, February 2007.

26. Interview with Annelie Kloppers, April 2007.

27. Interview with Ineke Leroux, April 2007.

28. Interview with Patsy Boshoff, April 2007.

29. Interview with Petronella Bekker, April 2007.

30. Interview with Jeanne Booysen, April 2007.

31. Interview with Ronel Kotze, May 2007.

32. Interview with Maretha Blignault, April 2007.

33. Interview with Zola Van der Walt, April 2007.

34. Interview with Dawid Botha, April 2007.

35. Interview with Sandra Witbooi.

36. Interview with Sandra Witbooi.

37. Interview with Sandra Witbooi.

38. Van der Westhuizen 2017.

39. Interview with Hendrik Louw, May 2007.

40. Interview with Carel Naude, April 2007.

41. Interview with Teron van Heerden, May 2007.

42. Interview with Carel Naude.

43. Interview with Jurie van Wyk, April 2007.

44. Interview with Jurie van Wyk.

45. Interview with Jaco Niekerk, May 2007.

46. Interview with Marie Mostert, May 2007.

47. Interview with Alex Strydom.

48. Interview with Le Roux Pienaar, May 2007.

49. Interview with Alex Strydom.

50. Interview with Chris Du Toit, May 2007.

51. Interview with Fanie Retief, May 2007.)

52. Interview with Rochelle Smit, May 2007.

Conclusion: Learning from South Africa

1. In 2018, it had a Gini coefficient of 63, compared to 59 in 1993. The United States has a coefficient of 41.5 (Sulla and Zikhali 2018).

2. Sulla and Zikhali 2018.

3. With the poverty line set at people who earn less than $83 per month. Things did change: the ANC government built more than 2 million new houses in townships and informal settlements, and access to basic services such as electricity, water, education, and health care have improved considerably since 1994.

4. In 2005, American political scientist Jennifer L. Hochschild suggested that the United States might follow a "South African" scenario, in which the nation is re-sorted into three groups: Whites and "honorary Whites" (most Asians, some Latinos, and some biracials), Coloureds (some Asians, most Latinos, some biracials, and a few Black people), and Black people (J. Hochschild 2005). Hochschild's "South African" scenario was similar to American sociologist Eduardo Bonilla-Silva's prediction in 2004 of the "Latin Americanization" of race relations in the

United States (Bonilla-Silva 2004). He also foresaw the United States moving away from a binary Black/White model toward a triracial model comprising three tiers: "Whites," "honorary Whites," and a "collective Black" category.

5. In *Marked Men*, American literary scholar Sally Robinson uses American novels to trace how the increasing visibility of White men leads to an identity crisis (Robinson 2000).

6. Whiteness scholars such as sociologists Karyn McKinney and Charles Gallagher have demonstrated that White students at elite universities are highly aware of their White racial identity and increasingly see this identity as a liability and themselves as victims (McKinney 2013). In 1997, Gallagher speculated specifically that Whiteness as an explicit cultural product might be taking on a life of its own, developing its own racial logics (Gallagher 1997).

7. The first American Whiteness conference at the University of California, Berkeley in 2000 was organized in part because of the conservative assault on affirmative action at the University of California (Rasmussen et al. 2001).

8. Bonilla-Silva 2006, 28.

9. Kaufmann 2018.

10. Koopmans 2018.

11. If we read his text, we find "majority" and "majority culture" consistently defined in opposition to immigrants; one of the main issues he mentions is the "majority right" for the racist blackface celebration of Sinterklaas. In the introduction, Koopmans writes: "In the context of immigration and associated increased cultural and religious diversity, minorities' claims for rights increasingly clash with sections of majority populations who wish to retain and defend 'national' cultural and religious traditions" (Koopmans 2018, 1). What Koopmans forgets is that most people protesting blackface are people with a Dutch nationality— they are not "immigrants."

12. Combahee River Collective 1983.

13. American historian Neil Ignatiev has argued that we must abolish Whiteness and that "treason to Whiteness is loyalty to humanity"(Garvey and Ignatiev 1997). His aim is to abolish a system that confers White privilege on people because of their color.

14. It cannot simply be "repudiated by a mere act of political will," as American sociologist Howard Winant writes (Winant 2001, 107).

Appendix

1. Willoughby-Herard 2015.

2. Magubane 1998.

3. Steyn 2001.

4. A. Hochschild 2016, 5.

5. Coles 1971.

6. Zuberi and Bonilla-Silva 2008.

7. Benjamin 2019.

8. Hartigan 2010.

9. Madison 2011.

10. Following Bonilla-Silva, I define a racial ideology as a political instrument, not an exercise in personal logic (Bonilla-Silva 2003, 66).

11. Lamont 2000.

12. Saito 1998; Perry 2002; McDermott 2006.

13. Du Bois and Eaton 1899; Drake and Cayton 1970.

14. Cramer 2016.

15. Anderson 2016; DiAngelo 2018.

16. Kruse and Sugrue 2006; Sugrue 1996; Theoharis 2018.

17. Bonilla-Silva 2006.

18. Du Bois and Eaton 1899; Drake and Cayton 1970.

19. The work of American sociologist Jonathan Rieder was an inspiration for this study. He studied residents of Canarsie, a neighborhood in Brooklyn, NY, in the 1980s. In *Canarsie: The Jews and Italians of Brooklyn against Liberalism*, he argues that the White grievances he mapped were not racism but rather a mindset of particular "placement in place." Rieder 1985; see also Steinberg 1988.

20. Goodwin and Schiff 1995.

21. Marcus 1995; 2009.

Works Cited

Adhikari, Mohamed. 2005. "Fiercely Non-racial? Discourses and Politics of Race in the Non-European Unity Movement, 1943–70." *Journal of Southern African Studies* 31:403–18.

Adorno, Theodor W. (1959) 1986. "'What Does Coming to Terms with the Past Mean?'" In *Bitburg in Moral and Political Perspective*, ed. Geoffrey H. Hartman, 114–29. Bloomington: Indiana University Press.

———. 2010. *Guilt and Defense: On the Legacies of National Socialism in Postwar Germany*. Cambridge, MA: Harvard University Press.

Ahmed, Sarah. 2004. *The Cultural Politics of Emotions*. London: Routledge.

———. 2007. "A Phenomenology of Whiteness." *Feminist Theory* 8:149.

Albertazzi, Daniele, and Duncan McDonnell. 2007. *Twenty-First Century Populism: The Spectre of Western European Democracy*. New York: Palgrave Macmillan.

Alexander, Neville. 2003. *An Ordinary Country: Issues in the Transition from Apartheid to Democracy in South Africa*. New York: Berghahn Books.

Anciano, Fiona. 2016. "A Dying Ideal: Non-racialism and Political Parties in Post-apartheid South Africa." *Journal of Southern African Studies* 42:195–214.

Anderson, Carol. 2016. *White Rage: The Unspoken Truth of Our Racial Divide*. New York: Bloomsbury.

Ansell, Amy E. 2006. "Casting a Blind Eye: The Ironic Consequences of Color-Blindness in South Africa and the United States." *Critical Sociology* 32:333–56.

Arnold, Millard W. 1978. *Steve Biko: Black Consciousness in South Africa*. New York: Random House.

Ashforth, Adam. 1990. *The Politics of Official Discourse in Twentieth-Century South Africa*. Oxford: Clarendon Press.

Asmal, Kader, Louise Asmal, and Ronald Suresh Roberts. 1997. *Reconciliation through Truth: A Reckoning of Apartheid's Criminal Governance*. New York: St. Martin's Press.

Asmal, Kader, Adrian Hadland, and Moira Levy. 2011. *Politics in My Blood*. Cape Town: Jacana Media.

Atkinson, Rowland, and Sarah Blandy. 2013. *Gated Communities: Interna-*

tional Perspectives. London: Routledge.

Avila, Eric. 2004. *Popular Culture in the Age of White Flight: Fear and Fantasy in Suburban Los Angeles*. Oakland: University of California Press.

Baldwin, James. 1964. *The Fire Next Time*. New York: Dell.

Bass, Orli, Kira Erwin, Amanda Kinners, and Gerhard Maré. 2012. "The Possibilities of Researching Non-racialism: Reflections on Racialism in South Africa." *Politikon* 39:29–40.

Beckert, Sven. 2003. *The Monied Metropolis: New York City and the Consolidation of the American Bourgeoisie, 1850–1896*. Cambridge: Cambridge University Press.

Bell, Morag. 2000. "American Philanthropy, the Carnegie Corporation and Poverty in South Africa." *Journal of Southern African Studies* 26:481–504.

Benjamin, Ruha. 2006. *Racism without Racists: Color-Blind Racism and the Persistence of Racial Inequality in the United States*. Lanham, MD: Rowman & Littlefield.

———. 2019. *Race after Technology: Abolitionist Tools for the New Jim Code*. London: John Wiley.

"Beweging stel Helpmekaarplan van R3, 5 miljard bekend." *Solidariteit/Solidarity* 6 (2015).

Bickford-Smith, Vivian. 1995. "South African Urban History, Racial Segregation and the Unique Case of Cape Town?" *Journal of Southern African Studies* 21:63–78.

Biko, Steve. 1972. *Black Viewpoint*. Durban, SA: Spro-Cas Black Community Programmes.

———. 1978. *I Write What I Like: Steve Biko—A Selection of His Writings*. Johannesburg: Picador Africa.

Blakely, Edward J., and Mary Gail Snyder. 1997. *Fortress America: Gated Communities in the United States*. New York: Brookings Institution Press.

Blaser, Thomas. 2004. "A New South African Imaginary: Nation Building and Afrikaners in Post-apartheid South Africa." *South African Historical Journal* 51:179–98.

Bond, Patrick. 2000. *Elite Transition: From Apartheid to Neoliberalism in South Africa*. London: Pluto Press.

———. 2003a. *Against Global Apartheid: South Africa Meets the World Bank, IMF, and International Finance*. Cape Town: University of Cape Town Press.

———. 2003b. "The Degeneration of Urban Policy after Apartheid." In *Confronting Fragmentation: Housing and Urban Development in a Democratising Society*, ed. Philip Harrison, Marie Huchzermeyerm, and Mzwanele Mayekiso, 40–56. Cape Town: University of Cape Town Press.

———. 2006. "Reconciliation and Economic Reaction: Flaws in South Africa's Elite Transition." *Journal of International Affairs* 60 (1):141–56.

Bonikowski, Bart. 2017. "Ethno-nationalist Populism and the Mobilization of

Collective Resentment." *British Journal of Sociology* 68:S181–S213.

Bonilla-Silva, Eduardo. 2003. "Racial Attitudes or Racial Ideology? An Alternative Paradigm for Examining Actors' Racial Views." *Journal of Political Ideologies* 8:63–82.

———. 2004. "From Bi-racial to Tri-racial: Towards a New System of Racial Stratification in the USA." *Ethnic and Racial Studies* 27:931–50.

———. 2006. *Racism without Racists: Color-Blind Racism and the Persistence of Racial Inequality in the United States*. Lanham, MD: Rowman & Littlefield.

Bonnett, Alastair. 2004. *The Idea of the West: Culture, Politics and History*. London: Palgrave.

Boraine, Alex, and Janet Levy, eds. 1995. *The Healing of a Nation?* Rondebosch, SA: Justice in Transition.

Boraine, Alex, and Robert Plummer. 2000. *A Country Unmasked*. Oxford: Oxford University Press.

Bosma, Martin. 2015. *Minderheid in eigen land: Hoe progressieve strijd ontaardt in genocide en ANC-apartheid*. Amsterdam: Bibliotheca Africana Formicae.

Botma, Gabriël J. 2008. "Paying the Field: The Cultural Economy of Afrikaans at Naspers." *Ecquid Novi: African Journalism Studies* 29:42–63.

Bottomley, Edward-John. 2017. "Governing Poor Whites: Race, Philanthropy and Transnational Governmentality between the United States and South Africa." PhD diss., University of Cambridge.

Bourdieu, Pierre. 1984. *Distinction: A Social Critique of the Judgement of Taste*. Cambridge, MA: Harvard University Press.

Brinkley, Alan. 1994. "The Problem of American Conservatism." *American Historical Review* 99 (2): 409–29.

Brits, J. P. 2008. "Thabo Mbeki and the Afrikaners, 1986–2004." *Historia* 53:33–69.

Brown, Barbara B. 1987. "Facing the 'Black Peril': The Politics of Population Control in South Africa." *Journal of Southern African Studies* 13 (2): 256–73.

Brubaker, Rogers. 2017. "Why Populism?" *Theory and Society* 46 (5): 357–85.

Caldeira, Teresa P. R. 2000. *City of Walls: Crime, Segregation, and Citizenship in São Paulo*. Oakland: University of California Press.

Carlin, John. 2008. *Playing the Enemy: Nelson Mandela and the Game That Made a Nation*. New York: Penguin.

Carter, Prudence L. 2012. *Stubborn Roots: Race, Culture, and Inequality in US and South African Schools*. Oxford: Oxford University Press.

Chanock, Martin. 2001. *The Making of South African Legal Culture 1902–1936: Fear, Favour and Prejudice*. Cambridge: Cambridge University Press.

Chisholm, Linda. 2003. "The State of South Africa's Schools." In *The State of the Union: South Africa 2004–2005*, ed. John Daniel, Adam Habib, and

Roger Southall, 268–89. Cape Town: HSRC Press.

Christie, Pam. 2006. "Changing Regimes: Governmentality and Education Policy in Post-apartheid South Africa." *International Journal of Educational Development* 26:373–81.

Christopher, Anthony J. 2001. "Urban Segregation in Post-apartheid South Africa." *Urban Studies* 38:449–66.

Coetzee, John M. 1988. *White Writing: On the Culture of Letters in South Africa.* New Haven, CT: Yale University Press.

Coles, Robert. 1971. "Understanding White Racists." *New York Review of Books* 17:71–74.

Combahee River Collective. 1983. "The Combahee River Collective Statement." In *Home Girls: A Black Feminist Anthology*, 264–74. New York: Kitchen Table—Women of Color Press.

Commission for Employment Equity (CEE). 1999. "Commission for Employment Equity, Annual Report 1999–2000." Pretoria: Department of Labour.

Cone, James H., and William Hordern. 1971. "Dialogue on Black Theology." *Christian Century* 88:1085.

Connell, R. W., and James W. Messerschmidt. 2005. "Hegemonic Masculinity: Rethinking the Concept." *Gender & Society Hegemonic Masculinity: Rethinking the Concept* 19:829–59.

Cornwell, Gareth. 1996. "George Webb Hardy's 'the Black Peril' and the Social Meaning of 'Black Peril' in Early Twentieth-Century South Africa." *Journal of Southern African Studies* 22 (3): 441–53.

Cramer, Katherine J. 2016. *The Politics of Resentment: Rural Consciousness in Wisconsin and the Rise of Scott Walker.* Chicago: University of Chicago Press.

Crapanzano, Vincent. 1985. *Waiting: The Whites of South Africa.* New York: Random House.

Crenshaw, Kimberle Williams, and Reform Race. 1988. "Retrenchment: Transformation and Legitimation in Antidiscrimination Law." *Harvard Law Review* 101 (7): 133187.

Cronjé, Geoffrey. 1934. *Egskeiding en huweliksen Gesinsontbinding.* Amsterdam: Nv Swets & Zeitlinger.

———. 1945. *'N Tuiste vir die nageslag: Die blywende oplossing van Suid-Afrika se rassevraagstukke.* Pretoria: Auspiciis Universitatis Pretoriensis.

———. 1947. *Regverdigte rasse-apartheid.* Pretoria: Christen-Studenteverenigingmaatskappy van Suid-Afrika.

Cronjé, Geoffrey, and Jacobus D. Venter. 1958. *Die Patriargale Familie: 'N Kultuursosiologiese Studie.* Cape Town: HAUM.

Davies, Rebecca. 2012. "Afrikaner Capital Elites, Neo-liberalism and Economic Transformation in Post-apartheid South Africa." *African Studies* 71:391–407.

Dawson, Michael C. 1994. "A Black Counterpublic? Economic Earthquakes,

Racial Agenda(s), and Black Politics." *Public Culture* 7:195–223.

DeGloma, Thomas. 2014. *Seeing the Light: The Social Logic of Personal Discovery*. Chicago: University of Chicago Press.

de Klerk, Willem. 2000. *Afrikaners: Kroes, kras, kordaat*. Kaapstad, SA: Human & Rousseau.

Derrida, Jacques. 1985. "Racism's Last Word." *Critical Inquiry* 12:290–99.

DiAngelo, Robin. 2018. *White Fragility: Why It's So Hard for White People to Talk about Racism*. New York: Beacon Press.

Distiller, Natasha, and Melissa E. Steyn, eds. 2004. *Under Construction: "Race" and Identity in South Africa Today*. Cape Town: Heinemann.

Dolby, Nadine. 2001a. *Constructing Race: Youth, Identity, and Popular Culture in South Africa*. Albany: SUNY Press.

———. 2001b. "White Fright: The Politics of White Youth Identity in South Africa." *British Journal of Sociology of Education* 22:5–17.

———. 2002. "Making White: Constructing Race in a South African High School." *Curriculum Inquiry* 32:7–29.

Dooling, Wayne. 2018. "'Cape Town Knows, but She Forgets': Segregation and the Making of a Housing Crisis during the First Half of the 20th Century." *Journal of Southern African Studies* 44:1057–76.

Drake, St. Clair, and Horace R. Cayton. 1970. *Black Metropolis: A Study of Negro Life in a Northern City*. Chicago: University of Chicago Press.

Du Bois, W. E. B. 1935. *Black Reconstruction in America: Toward a History of the Part Which Black Folk Played in the Attempt to Reconstruct Democracy in America, 1860–1880*. New York: Harcourt, Brace.

Du Bois, W. E. B., and Isabel Eaton. 1899. *The Philadelphia Negro: A Social Study*. Boston: Ginn.

Dubow, Saul. 1989. *Racial Segregation and the Origins of Apartheid in South Africa, 1919–36*. New York: St. Martin's Press.

———. 1992. "Afrikaner Nationalism, Apartheid and the Conceptualization of 'Race.'" *Journal of African History* 33:209–37.

———. 2001. "Scientism, Social Research and the Limits of 'South Africanism': The Case of Ernst Gideon Malherbe." *South African Historical Journal* 44:99–142.

———. 2014. *Apartheid, 1948–1994*. Oxford: Oxford University Press.

Dubow, Saul, and William Beinart, eds. 1995. *Segregation and Apartheid in Twentieth-Century South Africa*. London: Routledge.

Duncan, James, and Nancy Duncan. 2004. *Landscapes of Privilege: The Politics of the Aesthetic in an American Suburb*. New York: Routledge.

———. 2006. "Aesthetics, Abjection, and White Privilege in Suburban New York." In *Landscape and Race in the United States*, ed. Richard H. Schein, 157–85. New York: Routledge.

Du Pisani, Kobus. 2001. "Puritanism Transformed: Afrikaner Masculinities in the Apartheid and Post-apartheid Period." In *Changing Men in Southern*

Africa, ed. Robert Morrell, 157–75. Pietermaritzburg, SA: Natal University Press.

Du Preez, Max. 2004. *Pale Native: Memories of a Renegade Reporter*. Cape Town: Zebra.

Durrheim, Kevin, Xoliswa Mtose, and Lyndsay Brown. 2011. *Race Trouble: Race, Identity and Inequality in Post-apartheid South Africa*. New York: Lexington Books.

Du Toit, Andries, Sandra Kruger, and Stefano Ponte. 2008. "Deracializing Exploitation? 'Black Economic Empowerment' in the South African Wine Industry." *Journal of Agrarian Change* 8:6–32.

Du Toit, P. 1934. *Verslag van die Volkskongres oor die Armblankevraagstuk gehou te Kimberley, 2–5 Okt*. Cape Town: Nasionale Pers Beperk.

Duyvendak, Jan. 2011. *The Politics of Home: Belonging and Nostalgia in Europe and the United States*. London: Palgrave Macmillan.

Dyer, Thomas G. 1992. *Theodore Roosevelt and the Idea of Race*. Baton Rouge: LSU Press.

Essed, Philomena. 1991. *Understanding Everyday Racism: An Interdisciplinary Theory*. London: SAGE Publications.

Erasmus, Zimitri. 2017. *Race Otherwise: Forging a New Humanism for South Africa*. New York: NYU Press.

Everatt, David. 2009. *The Origins of Non-racialism: White Opposition to Apartheid in the 1950s*. New York: NYU Press.

Fanon, Frantz. 1952. *Black Skin, White Masks*. New York: Grove Press.

———. 1967. *Toward the African Revolution: Political Essays*. New York: Grove Press.

Feagin, Joe R. 2013. *The White Racial Frame: Centuries of Racial Framing and Counter-framing*. New York: Routledge.

Feagin, Joe R., and Kimberley Ducey. 2017. *Elite White Men Ruling: Who, What, When, Where, and How*. New York: Routledge.

Feagin, Joe R., and Sean Elias. 2013. Rethinking Racial Formation Theory: A Systemic Racism Critique. *Ethnic and Racial Studies* 36 (6): 9360.

Feagin, Joe R., and Eileen O'Brien. 2003. *White Men on Race: Power, Privilege and the Shaping of Cultural Consciousness*. New York: Beacon Press.

Feagin, Joe R., and Debra Van Ausdale. 2001. *The First R: How Children Learn Race and Racism*. Lanham, MD: Rowman & Littlefield.

Feagin, Joe R., and Hernan Vera. 1980. *Liberation Sociology*. Boulder, CO: Westview Press.

Fields, Karen E., and Barbara J. Fields. 2012. *Racecraft: The Soul of Inequality in American Life*. London: Verso.

Fleming, Crystal Marie. 2017. *Resurrecting Slavery: Racial Legacies and White Supremacy in France*. Philadelphia: Temple University Press.

Formisano, Ronald P. 2004. *Boston against Busing: Race, Class, and Ethnicity in the 1960s and 1970s*. Chapel Hill: University of North Carolina Press.

Frankenberg, Ruth. 1991. *White Women, Race Matters: The Social Construction of Whiteness*. London: Routledge.

Fraser, Nancy. 1990. "Rethinking the Public Sphere: A Contribution to the Critique of Actually Existing Democracy." *Social Text* 25/26:56–80.

Frederikse, Julie. 1990. *The Unbreakable Thread: Non-racialism in South Africa*. Bloomington: Indiana University Press.

Fredrickson, George M. 1982. *White Supremacy: A Comparative Study of American and South African History*. New York: Oxford University Press.

———. 1997. *The Comparative Imagination: On the History of Racism, Nationalism, and Social Movements*. Oakland: University of California Press.

———. 2015. *Racism: A Short History*. Princeton, NJ: Princeton University Press.

Frey, William H. 2018. *Diversity Explosion: How New Racial Demographics Are Remaking America*. New York: Brookings Institution Press.

Furlong, Patrick Jonathan. 1991. *Between Crown and Swastika: The Impact of the Radical Right on the Afrikaner Nationalist Movement in the Fascist Era*. Middletown, CT: Wesleyan University Press.

Gallagher, Charles A. 1997. "Redefining Racial Privilege in the United States." *Transformations: The Journal of Inclusive Scholarship and Pedagogy* 8:28–39.

Garvey, John, and Noel Ignatiev. 1997. "Toward a New Abolitionism: A Race Traitor Manifesto." In *Whiteness: A Critical Reader*, ed. Mike Hill, 346–49. New York: NYU Press.

Gest, Justin. 2016. *The New Minority: White Working Class Politics in an Age of Immigration and Inequality*. New York: Oxford University Press.

Gevisser, Mark. 1996. *Portraits of Power: Profiles in a Changing South Africa*. Cape Town: New Africa Books.

Gibson, James L. 2006. *Overcoming Apartheid: Can Truth Reconcile a Divided Nation?* New York: Russell Sage Foundation.

Giliomee, Hermann. 2003a. *The Afrikaners: Biography of a People*. Charlottesville: University of Virginia Press.

———. 2003b. "The Making of the Apartheid Plan, 1929–1948." *Journal of Southern African Studies* 29:373–92.

Giliomee, H., J. Myburgh, and L. Schlemmer. 2001. "Dominant Party Rule, Opposition Parties and Minorities in South Africa." *Democratization* 8:161–82.

Giordano, Peggy C. 2003. "Relationships in Adolescence." *Annual Review of Sociology* 29:257–81.

Godsell, Gillian. 1991. "Entrepreneurs Embattled: Barriers to Entrepreneurship in South Africa." In *The Culture of Entrepreneurship*, ed. Brigitte Berger, 85–97. San Francisco: ICS Press.

Goodwin, June, and Ben Schiff. 1995. *Heart of Whiteness: Afrikaners Face Black Rule in the New South Africa*. New York: Simon and Schuster.

Goodwin, Matthew, and Jocelyn Evans. 2012. *Far Right Extremism in Britain.* London: Searchlight Education Trust.

Gumede, W. M. 2007. *Thabo Mbeki and the Battle for the Soul of the ANC.* Cape Town: Struik.

Gunner, Liz. 2008. "Jacob Zuma, the Social Body and the Unruly Power of Song." *African Affairs* 108:27–48.

Habermas, Jurgen. 1991. *The Structural Transformation of the Public Sphere: An Inquiry into a Category of Bourgeois Society.* 6th ed. Cambridge, MA: MIT Press.

Habib, Adam, and Vishnu Padayachee. 2000. "Economic Policy and Power Relations in South Africa's Transition to Democracy." *World Development* 28:245–63.

Hacker, Andrew. 1993. "Two Nations: Black and White, Separate, Hostile." New York: Ballantine.

Hagerman, Margaret A. 2018. *White Kids: Growing Up with Privilege in a Racially Divided America.* New York: NYU Press

Hall, Stuart, Chas Critcher, Tony Jefferson, John Clarke, and Brian Roberts. 1978. *Policing the Crisis: Mugging, the State, and Law and Order.* New York: Holmes and Meier.

Harris, Cheryl I. 1993. "Whiteness as Property." *Harvard Law Review* 106 (8): 1707–91.

Harrison, David. 1983. *The White Tribe of Africa: South Africa in Perspective.* Oakland: University of California Press.

Harrison, Philip, Alison Todes, and Vanessa Watson. 2007. *Planning and Transformation: Learning from the Post-apartheid Experience.* London: Routledge.

Hart, Deborah M. 1988. "Political Manipulation of Urban Space: The Razing of District Six, Cape Town." *Urban Geography* 9:603–28.

Hart, Gillian. 2014. *Rethinking the South African Crisis: Nationalism, Populism, Hegemony.* Athens: University of Georgia Press.

Hartigan, John. 2010. *Race in the 21st Century: Ethnographic Approaches.* New York: Oxford University Press.

Harvey, David. 1985. *The Urban Experience.* Baltimore: Johns Hopkins University Press.

Hayner, Priscilla B. 2000. *Unspeakable Truths: Confronting State Terror and Atrocity.* New York: Routledge.

Henrard, Kristin. 2002. *Minority Protection in Post-apartheid South Africa: Human Rights, Minority Rights, and Self-determination.* Westport, CT: Greenwood Press.

Heribert, Adam, ed. 1971. *Politics in South Africa: Sociological Perspectives.* Oxford: Oxford University Press.

Hermann, Dirk Johannes. 2007. *The Naked Emperor: Why Affirmative Action Failed.* Pretoria: Protea Book House.

———. 2013. *Affirmative Tears: Why Representivity Does Not Equal Equality*. Cape Town: Kraal-Uitgewers.

Himmelstein, Jerome L. 1992. *To the Right: The Transformation of American Conservatism*. Oakland: University of California Press.

Hirschmann, David. 1990. "The Black Consciousness Movement in South Africa." *Journal of Modern African Studies* 28:1–22.

Hochschild, Arlie Russell. 2016. *Strangers in Their Own Land: Anger and Mourning on the American Right*. New York: The New Press.

Hochschild, Jennifer L. 2005. "Looking Ahead: Racial Trends in the United States." *Daedalus* 134:70–81.

Hook, Derek. 2005. "Affecting Whiteness: Racism as Technology of Affect." *International Journal of Critical Psychology* 16:74–99.

———. 2006. "Pre-discursive Racism." *Journal of Community & Applied Social Psychology* 16:207–32.

hooks, bell. 1984. *Feminist Theory: From Center to Margin*. Cambridge, MA: South End Press.

Horowitz, Donald L. 1992. *A Democratic South Africa? Constitutional Engineering in a Divided Society*. Oakland: University of California Press.

Hughey, Matthew. 2012. *White Bound: Nationalists, Antiracists, and the Shared Meanings of Race*. Stanford, CA: Stanford University Press.

Hunter, Mark. 2011. "Beneath the 'Zunami': Jacob Zuma and the Gendered Politics of Social Reproduction in South Africa." *Antipode* 43:1102–26.

Hyslop, Jonathan. 1999. "The Imperial Working Class Makes Itself 'White': White Labourism in Britain, Australia, and South Africa before the First World War." *Journal of Historical Sociology* 12:398–421.

Iheduru, Okechukwu C. 2004. "Black Economic Power and Nation-Building in Post-apartheid South Africa." *Journal of Modern African Studies* 42:1–30.

———. 2008. "Why 'Anglo Licks the ANC's Boots': Globalization and State–Capital Relations in South Africa." *African Affairs* 107:333–60.

Ioanide, Paula. 2015. *The Emotional Politics of Racism: How Feelings Trump Facts in an Era of Colorblindness*. Stanford, CA: Stanford University Press.

Jansen, Jonathan D. 2009. *Knowledge in the Blood: Confronting Race and the Apartheid Past*. Stanford, CA: Stanford University Press.

Jardina, Ashley. 2019. *White Identity Politics*. Cambridge: Cambridge University Press.

Jelin, Elizabeth. 2003. *State Repression and the Labors of Memory*. Minneapolis: University of Minnesota Press.

Johnstone, Anika. 2001. *The Politics of Apology and Acknowledgement: White Engagement with South Africa's Reconciliation Process—A Discussion Paper*. Johannesburg: Centre for the Study of Violence and Reconciliation.

Jung, Courtney. 2000. *Then I Was Black: South African Political Identities in Transition*. New Haven, CT: Yale University Press.

Kaltwasser, Cristóbal Rovira, Paul A. Taggart, Paulina Ochoa Espejo, and

Pierre Ostiguy, eds. 2017. *The Oxford Handbook of Populism*. Oxford: Oxford University Press.

Kaufmann, Eric. 2018. *Whiteshift: Populism, Immigration and the Future of White Majorities*. London: Penguin.

Kazin, Michael. 1998. *The Populist Persuasion: An American History*. Ithaca, NY: Cornell University Press.

Keegan, Timothy. 1986. *Rural Transformations in Industrialising South Africa*. Johannesburg: Ravan Press.

Kefalas, Maria. 2003. *Working-Class Heroes: Protecting Home, Community, and Nation in a Chicago Neighborhood*. Oakland: University of California Press.

Kempa, Clifford D., and Michael Shearing. 2000. "The Role of 'Private Security' in Transitional Democracies." In *Crime and Policing in Transitional Societies*, 205–14. Johannesburg: Jan Smuts House, University of the Witwatersrand.

Kendall, Diana. 2008. *Members Only: Elite Clubs and the Process of Exclusion*. Lanham, MD: Rowman & Littlefield.

Kendi, Ibram X. 2019. *How to Be an Antiracist*. New York: One World.

Khan, Shamus Rahman. 2011. *Privilege: The Making of an Adolescent Elite at St. Paul's School*. Princeton, NJ: Princeton University Press.

———. 2012a. "Elite Identities." *Identities* 19:477–84.

———. 2012b. "The Sociology of Elites." *Annual Review of Sociology* 38:361–77.

Kinder, Donald R., and David O. Sears. 1981. "Prejudice and Politics: Symbolic Racism versus Racial Threats to the Good Life." *Journal of Personality and Social Psychology* 40:414.

Klopper, Annie. 2011a. *Biografie van 'n bende: Die storie van Fokofpolisiekar*. Cape Town: Protea Boekhuis.

———. 2011b. "'In ferocious anger I bit the hand that controls': The Rise of Afrikaans Punk Rock Music." In *Reshaping Remembrance: Critical Essays on Afrikaans Places of Memory*, ed. Albert Grundlingh and Siegfried Huigen, 179–89. Amsterdam: Rozenberg.

Koopmans, Ruud. 2018. "Cultural Rights of Native Majorities between Universalism and Minority Rights." WZB Discussion Paper no. VI 2018–106.

Kretzer, Michael M., and Russell H. Kaschula. 2021. "Language Policy and Linguistic Landscapes at Schools in South Africa." *International Journal of Multilingualism* 18:105–27.

Krog, Antjie. 1999. *Country of My Skull: Guilt, Sorrow, and the Limits of Forgiveness in the New South Africa*. New York: Three River Press.

———. 2003. *Change of Tongue*. Cape Town: Penguin Random House.

———. 2009. *Begging to Be Black*. Cape Town: Penguin Random House.

Kruse, Kevin Michael, and Thomas J. Sugrue. 2006. *The New Suburban History*. Chicago: University of Chicago Press.

Kyratzis, Amy. 2004. "Talk and Interaction among Children and the Co-construction of Peer Groups and Peer Culture." *Annual Review of Anthropology*, 33:625–49.

Lake, Marilyn, and Henry Reynolds. 2008. *Drawing the Global Colour Line: White Men's Countries and the Question of Racial Equality*. Cambridge: Cambridge Univeristy Press.

Lamont, Michèle. 1992. *Money, Morals, and Manners: The Culture of the French and the American Upper-middle Class*. Chicago: University of Chicago Press.

———. 2000. *The Dignity of Working Men: Morality and the Boundaries of Race, Class, and Immigration*. Cambridge, MA: Harvard University Press.

Lamont, Michèle, Bo Yun Park, and Elena Ayala-Hurtado. 2017. "Trump's Electoral Speeches and His Appeal to the American White Working Class." *British Journal of Sociology* 68:S153–S180.

Landry, Bart, and Kris Marsh. 2011. "The Evolution of the New Black Middle Class." *Annual Review of Sociology* 37:373–94.

Lareau, Annette. 2003. *Unequal Childhoods: Class, Race, and Family Life*. Oakland: University of California Press.

Lemanski, Charlotte. 2004. "A New Apartheid? The Spatial Implications of Fear of Crime in Cape Town, South Africa." *Environment and Urbanization* 16:101–12.

Lemon, Anthony. 2005. "Shifting Geographies of Social Inclusion and Exclusion: Secondary Education in Pietermaritzburg, South Africa." *African Affairs* 104:69–96.

Lewis, Amanda E. 2003. *Race in the Schoolyard: Negotiating the Color Line in Classrooms and Communities*. New Brunswick, NJ: Rutgers University Press.

———. 2004. "'What Group?' Studying Whites and Whiteness in the Era of 'Color-Blindness.'" *Sociological Theory* 22:623–46.

Lipsitz, George. 2006. *The Possessive Investment in Whiteness: How White People Profit from Identity Politics*. Philadelphia: Temple University Press.

———. 2007. "The Racialization of Space and the Spatialization of Race: Theorizing the Hidden Architecture of Landscape." *Landscape Journal* 26 (1): 10–23.

———. 2011. *How Racism Takes Place*. Philadelphia: Temple University Press.

Lo, Clarence Y. H. 1982. "Countermovements and Conservative Movements in the Contemporary US." *Annual Review of Sociology* 8 (1): 107–34.

———. 1995. *Small Property versus Big Government: Social Origins of the Property Tax Revolt*. Oakland: University of California Press.

Lodge, Tom. 1983. *Black Politics in South Africa since 1945*. London: Longman.

———. 2007. *Mandela: A Critical Life*. Oxford: Oxford University Press.

———. 2011. *Sharpeville: An Apartheid Massacre and Its Consequences*. Oxford: Oxford University Press.

Lodge, Tom, and Bill Nasson. 1991. *All, Here, and Now: Black Politics in South Africa in the 1980s*. London: Hurst.

Lorde, Audre. 2007. "'The Master's Tools Will Never Dismantle the Master's House.'" In *Sister Outsider: Essays and Speeches*, 110–14. Berkeley, CA: Crossing Press.

Louw, C. 2001. *Boetman en die swanesang van die verligtes*. Kaapstad, SA: Human & Rosseau.

Love, Janice. 1985. *The US Anti-apartheid Movement: Local Activism in Global Politics*. New York: Praeger.

Low, Setha. 2004. *Behind the Gates: Life, Security, and the Pursuit of Happiness in Fortress America*. New York: Routledge.

Lubbe, Henriette J. 1997. "The Myth of 'Black Peril': Die Burger and the 1929 Election." *South African Historical Journal* 37 (1): 107–32.

Mabin, Alan. 1992. "Comprehensive Segregation: The Origins of the Group Areas Act and Its Planning Apparatuses." *Journal of Southern African Studies* 18:405–29.

Mabin, Alan, and Dan Smit. 1997. "Reconstructing South Africa's Cities? The Making of Urban Planning 1900–2000." *Planning Perspectives* 12:193–223.

MacDonald, Michael. 2006. *Why Race Matters in South Africa*. Cambridge, MA: Harvard University Press.

———. 2013. "Mandela's Non-racialism." *Logos* 12 (3):12.

Madison, D. Soyini. 2011. *Critical Ethnography: Method, Ethics, and Performance*. London: SAGE Publications.

Magubane, Zine. 1998. Review of *What Racists Believe* by Gerhard Schutte and *Ethnicity in Focus* by Simon Bekker. *Social Dynamics* 23:133–39.

———. 2008. "The American Construction of the Poor White Problem in South Africa." *South Atlantic Quarterly* 107:691–713.

Makovicky, Nicolette. 2013. "'Work Pays': Slovak Neoliberalism as 'Authoritarian Populism.'" *Focaal* 67:77–90.

Mamdani, Mahmood. 1998. *When Does Reconciliation Turn into a Denial of Justice?* Pretoria: HSRC.

———. 2015. "Beyond Nuremberg: The Historical Significance of the Post-apartheid Transition in South Africa." *Politics & Society* 43:61–88.

Mandela, Nelson Rolihlahla. 1995. *Long Walk to Freedom: The Autobiography of Nelson Mandela*. New York: Little Brown.

Mangcu, Xolela. 2012. *Biko: A Biography*. Cape Town: Tafelberg.

<3mc> ed. 2015. *The Colour of Our Future: Does Race Matter in Post-apartheid South Africa?* Johannesburg: Wits University Press.

<3mc> 2017. "Shattering the Myth of a Post-racial Consensus in South African Higher Education: 'Rhodes Must Fall' and the Struggle for Transformation at the University of Cape Town." *Critical Philosophy of Race* 5:243–66.

Marais, H. 1999. *South Africa: Limits to Change.* Cape Town: University of Cape Town Press.

———. 2011. *South Africa Pushed to the Limit: The Political Economy of Change.* Cape Town: Zed Books.

Marcus, George E. 1995. "Ethnography in/of the World System: The Emergence of Multi-sited Ethnography." *Annual Review of Anthropology* 24:95–117.

———. 2009. "Multi-sited Ethnography: Notes and Queries." In *Multi-sited Ethnography: Theory, Praxis, and Locality in Contemporary Research*, ed. Mark-Anthony Faldon, 181–96. New York: Routledge.

Maré, Gerhard. 2014. *Declassified: Moving beyond the Dead End of Race in South Africa.* Johannesburg: Jacana Media.

Marx, Anthony W. 1997. *Making Race and Nation: A Comparison of South Africa, the United States, and Brazil.* New York: Cambridge University Press.

Mattes, Robert. 2012. "The 'Born Frees': The Prospects for Generational Change in Post-apartheid South Africa." *Australian Journal of Political Science* 47:133–53.

Maylam, Paul. 1990. "The Rise and Decline of Urban Apartheid in South Africa." *African Affairs* 89:57–84.

———. 1995. "Explaining the Apartheid City: 20 Years of South African Urban Historiography." *Journal of Southern African Studies* 21:19–38.

McClintock, Anne. 1991. "'No longer in a future heaven': Women and Nationalism in South Africa." *Transition* 51: 104–23.

McDermott, Monica. 2006. *Working-Class White: The Making and Unmaking of Race Relations.* Oakland: University of California Press.

McDonnell, Terence E., Christopher A. Bail, and Iddo Tavory. 2017. "A Theory of Resonance." *Sociological Theory* 35:1–14.

McDowell, Linda. 2011. *Redundant Masculinities? Employment Change and White Working Class Youth.* Hoboken, NJ: John Wiley & Sons.

McGee, Timothy. 2017. "Against (White) Redemption: James Cone and the Christological Disruption of Racial Discourse and White Solidarity." *Political Theology* 18:542–59.

McKinney, Karyn D. 2013. *Being White: Stories of Race and Racism.* New York: Routledge.

Meiring, Pieter. 2014. *Chronicle of the Truth and Reconciliation Commission: A Journey through the Past and Present into the Future of South Africa.* Cape Town: Wipf and Stock.

Milazzo, M. 2015. "The Rhetorics of Racial Power: Enforcing Colorblindness in Post-apartheid Scholarship on Race." *Journal of International and Intercultural Communication* 8:7–26.

Miller, Jamie. 2016. *An African Volk: The Apartheid Regime and Its Search for Survival.* Oxford: Oxford University Press.

Miller, Roberta Balstad. 1993. "Science and Society in the Early Career of HF

Verwoerd." *Journal of Southern African Studies* 19:634–61.

Mills, C. Wright. 1956. *The Power Elite.* Oxford: Oxford University Press.

Minow, Martha. 1998. *Between Vengeance and Forgiveness: Facing History after Genocide and Mass Violence.* New York: Beacon Press.

———. 2015. "Forgiveness, Law, and Justice." *California Law Review* 103:1615.

Moodley, Kogila, and Heribert Adam. 2000. "Race and Nation in Post-apartheid South Africa." *Current Sociology* 48:51–69.

Morning, Ann. 2011. *The Nature of Race: How Scientists Think and Teach about Human Difference.* Oakland: University of California Press.

Morrell, Robert. 1998. "Of Boys and Men: Masculinity and Gender in Southern African Studies." *Journal of Southern African Studies* 24:605–30.

Morris, Edward W. 2006. *An Unexpected Minority: White Kids in an Urban School.* New Brunswick, NJ: Rutgers University Press.

Morrison, Toni. 1992. *Playing in the Dark: Whiteness and the Literary Imagination.* Cambridge, MA: Harvard University Press.

Motala, Enver, and Mala Singh. 2002. "Introduction." In *The State, Education and Equity in Post-apartheid South Africa*, ed. Enver Motala and John Pampallis, 1–13. Burlington, VT: Ashgate.

Mudde, Cas. 2007. *Populist Radical Right Parties in Europe.* Cambridge: Cambridge University Press.

———. 2016. *The Populist Radical Right: A Reader.* London: Taylor & Francis.

Nauright, John. 1998. "'The Mecca of Native Scum' and 'A Running Sore of Evil': White Johannesburg and the Alexandra Township Removal Debate, 1935–1945." *African Historical Review* 30:64–88.

Ndahinda, F. M. 2011. *Indigenousness in Africa: A Contested Legal Framework for Empowerment of "Marginalized" Communities.* Leiden: Springer.

Ndebele, Njabulo S. 2000. "'Iph'Indlela? Finding Our Way into the Future'— The First Steve Biko Memorial Lecture." *Social Dynamics* 26:43–55.

Nelson, Dana D. 1998. *National Manhood: Capitalist Citizenship and the Imagined Fraternity of White Men.* Durham, NC: Duke University Press.

Norris, Pippa, and Ronald Inglehart. 2019. *Cultural Backlash and the Rise of Populism: Trump, Brexit, and Authoritarian Populism.* Cambridge: Cambridge University Press.

Nuttall, Sarah. 2001. "Subjectivities of Whiteness." *African Studies Review* 44:115–40.

Nyamnjoh, Francis B. 2012. "Blinded by Sight: Divining the Future of Anthropology in Africa." *Africa Spectrum* 47:63–92.

Olick, Jeffrey K. 2005. *In the House of the Hangman: The Agonies of German Defeat, 1943–1949.* Chicago: University of Chicago Press.

O'Meara, Dan. 1983. *Volkskapitalisme: Class, Capital and Ideology in the Development of Afrikaner Nationalism, 1934–1948.* African Studies Series

34. Cambridge: Cambridge University Press.

Omi, Michael, and Howard Winant. 1994. *Racial Formation in the US: From the 1960s to the 1990s*. New York: Routledge.

Otter, Steven. 2012. *Khayelitsha: Umlungu in a Township*. Cape Town: Penguin Random House South Africa.

Parnell, Susan. 1988a. "Public Housing as a Device for White Residential Segregation in Johannesburg, 1934–1953." *Urban Geography* 9:584–602.

———. 1988b. "Racial Segregation in Johannesburg: The Slums Act, 1934–1939." *South African Geographical Journal* 70:112–26.

Paulle, Bowen. 2013. *Toxic Schools: High-Poverty Education in New York and Amsterdam*. Chicago: University of Chicago Press.

Pearson, Charles Henry. 1893. *National Life and Character: A Forecast*. New York: Macmillan.

Perry, Pamela. 2002. *Shades of White: White Kids and Racial Identities in High School*. Durham, NC: Duke University Press.

Pollock, Friedrich, and Theodor W. Adorno. 2011. *Group Experiment and Other Writings*. Cambridge, MA: Harvard University Press.

Pollock, Mica. 2009. *Colormute: Race Talk Dilemmas in an American School*. Princeton, NJ: Princeton University Press.

Ponte, Stefano, Simon Roberts, and Lance Van Sittert. 2007. "'Black Economic Empowerment': Business and the State in South Africa." *Development and Change* 38:933–55.

Posel, Deborah. 1991. *The Making of Apartheid, 1948–1961: Conflict and Compromise*. Oxford: Oxford University Press.

———. 1999. "Whiteness and Power in the South African Civil Service: Paradoxes of the Apartheid State." *Journal of Southern African Studies* 25:99–119.

———. 2013. "The ANC Youth League and the Politicization of Race." *Thesis Eleven* 115:58–76.

Ramphele, Mamphela. 2008. *Laying Ghosts to Rest: Dilemmas of the Transformation in South Africa*. Cape Town: Tafelberg.

Rasmussen, Birgit Brander, Eric Klinenberg, Irene J. Nexica, and Matt Wray. 2001. *The Making and Unmaking of Whiteness*. Durham, NC: Duke University Press.

Rassool, Ciraj. 2004. "The Individual, Auto/biography and History in South Africa." PhD diss., University of the Western Cape.

———. 2019. "The Politics of Nonracialism in South Africa." *Public Culture* 31:343–71.

Retief, Zed. 2013. "Unsettling Whiteness: Kipling's Boers and the Case for a White Subalternity." MS thesis, University of Cape Town.

Rieder, Jonathan. 1985. *Canarsie: The Jews and Italians of Brooklyn against Liberalism*. Cambridge, MA: Harvard University Press.

Robinson, C. J. 1983. *Black Marxism: The Making of the Black Radical Tradi-*

tion. London: Zed Press.

Robinson, Sally. 2000. *Marked Men: White Masculinity in Crisis.* New York: Columbia University Press.

Roediger, David R. 1999. *The Wages of Whiteness: Race and the Making of the American Working Class.* London: Verso.

Roos, Neil. 2015. "Alcohol Panic, Social Engineering, and Some Reflections on the Management of Whites in Early Apartheid Society, 1948–1960." *Historical Journal* 58:1167–89.

Rosa, Jonathan, and Yarimar Bonilla. 2017. "Deprovincializing Trump, Decolonizing Diversity, and Unsettling Anthropology." *American Ethnologist* 44 (2): 201–8.

Rothmann, Mimie E., J. R. Albertyn, Johann Friedrich Wilhelm Grosskopf, Ernst Gideon Malherbe, W. A. Murray, and Raymond William Wilcocks. 1932. *The Poor White Problem in South Africa: Report of the Carnegie Commission.* Cape Town: Pro Ecclesia Drukkery.

Rydgren, Jens. 2007. "The Sociology of the Radical Right." *Annual Review of Sociology* 33:241–62.

Sadie, Johannes L. 2002. "The Fall and Rise of the Afrikaner in the South African Economy." *University of Stellenbosch Annale 2002/01.*

Saito, Leland T. 1998. *Race and Politics: Asian Americans, Latinos, and Whites in a Los Angeles Suburb.* Champaign: University of Illinois Press.

Salmela, Mikko, and Christian von Scheve. 2017. "Emotional Roots of Right-Wing Political Populism." *Social Science Information* 56:567–95.

Salverda, Tijo, and Jon Abbink. 2013. "Introduction: An Anthropological Perspective on Elite Power and the Cultural Politics of Elites." In *The Anthropology of Elites,* ed. Jon Abbink and Tijo Salverda, 1–28. New York: Palgrave Macmillan.

Scott, David. 2004. *Conscripts of Modernity: The Tragedy of Colonial Enlightenment.* Durham, NC: Duke University Press.

Sears, David O., and Patrick J. Henry. 2003. "The Origins of Symbolic Racism." *Journal of Personality and Social Psychology* 85:259.

Sears, David O., James Sidanius, and Lawrence Bobo. 2000. *Racialized Politics: The Debate about Racism in America.* Chicago: University of Chicago Press.

Seekings, Jeremy. 2000. *The UDF: A History of the United Democratic Front in South Africa, 1983–1991.* Athens: Ohio University Press.

———. 2007. "'Not a Single White Person Should Be Allowed to Go Under': Swartgevaar and the Origins of South Africa's Welfare State, 1924–1929." *Journal of African History* 48 (3): 375–94.

———. 2008. "The Carnegie Commission and the Backlash against Welfare State-Building in South Africa, 1931–1937." *Journal of Southern African Studies,* 34:515–37.

Seekings, Jeremy, and Nicoli Nattrass. 2008. *Class, Race, and Inequality in*

South Africa. New Haven, CT: Yale University Press.

Sherman, Rachel. 2019. *Uneasy Street: The Anxieties of Affluence*. Princeton, NJ: Princeton University Press.

Simon, Jonathan. 2007. *Governing through Crime: How the War on Crime Transformed American Democracy and Created a Culture of Fear*. New York: Oxford University Press.

Sonn, Franklin. 1993. "Afrikaner Nationalism and Black Advancement as Two Sides of the Same Coin." In *Affirmative Action in a Democratic South Africa*, ed. C. Adams, 1–10. Cape Town: Juta Kenwyn.

Soske, Jon. 2015. "The Impossible Concept: Settler Liberalism, Pan-Africanism, and the Language of Non-racialism." *African Historical Review* 47:1–36.

Soudien, Crain. 2007. *Youth Identity in Contemporary South Africa: Race, Culture and Schooling*. Cape Town: New Africa Books.

———. 2012. *Realising the Dream: Unlearning the Logic of Race in the South African School*. Cape Town: HSRC Press.

Southall, Roger. 2004. "The ANC & Black Capitalism in South Africa." *Review of African Political Economy* 31:313–28.

Sparks, Allister. 1996. *Tomorrow Is Another Country: The Inside Story of South Africa's Road to Change*. Chicago: University of Chicago Press.

Steensland, Ann M. 2014. "Pathologizing the Bywoner: The Carnegie Commission Report's Diagnosis of 'Poor White Disease' in South Africa (1932)." PhD diss., George Mason University.

Steinberg, Stephen. 1988. "The Social Context of the White Backlash: A Critique of Jonathan Rieder's Carnarsie." *Ethnic and Racial Studies* 11:218–24.

Steyn, Melissa. 2001. *Whiteness Just Isn't What It Used to Be: White Identity in a Changing South Africa*. Albany: SUNY Press.

Stultz, Newell Maynard. 1974. *Afrikaner Politics in South Africa, 1934–1948*. Oakland: University of California Press.

Sugrue, Thomas J. 1995. "Crabgrass-Roots Politics: Race, Rights, and the Reaction against Liberalism in the Urban North, 1940–1964." *Journal of American History* 82 (2): 551–78.

———. 1996. *The Origins of the Urban Crisis: Race and Inequality in Postwar Detroit-Updated Edition*. Princeton, NJ: Princeton University Press.

Sulla, Victor, and Precious Zikhali. 2018. *Overcoming Poverty and Inequality in South Africa: An Assessment of Drivers, Constraints and Opportunities*. Washington, DC: World Bank.

Swart, Sandra 1998. "'A Boer and His Gun and His Wife Are Three Things Always Together': Republican Masculinity and the 1914 Rebellion." 24 24:737–51.

Taguieff, Pierre-André. 1990. "The New Cultural Racism in France." *Telos* 83:109–22.

———. 2001. *The Force of Prejudice: On Racism and Its Doubles*. Minneapolis: University of Minnesota Press.

Tangri, Roger, and Roger Southall. 2008. "The Politics of Black Economic Empowerment in South Africa." *Journal of Southern African Studies* 34:699–716.

Tayler, Judith. 1992. "'Our Poor': The Politicisation of the Poor White Problem, 1932–1942." *African Historical Review* 24 (1): 40–65.

Teeger, Chana. 2015. "'Both Sides of the Story': History Education in Postapartheid South Africa." *American Sociological Review* 80:1175–1200.

Telles, Edward Eric. 2004. *Race in Another America: The Significance of Skin Color in Brazil*. Princeton, NJ: Princeton University Press.

Tent, James F. 1982. *Mission on the Rhine: "Reeducation" and Denazification in American-Occupied Germany*. Chicago: University of Chicago Press.

Theissen, G. 1996. "Between Acknowledgement and Ignorance: How White South Africans Have Dealt with the Apartheid Past." Johannesburg: University of Witswaterrand Centre for the Study of Violence and Reconciliation.

Theissen, Gunnar, and Brandon Hamber. 1998. "A State of Denial: White South Africans' Attitudes to the Truth and Reconciliation Commission." *Indicator South Africa* 15:8–12.

Theoharis, Jeanne. 2018. *A More Beautiful and Terrible History: The Uses and Misuses of Civil Rights History*. New York: Beacon Press.

Thörn, Håkan. 2006. *Anti-apartheid and the Emergence of a Global Civil Society*. New York: Palgrave MacMillan.

TRC (Truth and Reconciliation Commission). 1998. *Truth and Reconciliation Commission of South Africa Report*. Cape Town: Juta.

Turok, Ivan. 1994. "Urban Planning in the Transition from Apartheid, Part 1: The Legacy of Social Control." *Town Planning Review* 65:243.

Tutu, Desmond Mpilo. 2009. *No Future without Forgiveness*. New York: Image.

UNU-WIDER. 2019. *Research Brief*. Johannesburg: UNU-WIDER.

Vandello, Joseph A., Jennifer K. Bosson, Dov Cohen, Rochelle M. Burnaford, and Jonathan R. Weaver. 2008. "Precarious manhood." *Journal of personality and social psychology* 95:1325.

van den Berghe, Pierre L. 1967. *Race and Racism: A Comparative Perspective*. New York: John Wiley & Sons.

van der Westhuizen, Christi. 2007. *White Power and the Rise and Fall of the National Party*. Cape Town: Zebra Press .

———. 2017. *Sitting Pretty: White Afrikaans Women in Postapartheid South Africa*. Pietermaritzburg, SA: University of KwaZulu–Natal Press.

van Kessel, Ineke. 2000. *Beyond Our Wildest Dreams: The United Democratic Front and the Transformation of South Africa*. Charlottesville: University Press of Virginia.

van Vugt, William E., and G. Daan Cloete. 2000. *Race and Reconciliation in South Africa: A Multicultural Dialogue in Comparative Perspective*. Lanham, MD: Lexington Books.

van Zyl-Hermann, Danelle. 2018a. "Race, Rumour and the Politics of Class in Late and Post-apartheid South Africa: The Case of Arrie Paulus." *Social History* 43:509–30.

———. 2018b. "Make Afrikaners Great Again! National Populism, Democracy and the New White Minority Politics in Post-apartheid South Africa." *Ethnic and Racial Studies* 41: 2673–92.

———. 2020. "White Workers and the Unravelling of Racial Citizenship in Late Apartheid South Africa." In *Rethinking White Societies in Southern Africa*, ed. Danelle van Zyl-Hermann and Duncan Money, 194–214. London: Taylor & Francis.

———. 2021. *Privileged Precariat: White Workers and South Africa's Long Transition to Majority Rule*. Cambridge: Cambridge University Press.

van Zyl Slabbert, Frederik. 1999. *Afrikaner Afrikaan: Anekdotes en analise*. Cape Town: Tafelberg.

Veblen, Thorstein. 1899. *The Theory of the Leisure Class*. New York: Macmillan.

Verhoef, Grietjie. 2016. "Innovation and Expansion: Product Innovation and Expansion in Insurance in South Africa. The Case of Sanlam, 1920–1998." *Historia* 61:66–91.

Verwey, Cornel, and Michael Quayle. 2012. "Whiteness, Racism, and Afrikaner Identity in Post-apartheid South Africa." *African Affairs* 111:551–75.

Viljoen, Shaun. 2001. "Non-racialism Remains a Fiction: Richard Rive's 'Buckingham Palace.' District Six and K. Sello Duiker's the Quiet Violence of Dreams." *English Academy Review* 18:46–53.

Visser, W. 2008. *Van MWU tot Solidariteit: Geskiedenis van die Mynwerkersunie 1902–2002*: Centurion, SA: Solidariteit.

Warikoo, Natasha Kumar. 2011. *Balancing Acts: Youth Culture in the Global City*. Oakland: University of California Press.

Warren, Mark R. 2010. *Fire in the Heart: How White Activists Embrace Racial Justice*. Oxford: Oxford University Press.

Wasserman, Herman, and Arnold S. de Beer. 2009. "Afro-Optimism/Afro-Pessimism and the South African Media." *Critical Arts: A Journal of South-North Cultural Studies* 23:377–95.

Wasserman, Herman, and Sean Jacobs. 2003. *Shifting Selves: Post-apartheid Essays on Mass Media, Culture, and Identity*. Cape Town: Kwela.

Weis, Lois. 2004. *Class Reunion: The Remaking of the American White Working Class*. New York: Routledge.

Wellman, David T. 1977. *Portraits of White Racism*. Cambridge: Cambridge University Press.

Willoughby-Herard, Tiffany. 2007. "South Africa's Poor Whites and Whiteness Studies: Afrikaner Ethnicity, Scientific Racism, and White Misery." *New Political Science* 29:479–500.

———. 2015. *Waste of a White Skin: The Carnegie Corporation and the Racial*

Logic of White Vulnerability. Oakland: University of California Press.

Wilson, Richard. 2001. *The Politics of Truth and Reconciliation in South Africa: Legitimizing the Post-apartheid State.* Cambridge: Cambridge University Press.

Winant, Howard. 1998. "Racism Today: Continuity and Change in the Post–Civil Rights Era." *Ethnic and Racial Studies* 21:755–66.

———. 2001. "White Racial Projects." In *The Making and Unmaking of Whiteness,* ed. Birgit Brander Rasmussen, Eric Klinenberg, Irene J Nexica, and Matt Wray, 97–112. Durham, NC: Duke University Press.

Wolpe, Harold. 1972. "Capitalism and Cheap Labour-Power in South Africa: from Segregation to Apartheid." *Economy and Society* 1:425–56.

Zuberi, Tukufu, and Eduardo Bonilla-Silva. 2008. *White Logic, White Methods: Racism and Methodology.* Lanham, MD: Rowman & Littlefield.

Index

CPSIA information can be obtained
at www.ICGtesting.com
Printed in the USA
JSHW020858291221
21619JS00004B/4

9 781503 627789